IMAGES
of America

FAIRHOPE IN THE ROARING TWENTIES

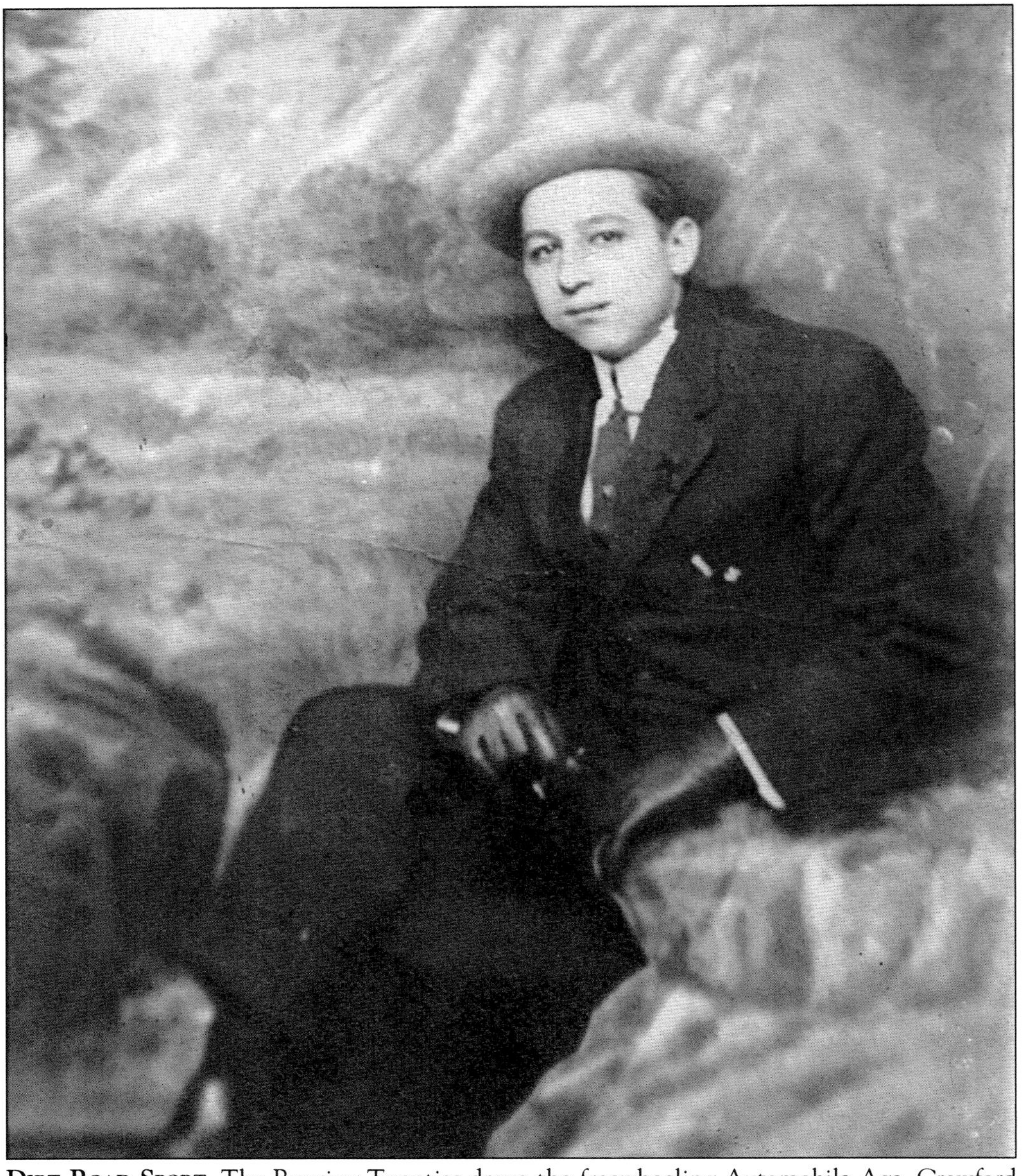

DIRT ROAD SPORT. The Roaring Twenties drove the freewheeling Automobile Age. Crawford "Cotton" Ziegler, wearing spiffy touring gloves, loved fine cars and would drive down from Big Bend Plantation, 200 miles up the Alabama River, for the Eastern Shore's attractions. He visited family and friends like Fairhope tycoon Thomas Molton, who had started out as Ziegler's grandfather's overseer. (Courtesy of Cathy Donelson.)

ON THE COVER: "The world's mine oyster" could be the theme of this 1920s oyster party under moss-hung oaks on the shimmering Mobile Bay beach in Fairhope. The fashionable pleasure resort, located on what was called the "American Riviera," was famous for its succulent seafood. The country's finest oyster reefs also drew visitors to the area. (Courtesy of the Fairhope Museum of History.)

IMAGES
of America

Fairhope in the Roaring Twenties

Cathy Donelson

ARCADIA
PUBLISHING

ISBN 978-0-7385-9892-5

Published by Arcadia Publishing
Charleston, South Carolina

Printed in the United States of America

Library of Congress Control Number: 2012954027

For all general information, please contact Arcadia Publishing:
Telephone 843-853-2070
Fax 843-853-0044
E-mail sales@arcadiapublishing.com
For customer service and orders:
Toll-Free 1-888-313-2665

Visit us on the Internet at www.arcadiapublishing.com

To my grandparents Crawford and Elizabeth Veronica Ziegler, who introduced me to the Roaring Twenties

Contents

ACKNOWLEDGMENTS

Voices from the past echo through this book like the bittersweet fade of a jazz saxophone. They come from the great writers, musicians, filmmakers, and storytellers of the 1920s, whose catchy slang and titles contributed to many of the photographic captions herein.

My first dance was the Charleston, taught to me by my grandmother in her big kitchen. As I grew older, I learned of my grandparents black-bottoming at Harlem's Cotton Club during Prohibition and the scandalous tale of how they met.

My grandfather, a seventh-generation planter and unlikely mechanical genius, was occasionally lured north in the winters to invent processes for the growing automotive industry. In the early 1920s, after the cotton was in, he headed out for the bright city lights in his treasured Cole Eight.

My bluestocking Yankee grandmother met him pushing a tire heiress—who was sucking gin from a baby bottle—down a snowy Cleveland sidewalk in a baby carriage and decided he needed reforming. She succeeded, to some extent.

He liked her foxy walk, and after the prerequisite Niagara Falls honeymoon, he brought her "down home," where I grew up with their memories.

Other stories that influenced this book came from old Fairhopers, Faulkner, Fitzgerald, and *Stars Fell on Alabama* by Carl Carmer, who wrote, "No people of the world give more thought to social enjoyment than the Alabamians."

Fairhope was neither Northern nor Southern, but an intriguing mélange of the best of both, where dancers did their "Alabama stepping" around pavilions in the soft, moonlit bay breezes.

I also am deeply indebted to the new Fairhope Museum of History and its generous donors and staff, especially director Donnie Barrett, who graciously and enthusiastically shared its collections for reproduction, along with others credited.

Thanks also go to my great-great-grandparents James and Janet McAdams, who settled after the Civil War on the shores of Mobile Bay, in what is now part of Fairhope. When I was a little girl, we would visit relatives on the Eastern Shore, which I thought was the most elegant place in the world.

I still do.

INTRODUCTION

Pleasure-seekers and some of the deep thinkers of the Roaring Twenties all converged in the experimental town of Fairhope, which had just celebrated its first quarter century at the beginning of the decade. Most of the great hallmark themes of the 1920s—art, evolution, Prohibition, politics, literature, and liberalism—played out in the tiny coastal Alabama town. Remarkably, this isolated enclave on the Eastern Shore of Mobile Bay became a microcosm of the decade. Called "Alabama's favorite outing place" by the weekly newspaper, its wharf greeted visitors with the strains of jazz floating across the waterfront from the large casino and dance pavilion.

The profound social and cultural changes that would transform the nation during the coming decade are illustrated by the two leading front-page items in the January 2, 1920, *Fairhope Courier*. One is a report of a Christmas Eve automobile wreck that was deemed a lesson on driving in the dark without lights. The other reports that cattleman Thomas Wilson had freed his herd to run loose in defiance of new stock laws. Wilson, who according to the newspaper "had been quite resentful of the town stock ordinance," broke down the marshal's impoundment and released his cows. A showdown was predicted for the next town council meeting. The town won on the corral issue, thus beginning a new era with the automobile dominating the local scene instead of livestock.

Soon, there would be more mavericks on the streets as Fairhope became a refuge for some of the country's most famous and infamous characters. Little more than a village, with a population of only 853 in 1920, Fairhope would leave its mark in history as the next few years brought the town into national prominence with a stream of celebrity visitors and cosmopolitan residents. The mile of glistening golden beaches and the utopian ideals of the community's founding drew everyone from artists to agitators. They came by water because Fairhope was accessible only by boat from Mobile, where the biggest bootlegging outfit in the country during Prohibition operated under the protection of the sheriff and local leaders.

From its unique beginnings, Fairhope was never a typical Southern town. It was founded by idealists in 1894 as an intentional community on an isolated Mobile Bay bluff populated by free-range cattle roaming through stands of turpentine pines. Despite its relative infancy at the beginning of the 1920s, Fairhope was a lively miniature metropolis. The first week of the new decade featured a basketball game at the Magnolia Beach Pavilion and the regular Sunday afternoon monthly Fairhope Socialist Local meeting. By that time, the town had become a summer and winter resort, catering to different kinds of guests. Notables from over the country wintered there, enjoying the mild Gulf Coast climate, and many wealthy and liberal-minded parents enrolled their children in the town's well-known progressive Marietta Johnson School of Organic Education, also called the Organic School.

Fairhope, almost an island, was a retreat for many, and bay steamers carried people from Mobile, where rail lines converged. The railroads were at their peak, and the era of classy new passenger trains with full-service dining cars brought visitors overnight from snow to sunshine. Others came by automobile on the old Dixie Bee Line highway from places like Chicago. All were drawn by Fairhope's amusements, natural attractions, intellectual freedom, and connections to the larger world.

Before it was a place, Fairhope was a name and a dream. A group of Populist idealists and reformers based in Des Moines, Iowa, believing their Utopian colony would have a "fair hope" of succeeding, began a search for a location to begin a model community based on cooperative individualism. From the beginning, the Fairhope colony's selection committee envisioned an inviting resort. They found their site on a spectacular rise on the eastern shore of a beautiful wide bay, an area that had been a summer retreat for Mobilians and visitors since the early 1800s. Before the War of 1812, the area had been a British colony. "There is probably no other place that we could secure where so many friends from the north would be interested in visiting us and in spending the winters for pleasure and health," one committee member wrote.

The first group of 28 settlers, including nine children, arrived in November 1894 and soon purchased 135 acres with a half mile of bay frontage to begin their experiment in communal living. All colony property belonged to the association, with each member leasing land. Newspaper editor and colony founder Ernest B. Gaston wrote, "We came to what then seemed to be an out-of-the way corner of the world and secured a tract of land which then practically worthless upon which to demonstrate the virtues of a well-defined policy."

The venture became the Fairhope Single Tax Corporation (FSTC) in 1904 and operated as a single-tax colony based on the land reform theories of Henry George, the leading social economist of the 1800s and proponent of land value tax. His book *Progress and Poverty* inspired the Fairhope single-tax demonstration, and "true-hearted reformers" were invited to join. By 1908, when the town incorporated with a municipal government, the corporation owned 4,000 acres. It would become the world's oldest and most successful single-tax colony.

The colony's law of equal freedom that said "everyone has freedom to do all that he wills provided he infringes not the equal freedom of any other" drew a variety of freethinkers and bohemians, including free-love advocates like Marie Howland. A Socialist and feminist author of the labor novel *Papa's Own Girl,* Howland became associate editor of the *Courier* and established the town's library with her rare book collection. She was also fond of swimming and rowing her boat in the nude. Several groups and families in the community were dedicated nudists, believing in the open-air benefits of bathing in the bay.

Socialists, Communists, leftist-leaning "parlor pinks," and Wobblies (members of the Industrial Workers of the World) and others involved in the changing politics of the 1920s also gravitated to Fairhope. Iconoclasts and individuals contentious by national and world standards, let alone Southern conservative mores, were drawn to the colony—a cauldron of reformists, cutting-edge writers, sexual and social renegades, and artists.

Clarence Darrow, the nation's best-known lawyer, came to rest and recuperate after the famed Scopes "Monkey Trial," which likely killed his Christian opponent, noted orator William Jennings Bryan. Bryan, "the Great Commoner," died in his sleep within a week of the trial. *Baltimore Sun* journalist H.L. Mencken, who had satirized the South and the landmark case about teaching evolution, wrote, "God aimed at Darrow, missed, and hit Bryan instead."

Ironically, both Darrow and Bryan, despite their other differences, were single-taxers and supportive of the Fairhope colony. The agnostic Darrow, made a household name by the radio broadcast of the provocative trial, had several speaking engagements in Fairhope and across the bay during his stay during the winter of 1927. He and the nation's leading evangelist, Billy Sunday, who was drawing crowds of up to 40,000 in many places across the country, spoke in Mobile on the same night—Darrow at the downtown Lyric Theater, and Sunday in a large tent. Both spoke later in Fairhope during the same week, making history in the small town. Darrow aroused the ire of the local Ku Klux Klan after he made a civil rights speech at a black school near Fairhope.

A *Time* magazine article titled "Negroes: Darrow v. Klan" reports that afterward, amid threats of tarring and feathering, he fled on a noon train to Chattanooga.

During the turbulent social shifts of the 1920s, the KKK grew into a political power in Alabama as well as across the nation. Klan support helped Bibb Graves win the election as Alabama governor in 1926, and there were rumors he was the exalted cyclops of its Montgomery chapter. He eventually rejected the organization as it became violent and would later be remembered as one of the South's most progressive governors. Despite its egalitarian roots, Fairhope had its own Invisible Empire. Birmingham millionaire and hotel owner Thomas Hunt Molton, who had a retreat named Lone Pine in Fairhope, decried the Klan outrages in 1924. "Not long ago, under the cover of darkness someone, supposedly members of the Klan, put up in the very heart of our little town several fiery crosses to frighten someone, I know not who. Our Northern visitors must feel their lives are unsafe here," he wrote in a letter to the newspaper editor. Molton complimented the newspaper for approving Alabama presidential candidate Oscar W. Underwood's bold stand against the Klan and Prohibition. Underwood would be featured in John F. Kennedy's *Profiles in Courage*. However, as late as 1927, the Fairhope Klan No. 127 sponsored a space in the high school *Bay Breeze* yearbook.

Darrow, another KKK opponent, was known for defending underdogs and liberal causes. He had represented a main defendant when 100 Wobblies, including radical IWW founder William "Big Bill" Haywood, were convicted for violating the federal Espionage Act. Haywood served a year of a 20-year sentence at Leavenworth Prison before being released on bail to await the appeal of his conviction. His bond was the home of Mary Marcy, a longtime friend of Darrow, who spent several winters in Fairhope writing poetry and propaganda. Haywood jumped bail and fled to Soviet Russia in 1921, and Marcy, having lost her home, committed suicide. In a memorial pamphlet illustrated by a Wharton Esherick woodcut, Wobblie founder Eugene Debs calls her "the brainiest woman" in the American labor movement.

Marcy's friend Wharton Esherick, an artist and sculptor who had studied on scholarship at the Philadelphia Academy of Fine Arts, accepted a job in 1919 as art teacher at Fairhope's Organic School. Soon, he became immersed in woodcuts and block printing, using a set of chisels given to him by author Sherwood Anderson, a lifelong friend whom he had met in Fairhope. Esherick's exhibits of his "modern" art in Fairhope drew mixed reactions, with one reviewer noting the pictures were attractively framed and hung, while a printed catalogue helped art lovers recognize many of the pictures as Fairhope scenes. At the Organic School, he also became interested in movement and dance and often took his young family to the beach, where they swam naked with the Andersons.

Esherick's friend Sherwood Anderson was among the many Fairhopers influenced by the so-called Chicago Renaissance of the 1920s. He, Marcy, Darrow, and many other Fairhope visitors were habitués of the famed Dill Pickle Club, a bohemian speakeasy and underground theater on a Chicago back alley that attracted a mix of hoboes, anarchists, attorneys, artists, and noted speakers.

Poets such as Carl Sandberg and Vachel Lindsay and writers including Anderson and Pulitzer Prize winner Upton Sinclair were regulars. Sinclair, having won national fame for his muckraking novel *The Jungle*, about the meatpacking industry, moved his family to Fairhope during the winter of 1910. They lived in a bay-front cottage while Sinclair wrote *Love's Pilgrimage* in a tent. A health food faddist, Sinclair wrote about swimming daily in the icy bay. An advocate of communal living, he wrote more favorably about the Fairhope colony than did Anderson. Anderson moved there to escape from both the critical acclaim of his *Winesburg, Ohio,* considered one of the best novels of the last century, and his second wife, Tennessee Mitchell. In a 1921 journal, Anderson wrote that he lived in the Alabama enclave for six months. "From the bay I turned inland at a little place where northerners, well to do men from O[hio], ILL had come to the far s[outh] place to make themselves homes for certain winter months," he wrote. "How ugly and smug the little houses were and what ugly names they had. The Dovecote. Westwood. Idlehours, Moss Manor etc.," Anderson wrote. "The names were painted on board and stuck up over frail cheaply flung together verandahs on which tired old men sat staring with vacant eyes from MM into the staring windows of Westwood." Perhaps he was disgruntled because Tennessee, an artist and piano teacher, joined him in Fairhope and began creating sculptures to illustrate his next book.

The 1920s opened a new era of opportunity for women, and many began to assert their independence by smoking, drinking shinny, dancing the shimmy, and voting under the newly ratified Nineteenth Amendment. Hemlines rose and morals loosened, with one new magazine called *Flapper* advertising that it was "Not for Old Foggies." In Alabama, women voted for the first time in 1920. They had always been active in Fairhope's leadership, though, and in 1924 new FSTC president pro tem Minnie Brown presided over the anniversary dinner attended by 200 members.

Marietta Johnson, founder of the Organic School, also helped put Fairhope on the map with her national and international speaking engagements on progressive education, and many prominent families sent their children to her Fairhope school. Among them were some authentic mavericks, such as Lola Maverick Lloyd, a wealthy world-peace activist from a Texas cattle-baron family. Her grandfather Samuel Maverick famously refused to brand his cattle. Her husband, William Bross Lloyd, helped found the Communist Party of the United States in 1919, becoming its first millionaire. The couple's youngest daughter, Georgia, who was graduated from the Organic School in 1930, went on to become a peace worker herself, directing the Campaign for World Government until her death at age 85. Charles H. Ingersoll of New York, wealthy maker of the dollar watch, also sent his son to the school, as did the vice president of Ford Motor Company and other national leaders.

The Organic School also offered what was called the Winter Course for adults who came to Fairhope. Albert W. Fuchs, a Chicago real estate magnate and philanthropist, came for the winter of 1924 to take the classes, as did both former Connecticut governor Thomas M. Waller and American Ophthalmological Society president Dr. Myles Standish of Boston.

In 1920, Col. H. Martin Williams, the former reading clerk of the US House of Representatives, Henry George adherent, and a nationally prominent lecturer, visited and attended the Winter Course. While in town, Williams addressed the regular Fairhope Forum, a popular speaking venue. His remarks went unrecorded, but apparently were stirring enough to gain the government's attention. "He made a speech which was thought to be too radical for some, and led to some inquiry by federal authorities in Mobile (this being just after the close of the war when some patriots were very sensitive to criticism of the government)," the newspaper reports.

But Fairhope was a radical town and reflected the revolutionary changes that the decade was having on the nation. In the mid-1920s, Albert M. Troyer, a local citrus grower and agricultural expert, was elected president of the colony. A Socialist, he later emigrated to Soviet Russia, where he disappeared into a gulag.

And the Roaring Twenties in Fairhope became only a faint but fond memory of the Lost Generation, now recaptured in the faded sepia photographs of this book.

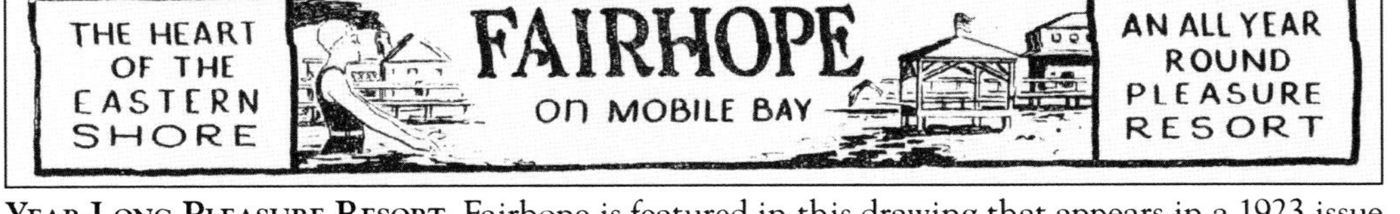

Year-Long Pleasure Resort. Fairhope is featured in this drawing that appears in a 1923 issue of the *American Riviera Review*, which touts the attractions of the upper Gulf Coast. "Fairhope is much more than a resort," the magazine says. (Courtesy of the Mobile Public Library.)

One

Mavericks of Fairhope

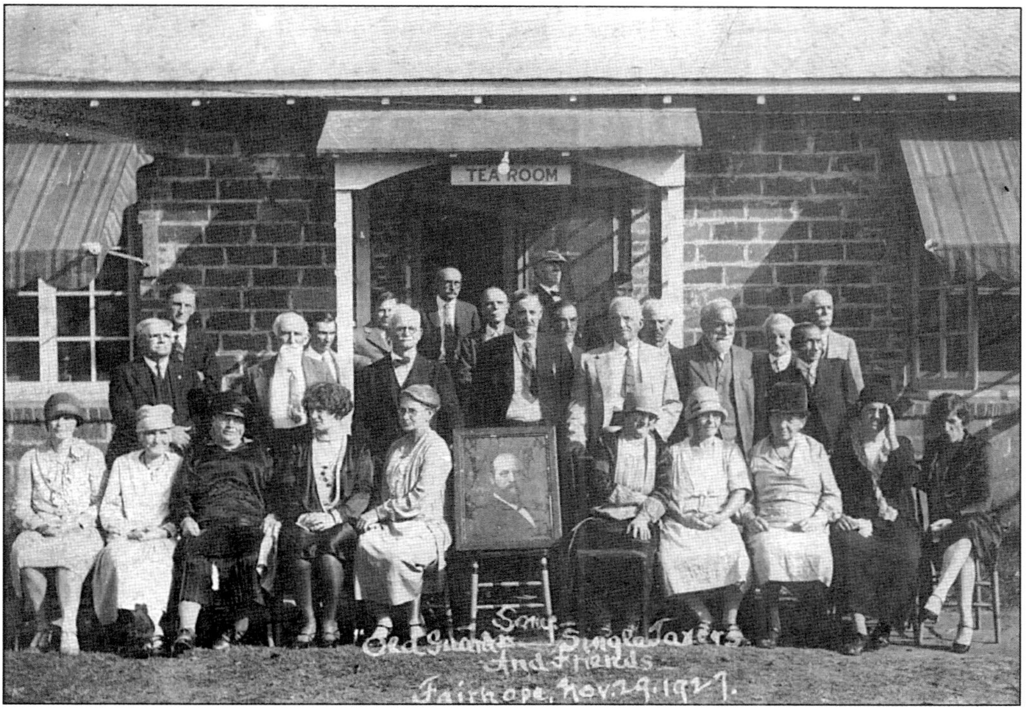

Old Guard Single-Taxers. Fairhope was a thriving town when this group of dedicated single-taxers gathered in November 1927 to observe the colony's 33rd anniversary. These earnest reformers surround a portrait of their inspiration, economist Henry George. A band was booked for the celebration, but, as the newspaper observed, the attendees were not a dancing crowd. (Courtesy of the FMH.)

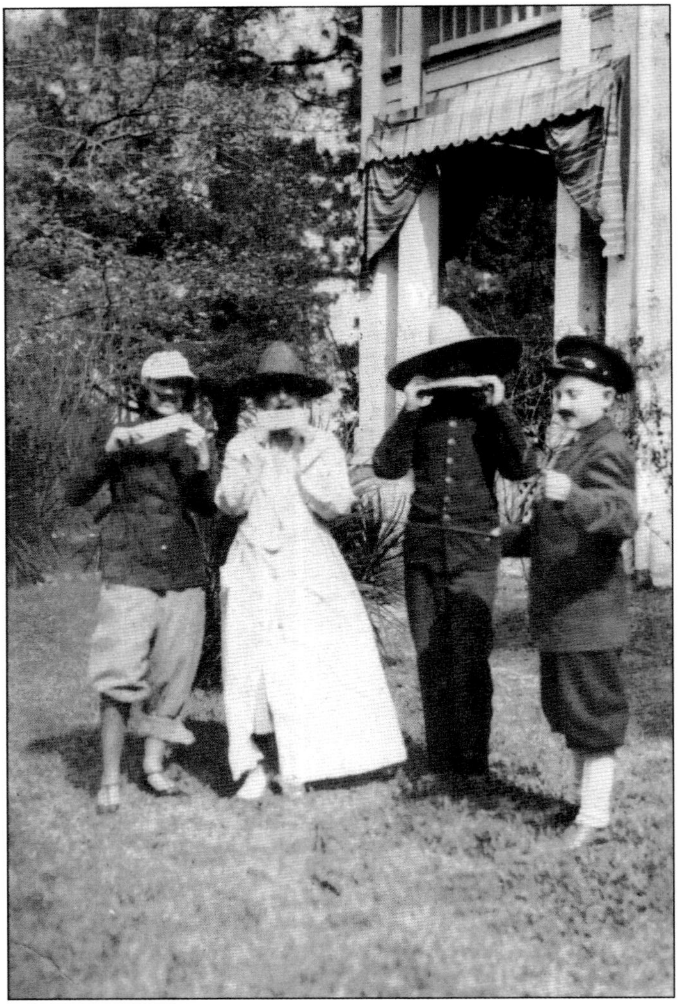

A War Party. Youngsters wearing old World War I uniforms make homemade music in front of the Colonial Inn resort to celebrate the war's end. Their lives would change greatly over the coming decade, and technological advances would afford them new luxuries, like the ability to listen to music on inventions like the radio. (Courtesy of WOFC.)

Flags in the Dust. With flags flying, townspeople crowded Fairhope Avenue, the sandy main street, for an Armistice Day parade on November 11, 1918, upon hearing the news that the war to end all wars was finally over. In the not-to-distant future, the celebrants would be ringing in a distinctive new era called the Jazz Age. (Courtesy of FMH.)

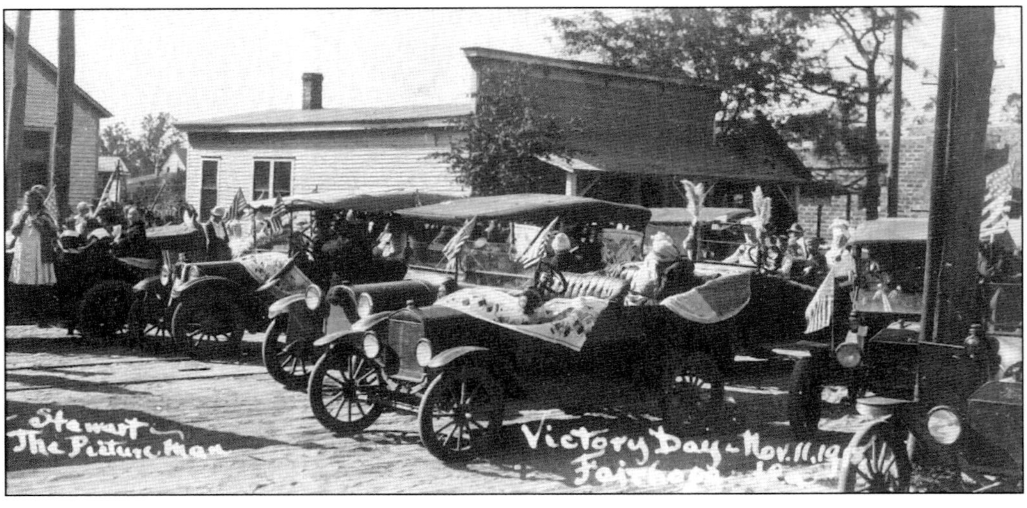

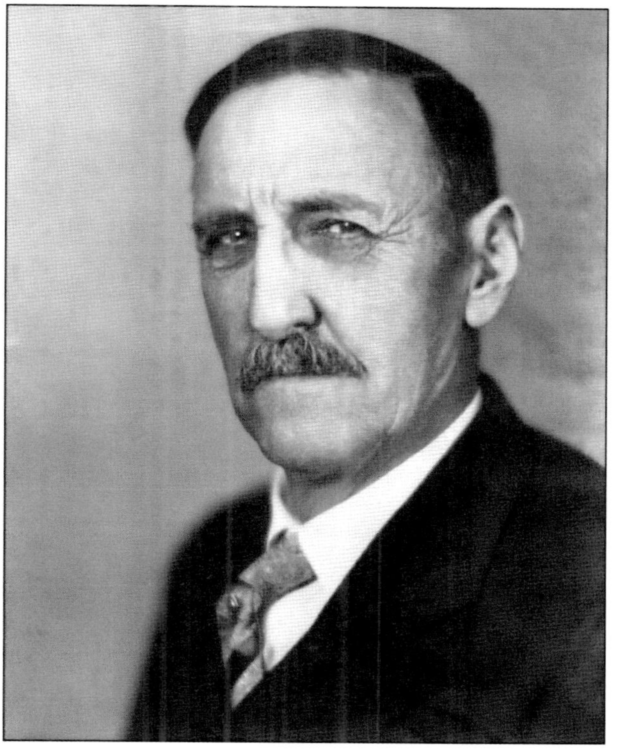

COLONY'S GUIDING FORCE. Ernest B. Gaston, the colony's main founder, who led the first settlers to the raw land that would become Fairhope, served as colony secretary and editor of the *Fairhope Courier* newspaper for four decades. By the 1920s, the community he had helped create was at the height of its fame, drawing visitors from over the country. (Courtesy of Rusty Godard.)

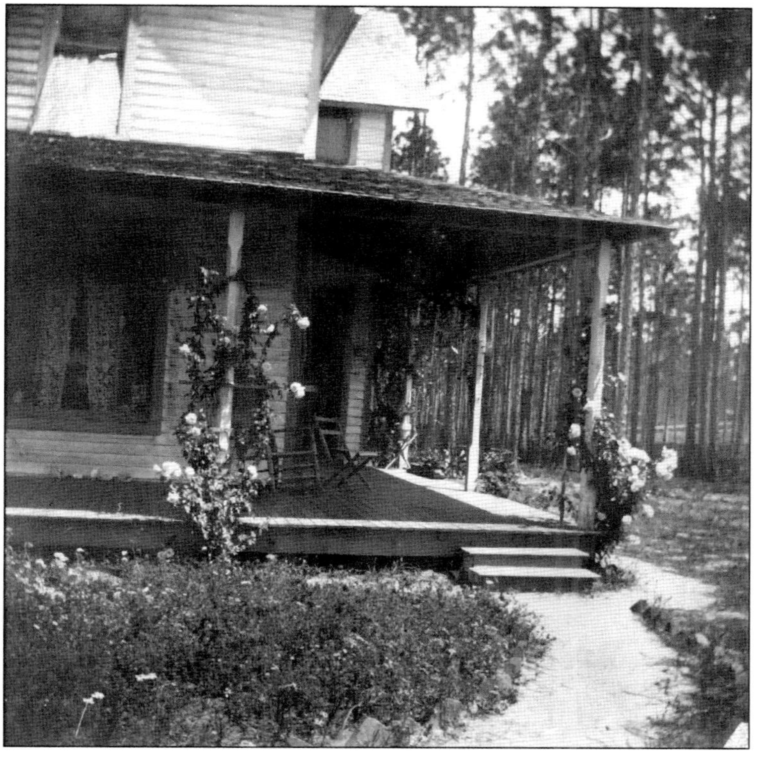

REMEMBRANCE OF THINGS PAST. Gaston was proud of saying he built his family's first Fairhope home for $2.50. His second house, still standing on Magnolia Avenue, was more substantial, though also modest. Townsfolk considered ostentatious houses vulgar, and Gaston once wrote, "In this country, it is hard to tell which ones are of the most importance, rooms or galleries." (Courtesy of Rusty Godard.)

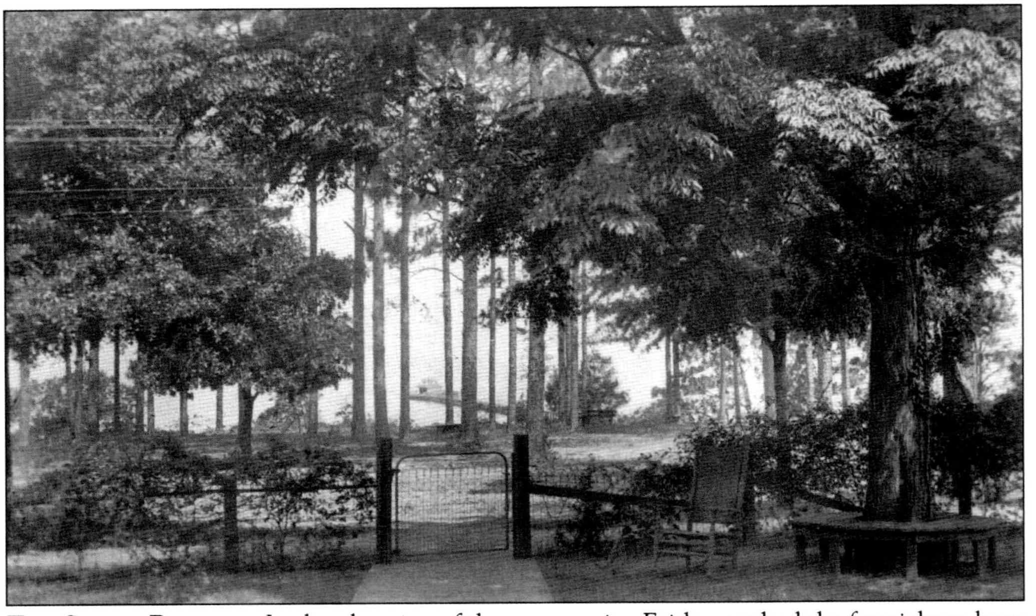

This Side of Paradise. In the planning of the community, Fairhopers had the foresight to keep their lovely waterfront publicly accessible. The pine bluffs offered spectacular views of the bay and of sunsets over the utopian settlement. While many looked upon the colonists as "freaks," Gaston wrote, "On further acquaintance with us, however, they find us to be a broad-minded, cultured, energetic people." (Courtesy of Reed Myers.)

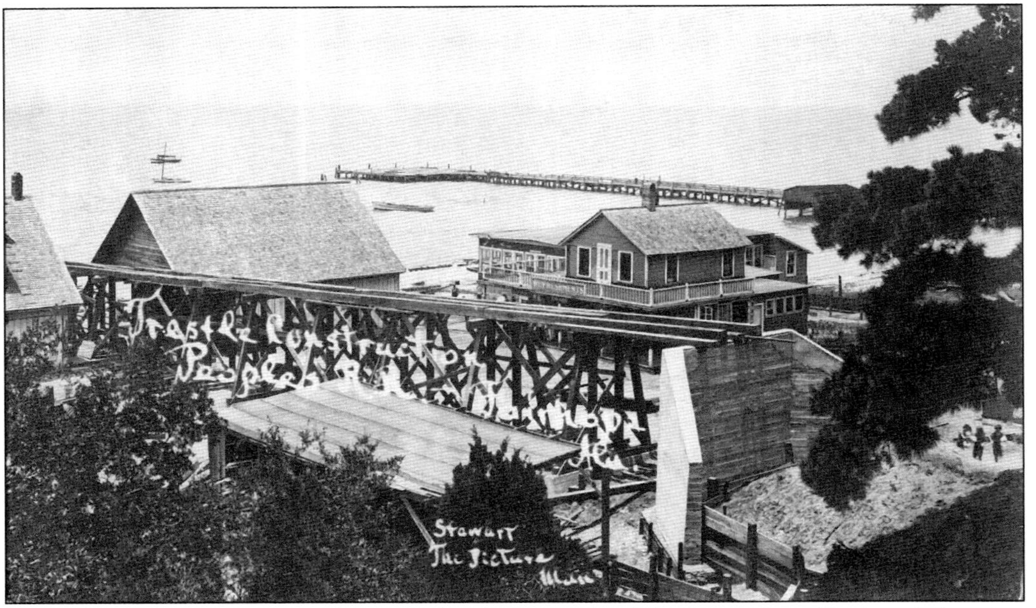

Link to Outside World. Within months of securing land for their colony, Fairhope's founders started constructing their public wharf. Operated at a profit by the colony, it was used to ship orange crops across the bay. It soon gained rails to bring passengers and goods up the steep Wharf Hill to the commercial area. Though a railroad was planned through Fairhope, it never materialized beyond the first mile. (Courtesy of Cathy Donelson.)

FREE LOVER FINDS FAIRHOPE. Another nonconformist, feminist and free-love author Marie Howland wrote, "I am still determined as soon as my circumstances will permit to 'seek refuge' in a Cooperative society and with full knowledge of the hardships and anxiety necessarily attending the attempt to found a new one." She came from a Socialist colony in Mexico in 1899. (Courtesy of Fairhope Public Library.)

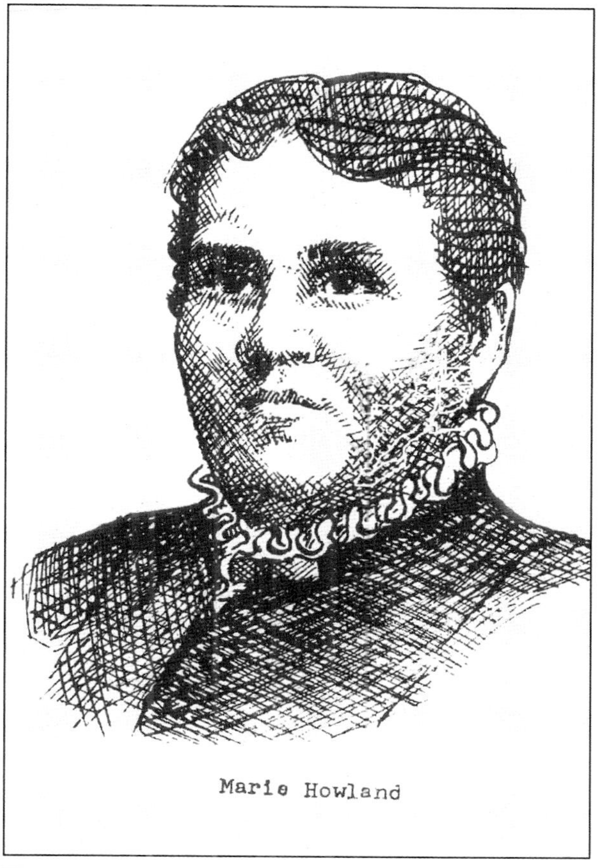

FAIRHOPE'S FIRST LIBRARY. Howland, who had inherited her late husband's collection of 2,000 rare books from all over the globe, maintained a lending library in her home. In 1906, the Single Tax Colony built this structure, which still stands at 10 North Summit Street, since incorporated into a larger building as the library expanded. Today, a new library operates at a third location. (Courtesy of Pinky Bass.)

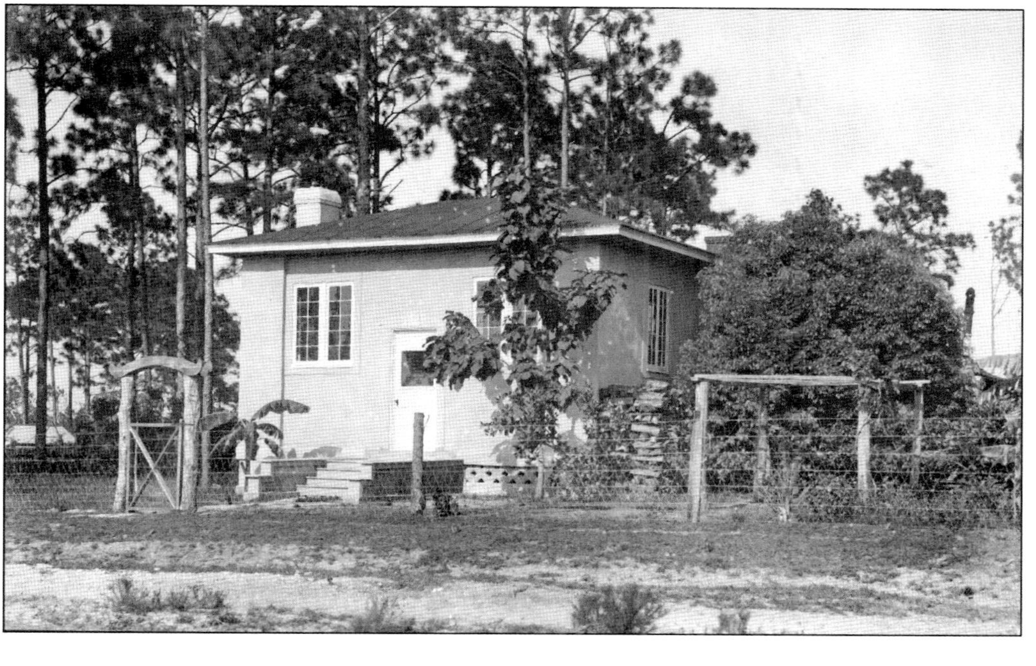

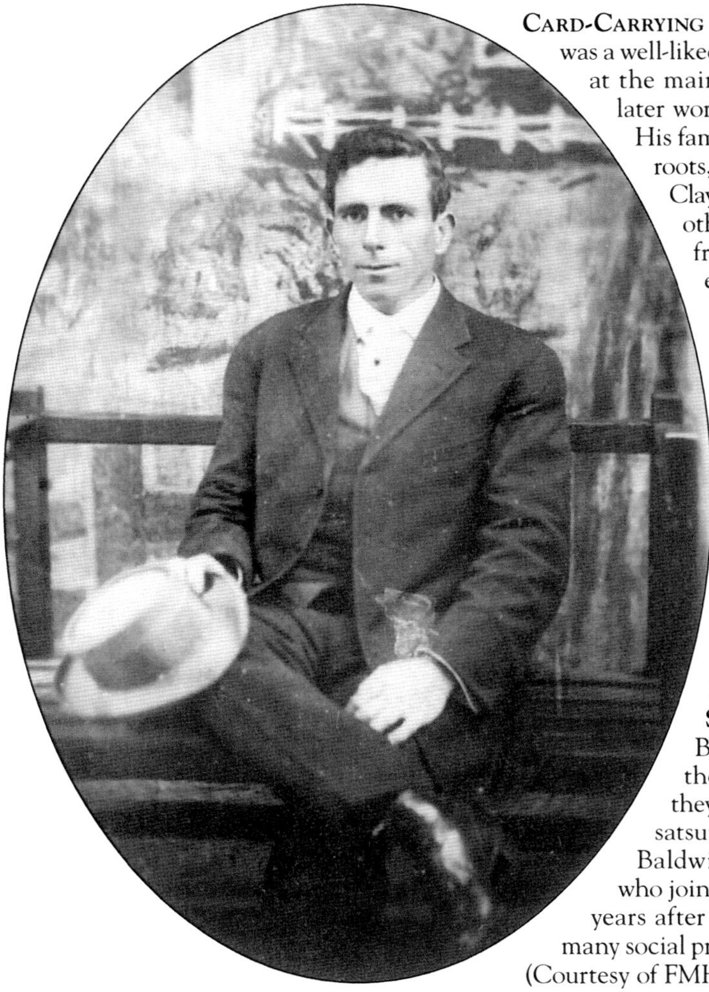

Card-Carrying Socialist. Clayton Baldwin was a well-liked fellow around town, clerking at the main corner hardware store and later working as a Ford car salesman. His family, which had deep Socialist roots, had moved to Fairhope when Clayton was a youngster. Like many others, they were attracted by the freedom of expression that gave everyone a voice. (Courtesy of Harriet Swift.)

Pastoral Side of Red Scare. The large, Socialist Baldwin family lived here at the outskirts of Fairhope where they had prizewinning orange and satsuma orchards. Patriarch C.A. Baldwin was a Civil War veteran who joined the Fairhope venture a few years after its founding. He was one of many social progressives drawn to the town. (Courtesy of FMH.)

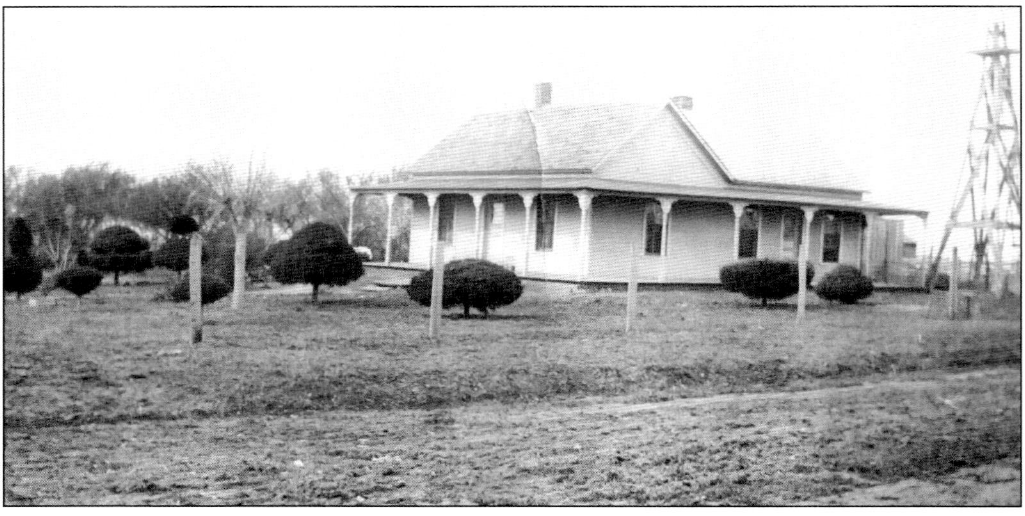

Socialist Party Card. A brother, Ernest Baldwin, saved his bright red Socialist Party of America membership card. The Socialists in Fairhope were comrades who held regular meetings on the first Sunday each month and addressed each other as "brother" and "sister." Their meeting sites varied from the country club to the Citrus Growers' Hall, because many of the members were farmers. (Courtesy of FMH.)

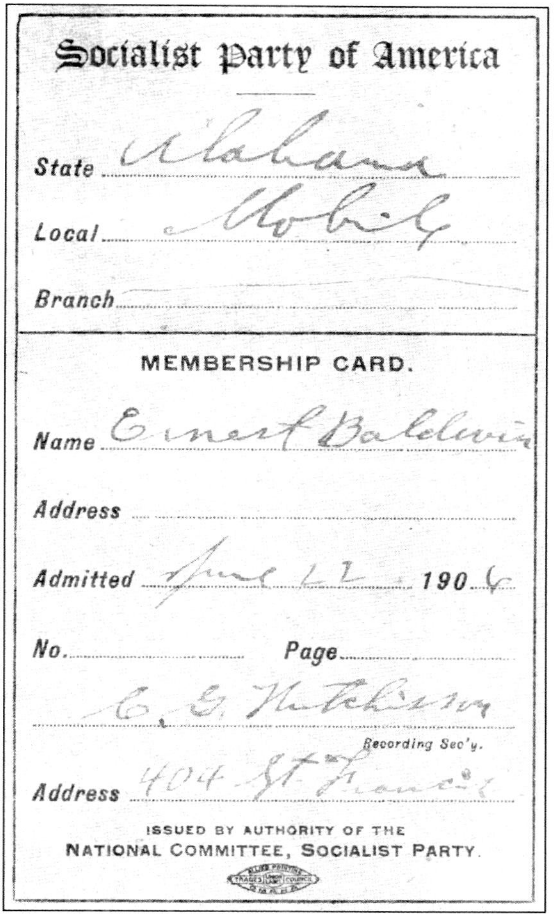

Socialist Party of America

State Alabama

Local Mobile

Branch

MEMBERSHIP CARD.

Name Ernest Baldwin

Address

Admitted June 22 1906

No. Page

C. G. Hutchinson

Recording Sec'y.

Address 404 St. Francis

ISSUED BY AUTHORITY OF THE
NATIONAL COMMITTEE, SOCIALIST PARTY.

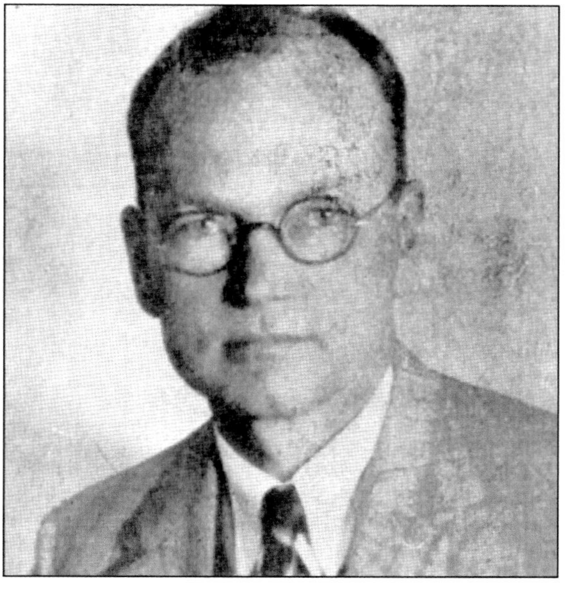

Radical Schoolteacher. Willard H. Edwards, a wealthy Chicago Socialist who brought his family to Fairhope in 1924, taught at the Organic School with his wife. After the Crash of 1929, he took the family to Soviet Russia and later abandoned them there. All were eventually able to get back to the United States, with the exception of one son. (Courtesy of MJM.)

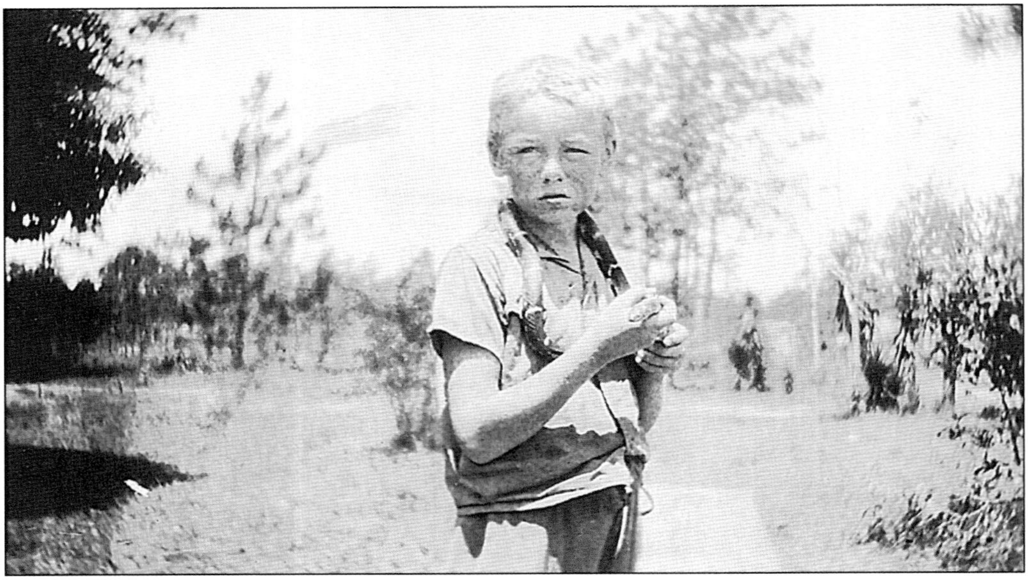

Left Behind in Russia. Kenneth "Dan" Edwards (holding a five-foot king snake during an Organic School nature class), had two siblings adopted by the Edwards from Jane Addams's Hull House in Chicago. His biological parents left him in Russia, where he became an engineer and lived the rest of his life. He was later reunited with his foster sister, whom he often visited in Fairhope. (Courtesy of MJM.)

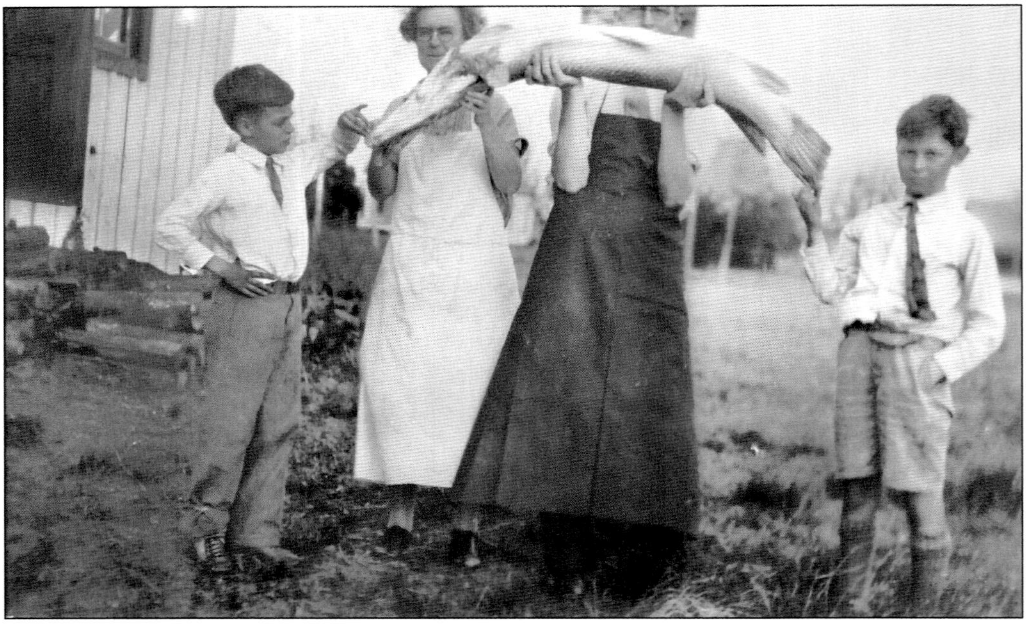

Socialites Turned Socialists. Helen and Willard Edwards display an alligator gar to two admiring 10-year-olds at Fairhope's School of Organic Education, where they taught. Helen, a naturalist, was a bird bander for the US Biological Survey for years. Their stay in Russia, where her husband went to teach, turned out to be a disappointment. (Courtesy of MJM.)

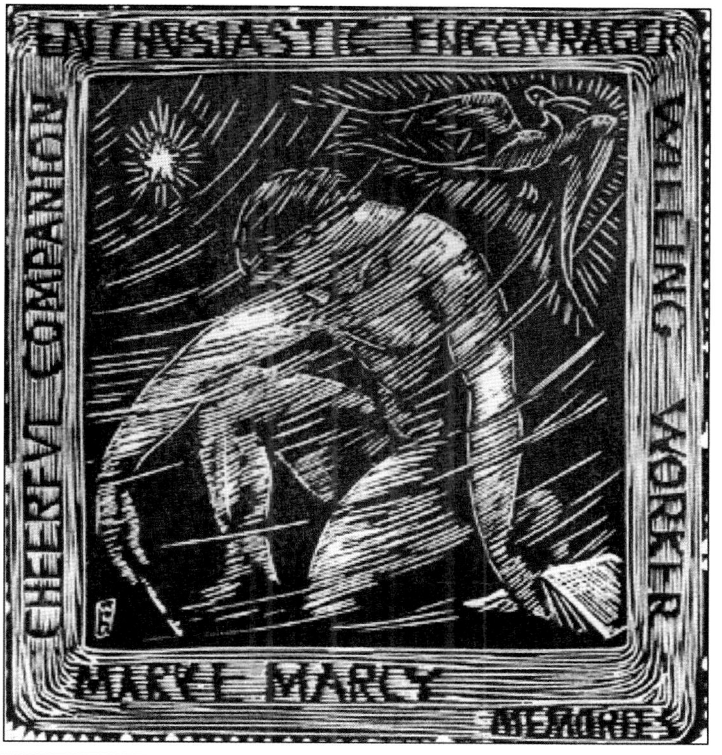

MARY MARCY MEMORIALIZED. Famed American artist Wharton Esherick memorialized his friend Mary Marcy, who spent her winters in Fairhope, with a woodcut after her death in 1922. Marcy lost her home when Wobblie leader "Big Bill" Haywood skipped bail and fled to Soviet Russia in 1921. Homeless and demoralized, Marcy committed suicide upon returning to Chicago. (Courtesy of MJM.)

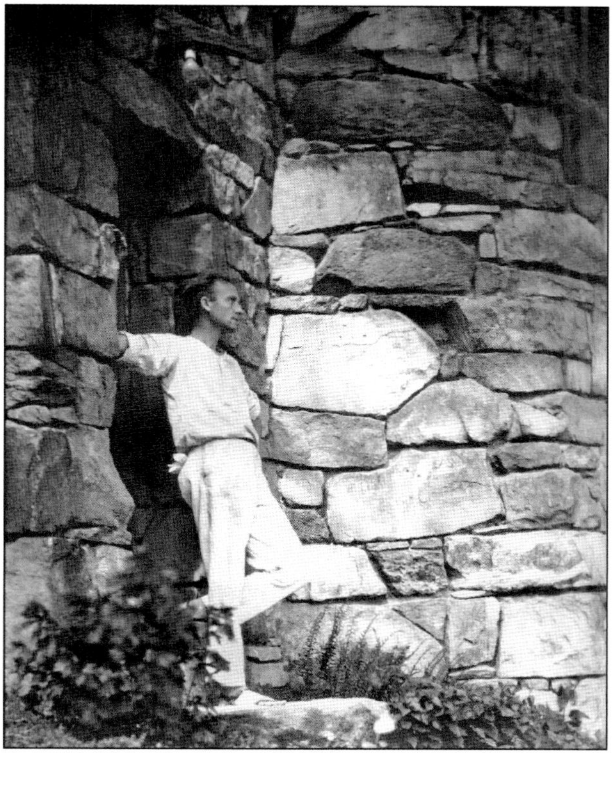

AMERICA'S PREMIER WOODCARVER. Esherick, known as the "dean of American craftsmen," excelled in the organic forms of the later Arts and Crafts movement. He began his noted career in woodcarving and art while teaching at Fairhope's Organic School in the early 1920s. His home in Paoli, Pennsylvania, is a National Historic Landmark, remarkable for its sculptured wood features. (Courtesy of the Wharton Esherick Museum.)

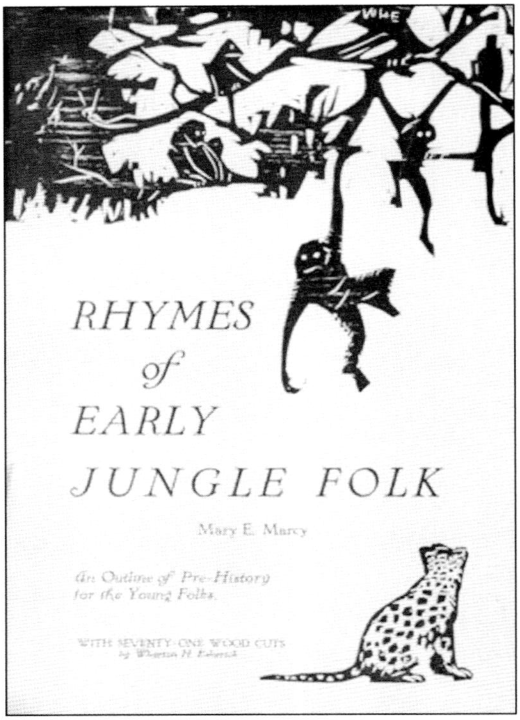

CONTROVERSIAL CHILDREN'S RHYMES. Mary Marcy, a frequent Fairhope visitor who was editor of the *International Socialist Review,* wrote a children's book about evolution titled *Rhymes of Early Jungle Folk.* The book, which turned out to be controversial, was illustrated with woodcuts by Esherick, whose impressionistic designs later won him many other commissions from leading publications. (Courtesy of MJM.)

EARLY FAIRHOPE BOHEMIAN. Frances Mitchell, another local free spirit, had three sons by three different men and often left them in Fairhope to be reared by her mother, Lou Mitchell, and her grandmother. Many Fairhopers traveled to New York where Frances, an early hippie, once had a vegetable juice stand in Greenwich Village. (Courtesy of Claire Gray.)

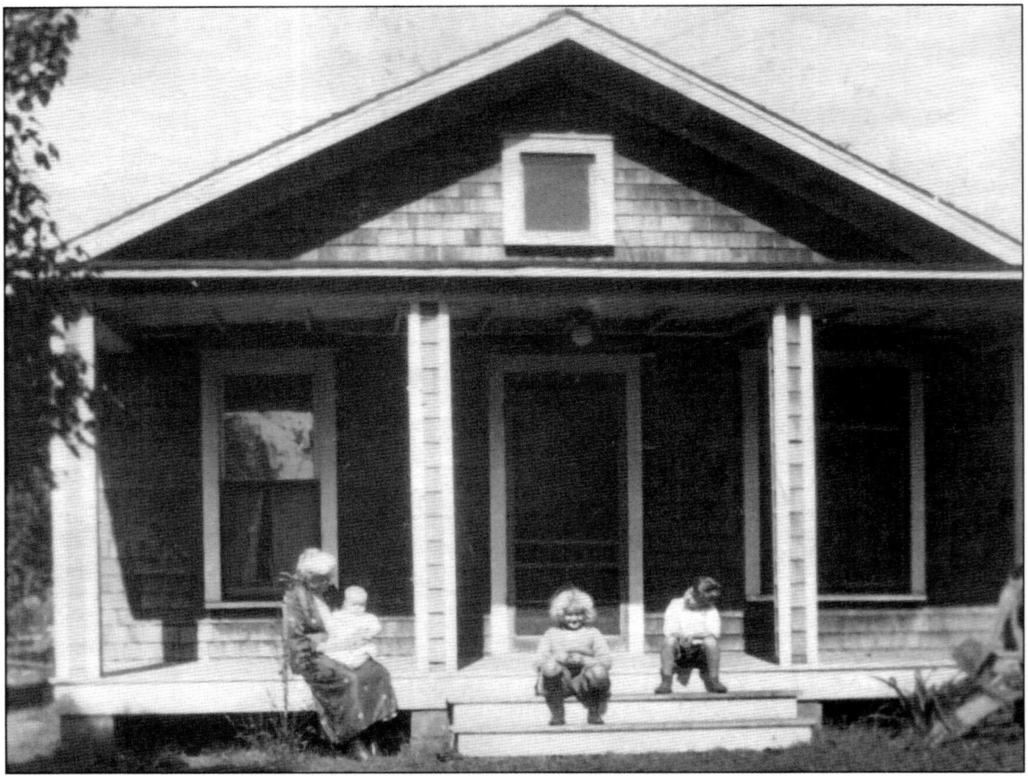

Two

I'M ALABAMY BOUND

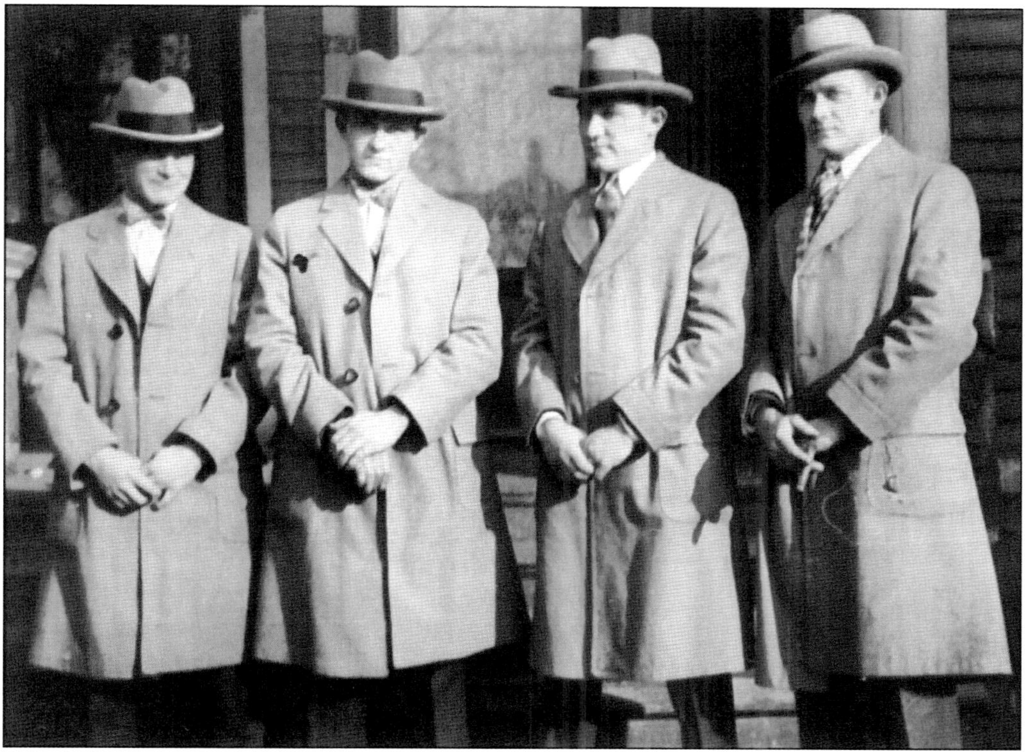

BOUND FOR ALABAMA. The four Funk brothers confidently pose as they prepare to leave Indiana in 1921 to seek their fortunes in Fairhope. Pictured are, from left to right, Clyde, Harold "Bub", Joseph, and William. They are wearing smart hats and matching coats that were called "floggers" at the time. The term *Chicago overcoat* would soon become slang for "coffin" as gangsters took over northern cities during the Prohibition gangland wars. (Courtesy of FMH.)

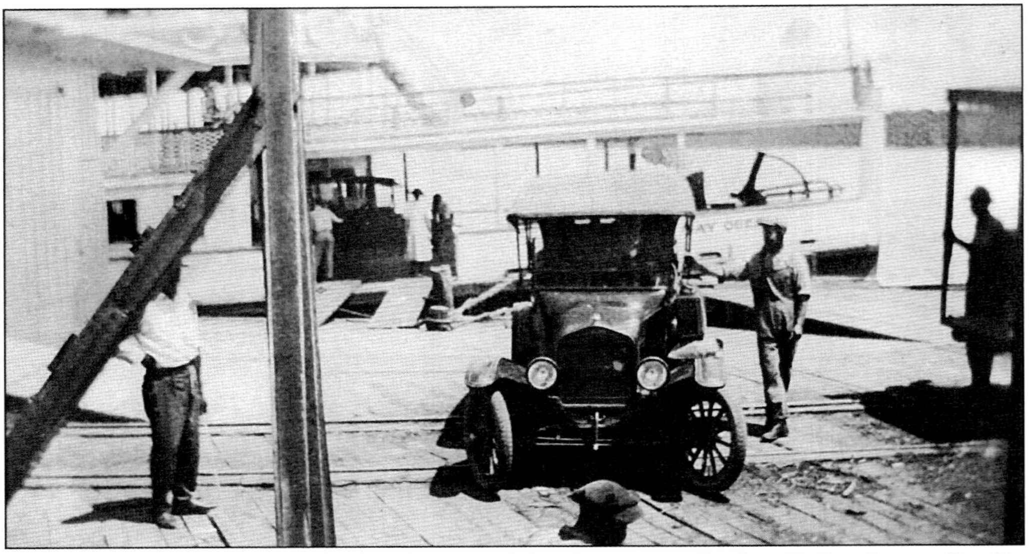

Wharf Handles Wheels. The family automobile of contractor Reuben E. Sundberg rolls off a bay boat in Fairhope after making the trip over from Mobile. Sundberg's wife, Lois, a photographer, probably captured the moment. Early in the century, the steamers had to make adjustments from carrying passengers and freight to handling the new automobiles. (Courtesy of Pinky Bass.)

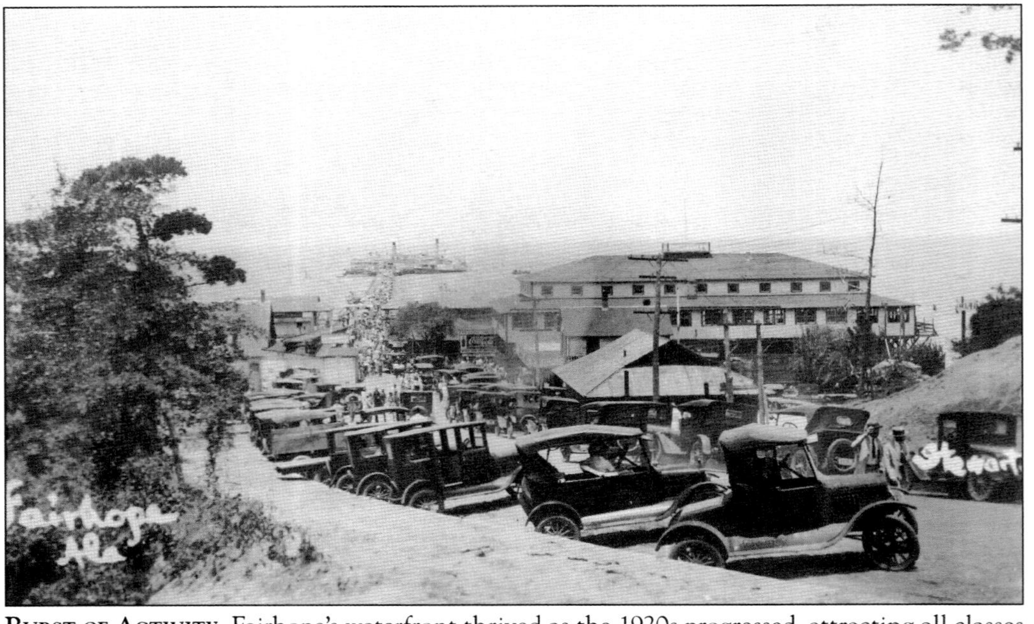

Burst of Activity. Fairhope's waterfront thrived as the 1920s progressed, attracting all classes to the so-called American Riviera. Many were vacationers, and others came for business. As this 1924 view shows, the pier was the center of activity where everyone went to see who arrived on the boats. Even today, Fairhope has a sign there identifying it as the "town square." (Courtesy of Edwin Skinner.)

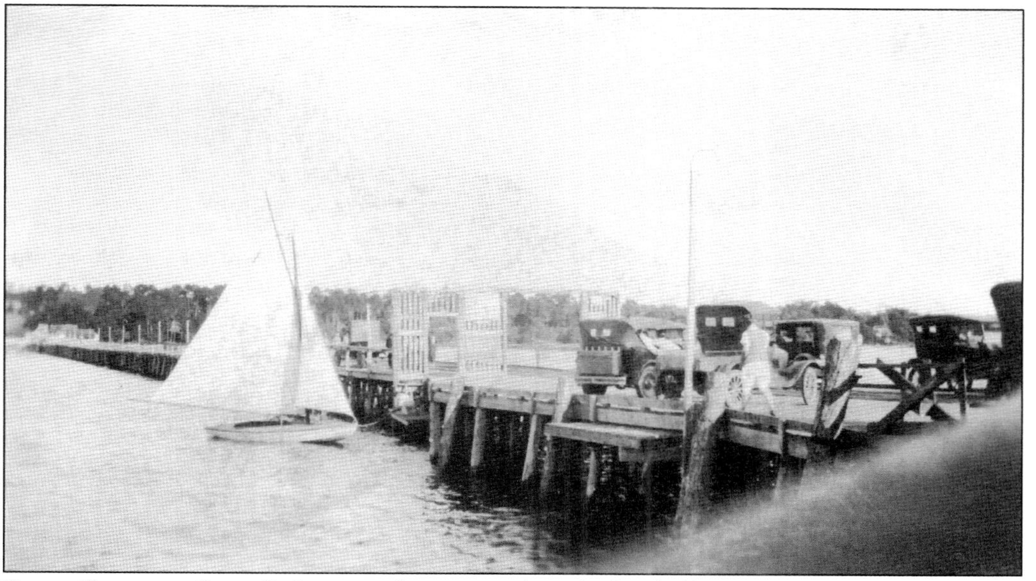

Steam Replaced Sail. Sailing vessels continued to ply the shallow Mobile Bay waters, but bay steamers served the Fairhope wharf until they stopped running during the 1930s. The colony built its own bay boats early in the century, each named *Fairhope*. However, the first one burned in 1905, and the next was dismantled. Many of the steam-powered boats were casualties of fire. (Courtesy of Pinky Bass.)

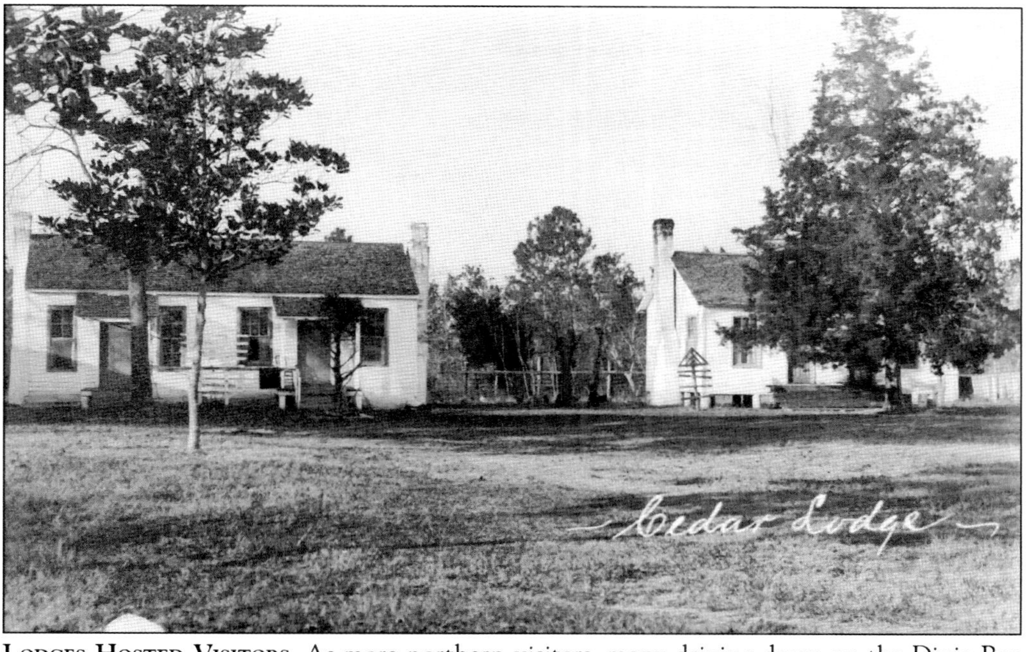

Lodges Hosted Visitors. As more northern visitors, many driving down on the Dixie Bee Line route from Chicago, began arriving to spend their winters on the bay, Fairhope began building accommodations for them. Cedar Lodge is an example of some of the rental tourist lodgings offered in the early days when Fairhope cottages had names, not addresses. (Courtesy of Cathy Donelson.)

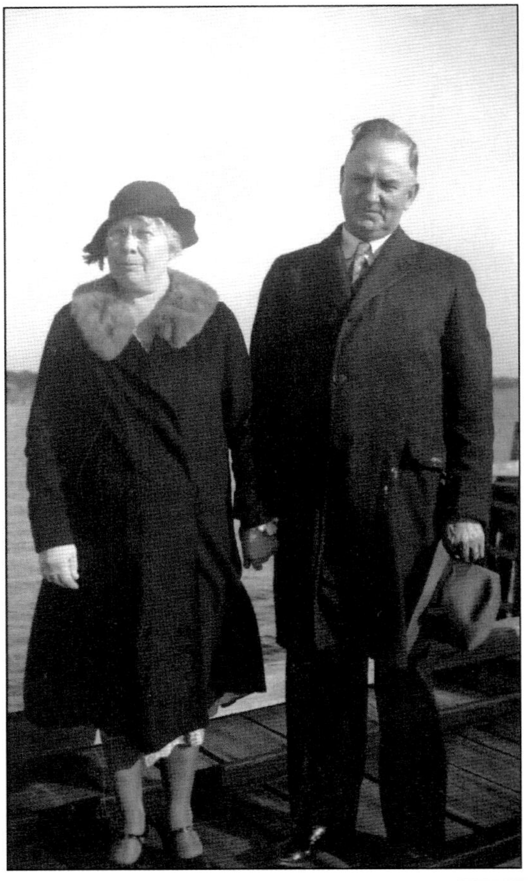

Welcome to Tourists. Peter A. Grassfield, with his wife, Helen, was the "official greeter" for the Fairhope Tourist Club. Their daughter Dorothy would become a central figure in a sensational love-triangle murder in which her husband, prominent Fairhope contractor Raymond Dyson, would kill her lover in 1932 after luring him to the Battle House hotel in Mobile. (Courtesy of Evelyn Evans.)

Fairhope's Premier Resort. The Colonial Inn was the town's most prestigious resort hotel. The imposing structure reigned on the bluff overlooking the bay until being razed in 1992. Built in 1909, it advertised fine dining and gracious service and was a Fairhope social center in addition to catering to visitors from across the country. In later years, it was operated by Ed and Julia Overton. (Courtesy of Edwin Skinner.)

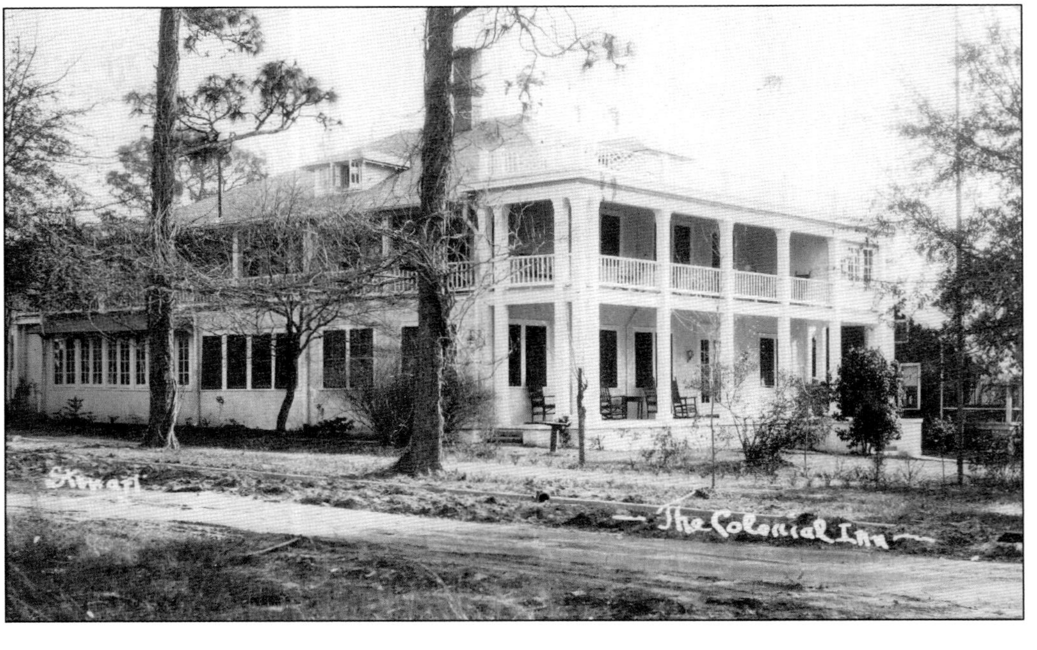

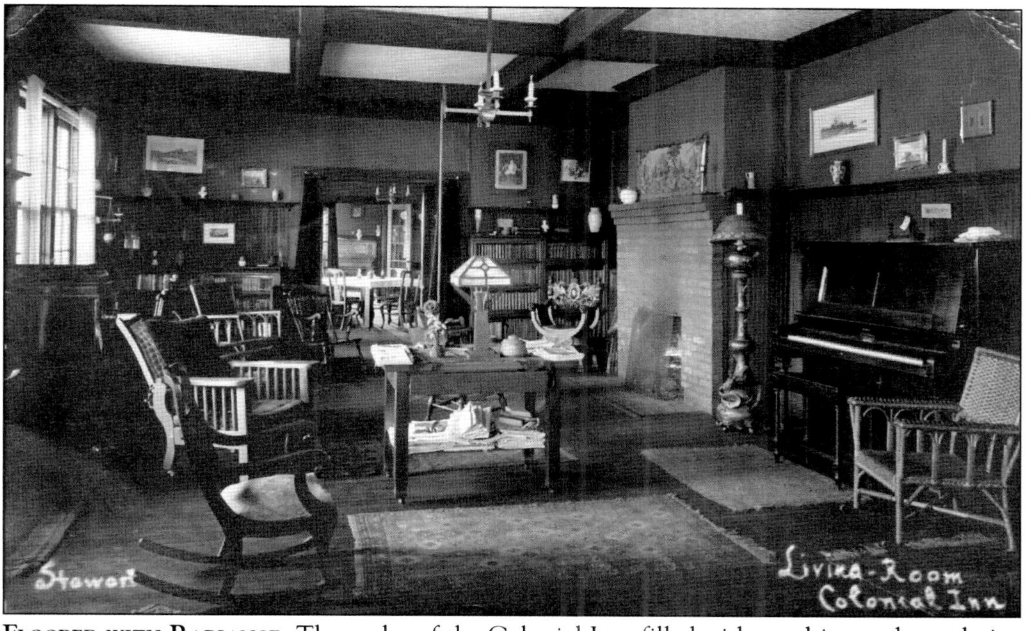

FLOODED WITH RADIANCE. The parlor of the Colonial Inn, filled with sunshine and armchairs, served as a retreat for guests. It also offered a large library for their indoor activity. In the rear was the family-style dining room, where waiters wearing white jackets served the visitors three meals a day. (Courtesy of Edwin Skinner.)

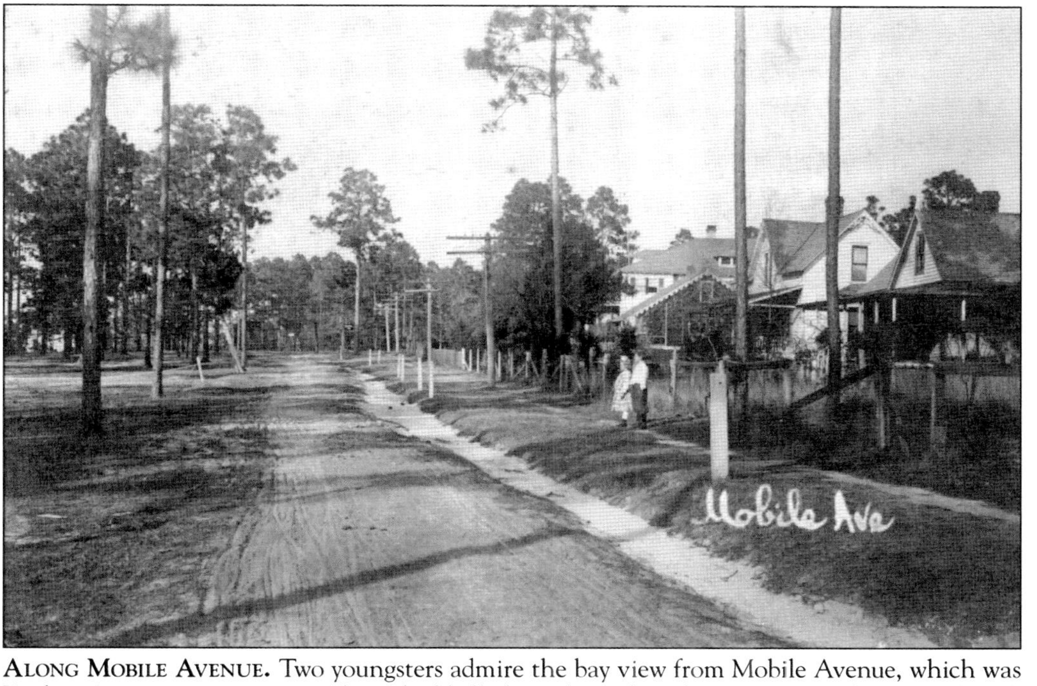

ALONG MOBILE AVENUE. Two youngsters admire the bay view from Mobile Avenue, which was Fairhope's main street running along the bluff where the Colonial Inn was located. The bluff park featured the area's distinctive pine trees, which became a symbol of the community, providing building materials and contributing to the turpentine industry. (Courtesy of FMH.)

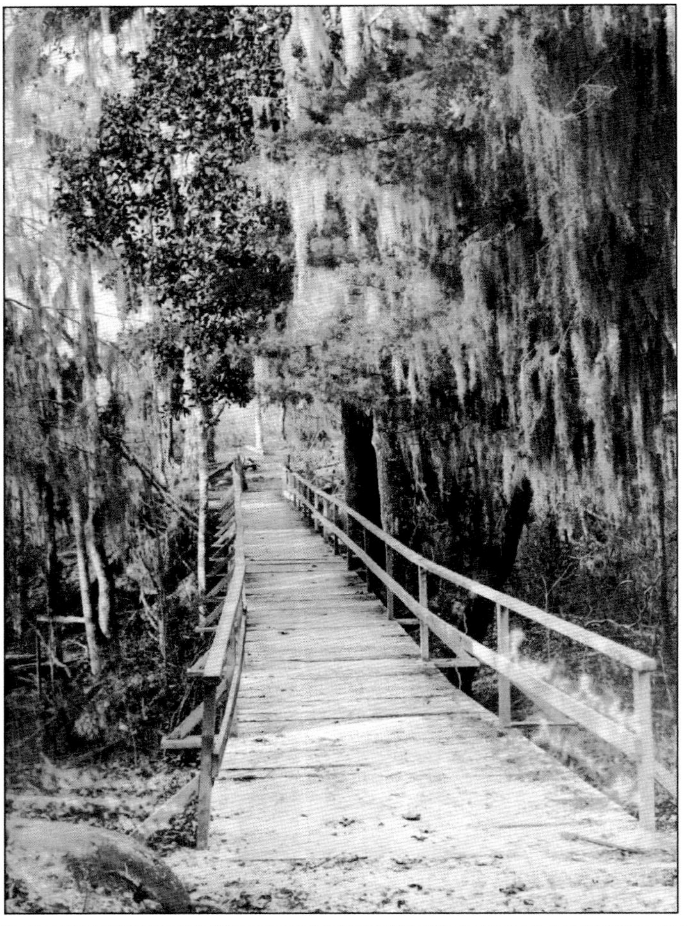

Gullies Considered Beautiful. Fairhopers regarded the waterfront gullies as part of the natural waterfront landscape. They named their gullies and built wooden walkways across them. Everyone strolled "through verdurous glooms and winding mossy ways," as Keats writes in "Ode to a Nightingale." (Courtesy of Reed Myers.)

Footloose in Fairhope. The town's distinctive gullies, which carried rainwater to the bay, also were a means of travel. Most were crossed by footbridges, some more sturdy than others. Here, a woman confidently strides across a narrow boardwalk over Stack's Gully. Fairhope's more reckless young people liked to walk the railings. (Courtesy of WOFC.)

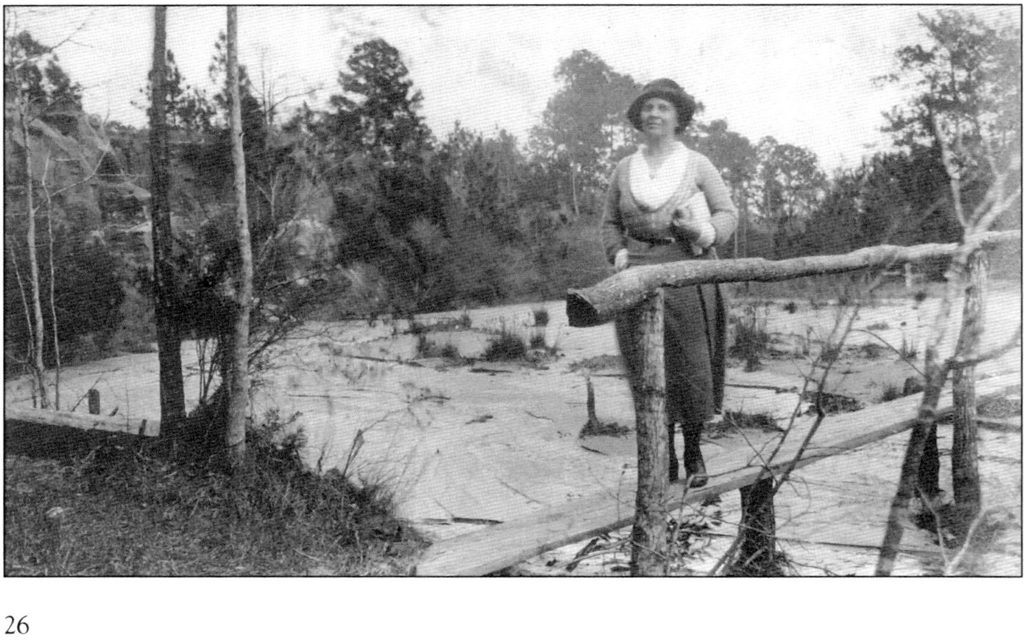

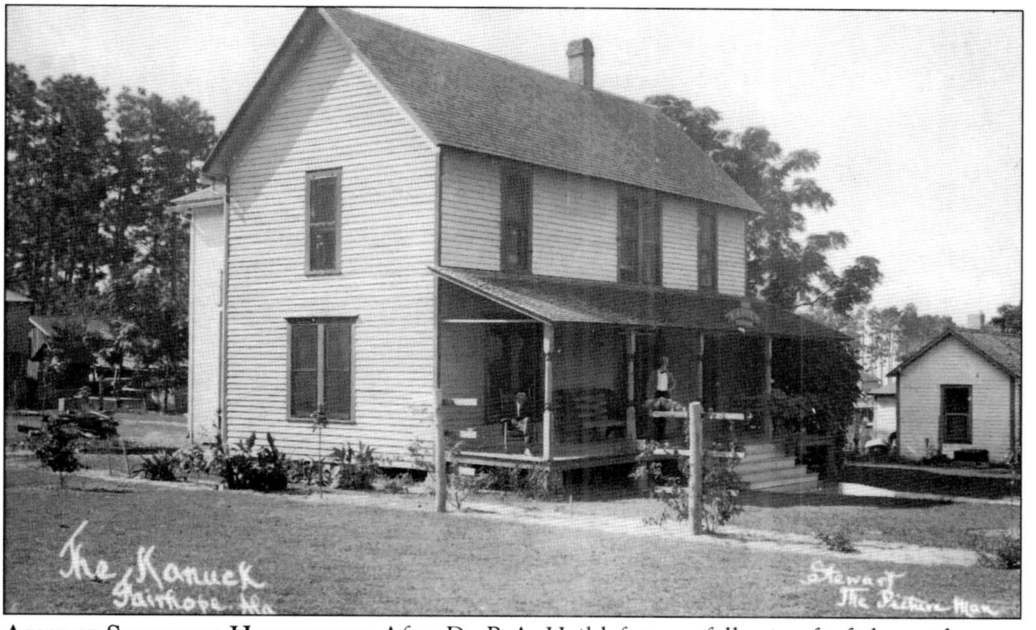

ARMS OF SOUTHERN HOSPITALITY. After Dr. R.A. Hail left town following fistfights with some single-tax leaders over philosophical differences, he sold his home on Fairhope Avenue. It opened as the Kanuck Hotel in 1914, with its name probably chosen to appeal to Canadian guests. Here, some visitors, who paid $1 a day for their stay, lounge on the front porch. (Courtesy of Reed Myers.)

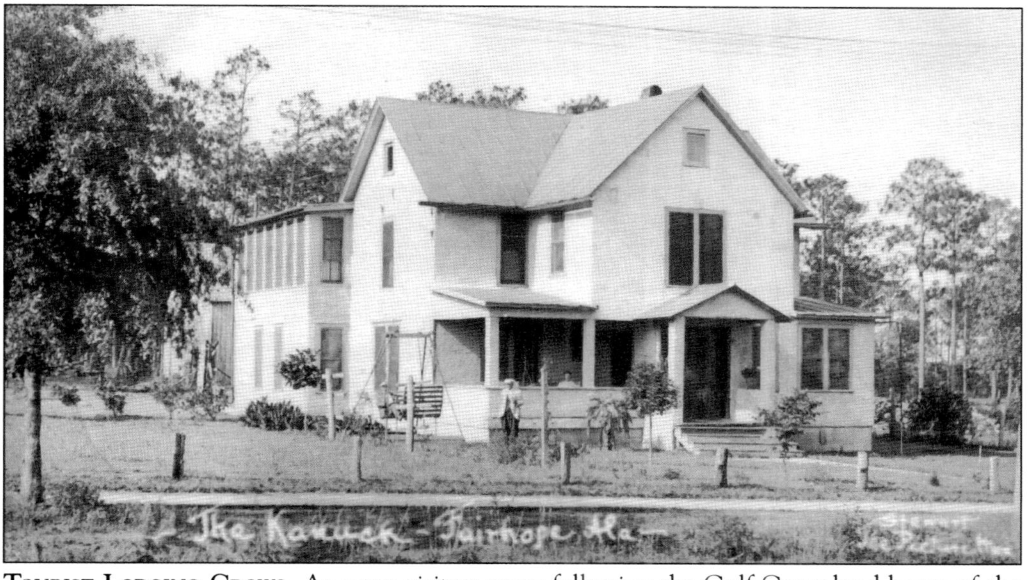

TOURIST LODGING GROWS. As more visitors came following the Gulf Coast land boom of the prosperous 1920s, Fairhopers opened their homes to boarders, and more hotels opened. The Kanuck was expanded with large additions in the front and rear and was coated with the trendy new stucco. (Courtesy of Reed Myers.)

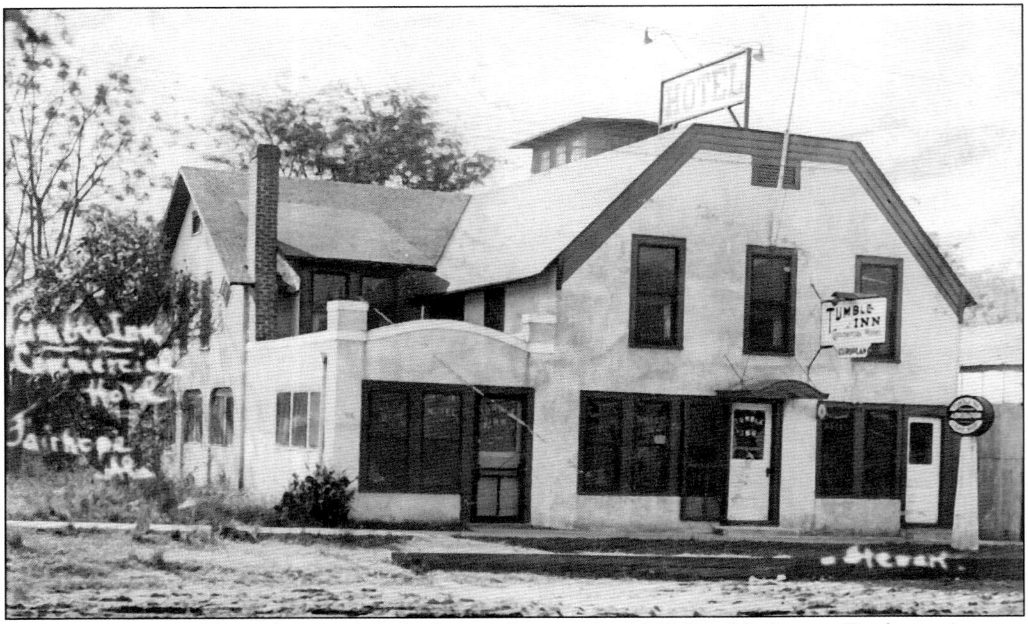

Oldest Hotel in Town. Located in the heart of town, the 1903 Tumble Inn on Fairhope Avenue was the oldest commercial building in Fairhope. It operated as a restaurant for over a century before being demolished in recent years to make way for new construction. Pictured here in 1923, it advertised specials for commercial travelers and offered Sunday dinner for $1. (Courtesy of Cathy Donelson.)

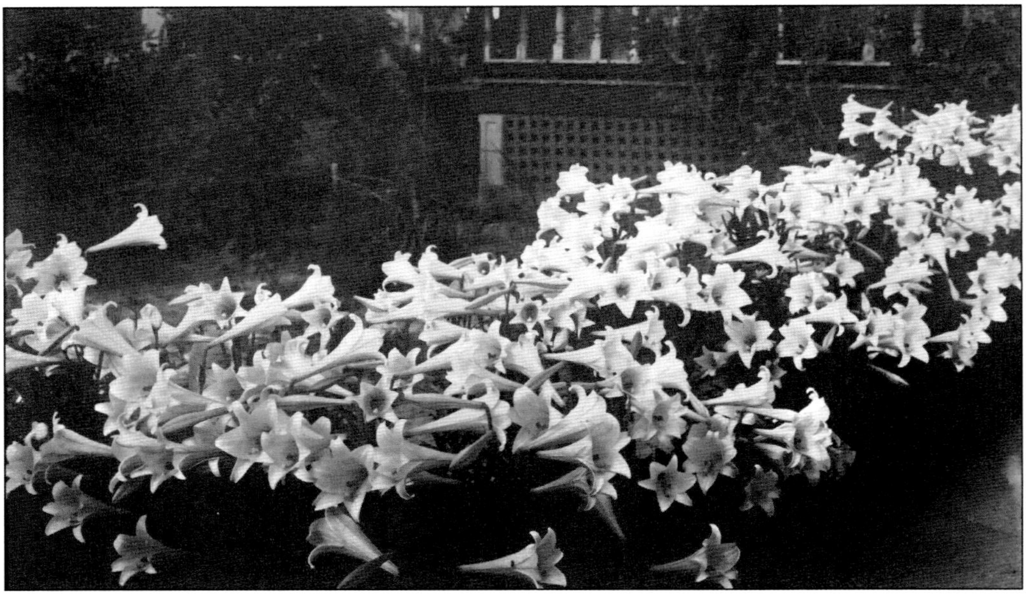

The Pleasure Garden. Part of Fairhope's appeal, besides the large parks and "beautified lands" provided for in the colony's constitution, was its abundance of flowers. From the beginning, the founders were dedicated to having a landscaped city and planted azaleas and trees along the wide streets. Residents vied to have the best gardens, and many growers shipped their cut flowers to northern markets. (Courtesy of Reed Myers.)

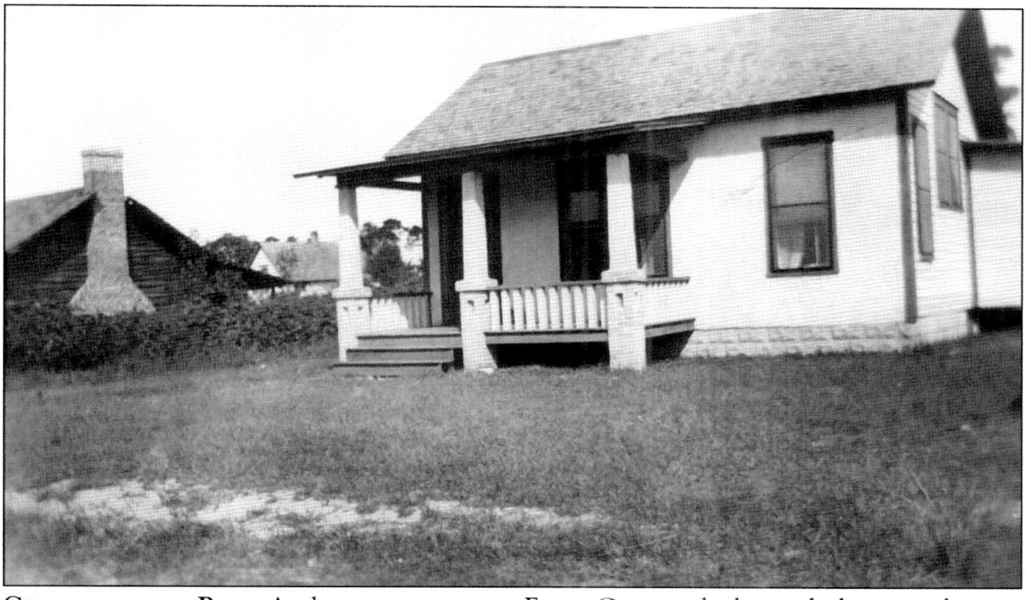

GUESTHOUSES FOR RENT. As the resort town grew, Ernest Gaston, who began dealing in real estate, moved a family residence from Fairhope Avenue back to Delamare Avenue as a rental cottage for newcomers. The log clubhouse in the background was used for community gatherings. The street was previously called "Pig Alley" because of the hogs that ran there. (Courtesy of Claire Gray.)

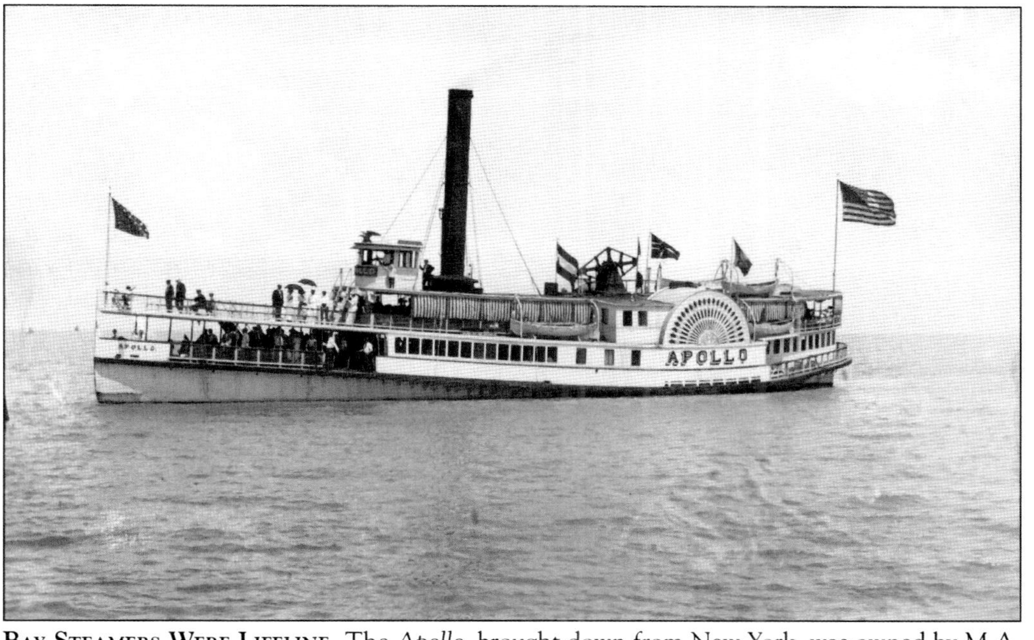

BAY STEAMERS WERE LIFELINE. The *Apollo*, brought down from New York, was owned by M.A. Bowen, who operated the Bayside Casino, and Capt. Ed Roberts. It made daily runs between the Fairhope Wharf and the foot of Dauphin Street in Mobile, where many Chicago tourists disembarked because the railroads offered special excursion rates heading south. (Courtesy of Pinky Bass.)

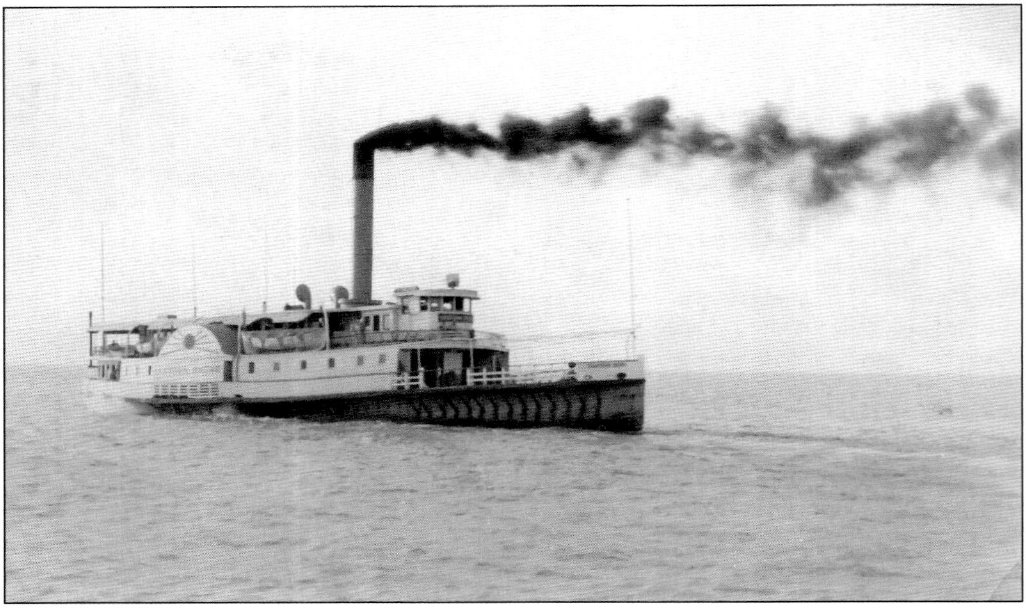

Another New Arrival. The *Eastern Shore*, another bay steamer, was operated by the Fairhope Transportation & Excursion Company starting in 1923. Its deck had to be widened to handle passengers with automobiles—as the famed American jurist Clarence Darrow described them, "Those who had driven their Fords down South to escape the rigors and coal bills of our Northern winters." (Courtesy of MJM.)

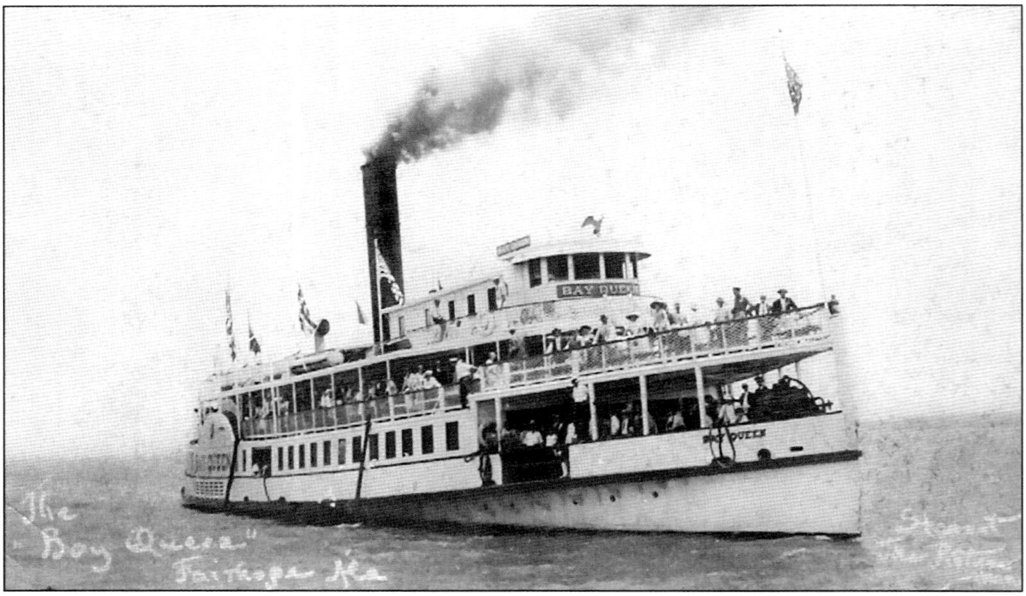

Queen of Mobile Bay. The *Bay Queen* was the biggest and prettiest bay boat, called "as handsome as a bride" by the Fairhope newspaper, which noted in 1922, "Dancing was enjoyed going and coming." The editor's son, Arthur Fairhope Gaston, who had been the first boy born in the new colony, was employed as the first purser. (Courtesy of FMH.)

Three

A Monkey's Uncle

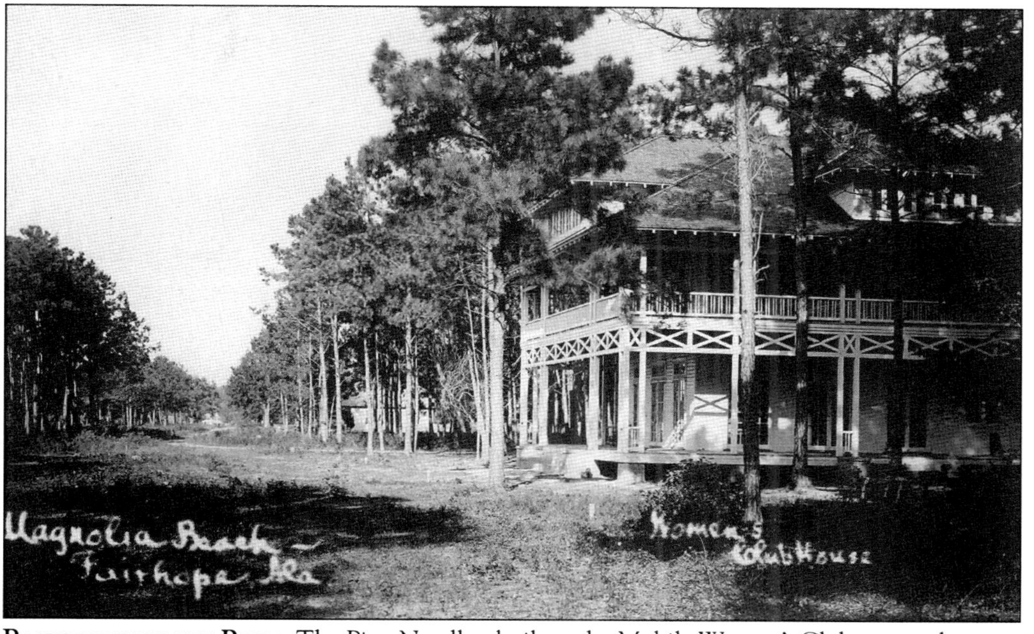

Prohibition in the Pines. The Pine Needles, built as the Mobile Women's Club retreat, became a so-called gentlemen's club in the Roaring Twenties, replete with private rooms and third-story boxing ring. Fairhope did not have any saloons during the Prohibition era, but the liquor flowed freely at many private parties in town. This century-old landmark at 700 South Mobile Street is now the American Legion Post No. 199. (Courtesy of Claire Gray.)

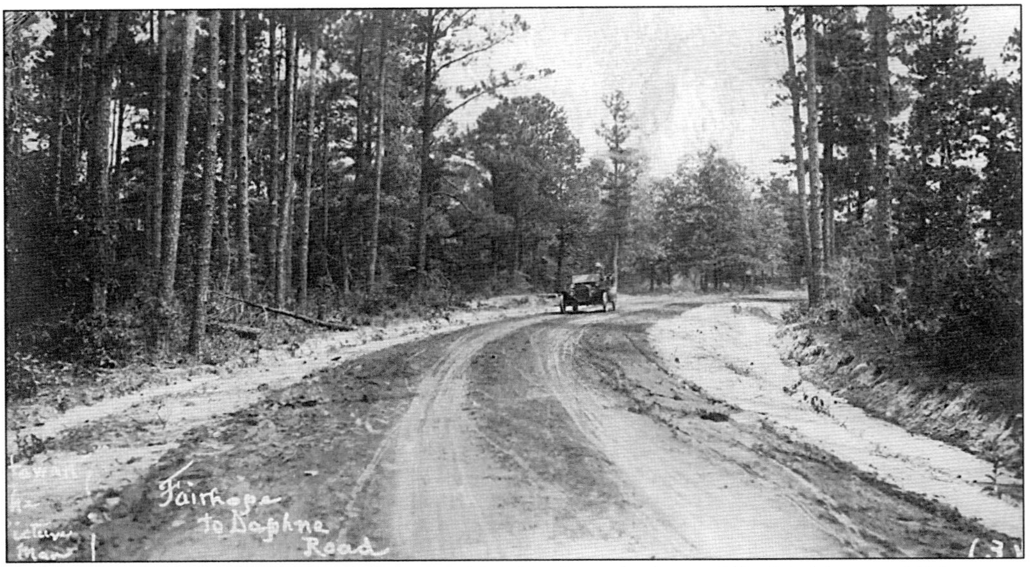

How Dry I Am. Even before Prohibition in 1919, Fairhope had no public drinking establishments. However, alcohol was always available just up the road on the outskirts of town at dance clubs like the Pink Elephant, which later became the Blue Light service station and now operates as a restaurant. Back then, the club also had nightly cabin rentals on its grounds. (Courtesy of Reed Myers.)

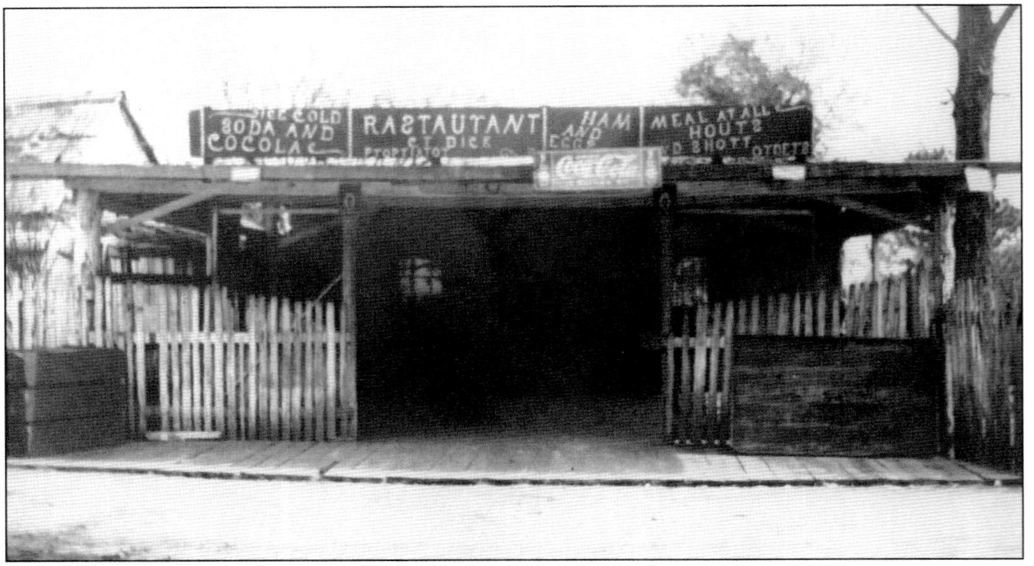

Down Home Speakeasy. Moonshine also could be obtained at rural shot houses offering jazz and blues, like Cuf Dick's honky-tonk restaurant in nearby Daphne. The manufacture and sale of alcohol was illegal, but people often distilled at home. Alabama had outlawed liquor in 1915, along with any beverage that even looked like beer. (Courtesy of George DuBrock collection.)

Hoisting a Toast. Not everyone depended on the massive regional smuggling during the Prohibition era. Here, a dapper young William Jefferson Hearin toasts with a Cuba libre in Havana. The future newspaper publisher had a summer place near Fairhope on the Eastern Shore, as did many well-to-do Mobilians who came over the bay to drink in the resort atmosphere. (Courtesy of Ann Hearin.)

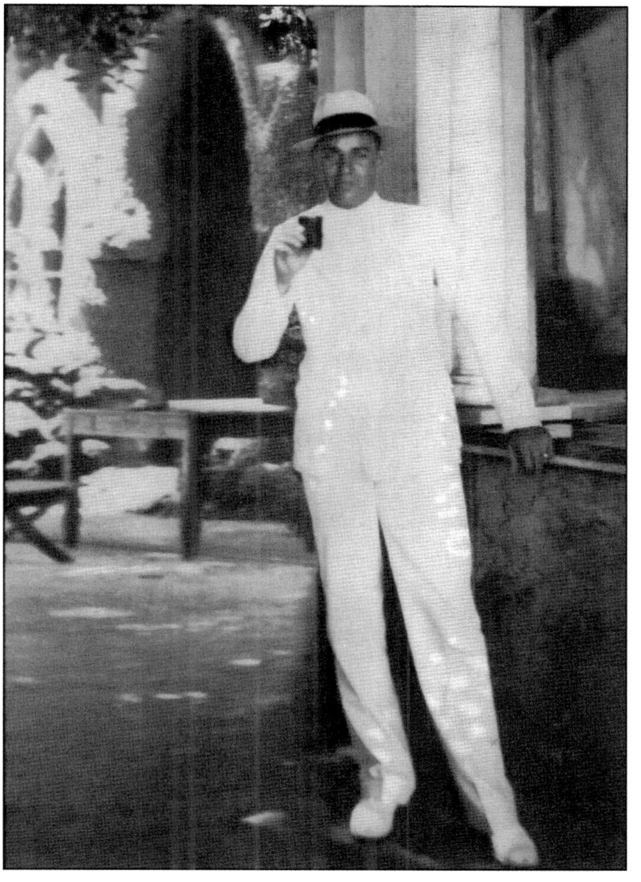

The Offshore Pirate. Fishermen also savored the free-flowing booze along the Gulf Coast, where rumrunners brought it to the three-mile international "Rum Line" to be offloaded to bootleggers. The area was called Rum Row when federal revenuers busted the country's biggest "vicious, lawless" whiskey ring in 1923, confiscating more than 10,000 quarts and arresting the Mobile police chief, sheriff, and 100 others. (Courtesy of Reed Myers.)

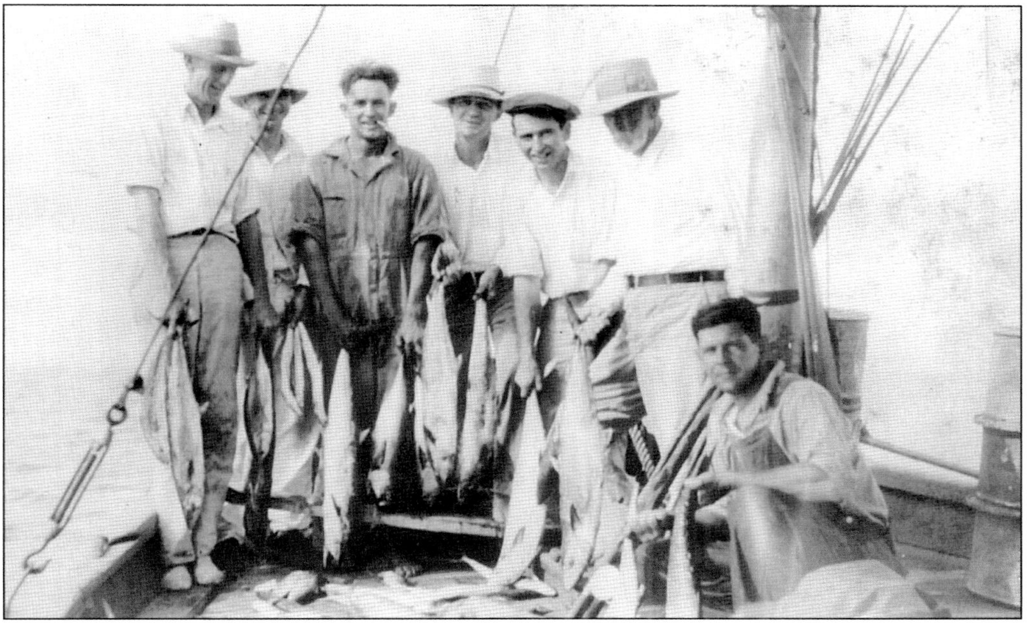

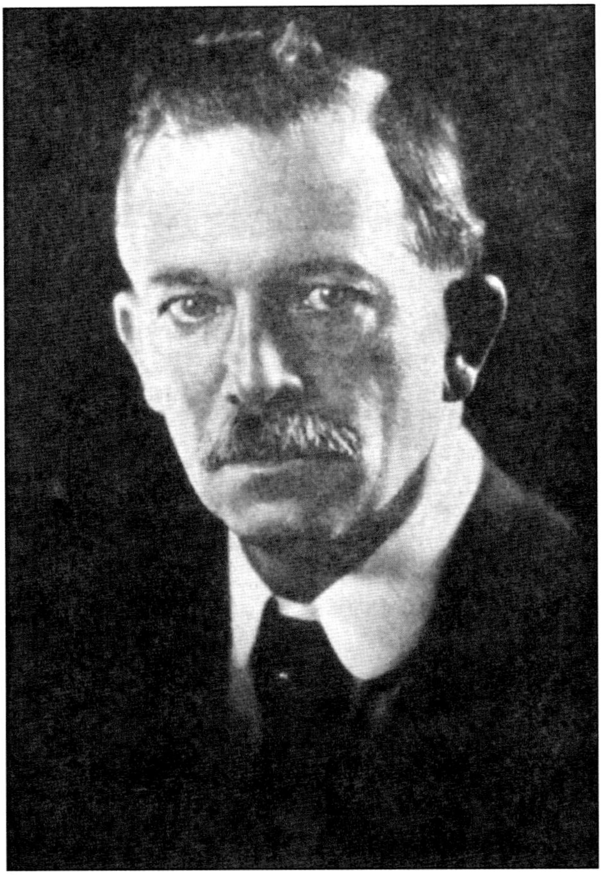

"Dry" Governor Arrested. Deputy Sheriff Barney Wiggins arrested Gov. William "Plain Bill" Brandon in 1926 at a nearby fish camp with a dozen quarts of "fine liquor" and several bottles in a suitcase behind the chair where he sat playing poker. His servant Henry took the rap, but was immediately pardoned by the governor, who had run on a Prohibition ticket. (Courtesy of Marie Bankhead Owen collection.)

Ol' Man River. Area rivers provided cover for rumrunners, and it was on the Magnolia River at McQueen's Fish Camp that the governor's party was busted. "Boys, if you're convicted, all I can do is parole you," Brandon told his companions. Over in Mobile, prosecutors accused future US congressman Frank Boykin of shipping whiskey to the White House and of smuggling a trainload to Chicago, hidden in pine tar barrels. (Courtesy of Cathy Donelson.)

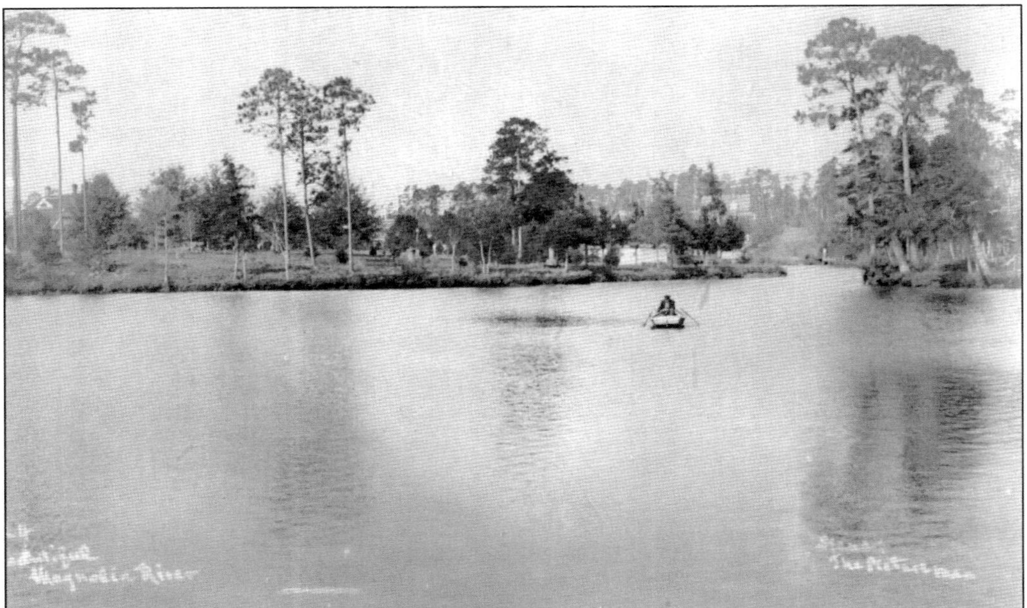

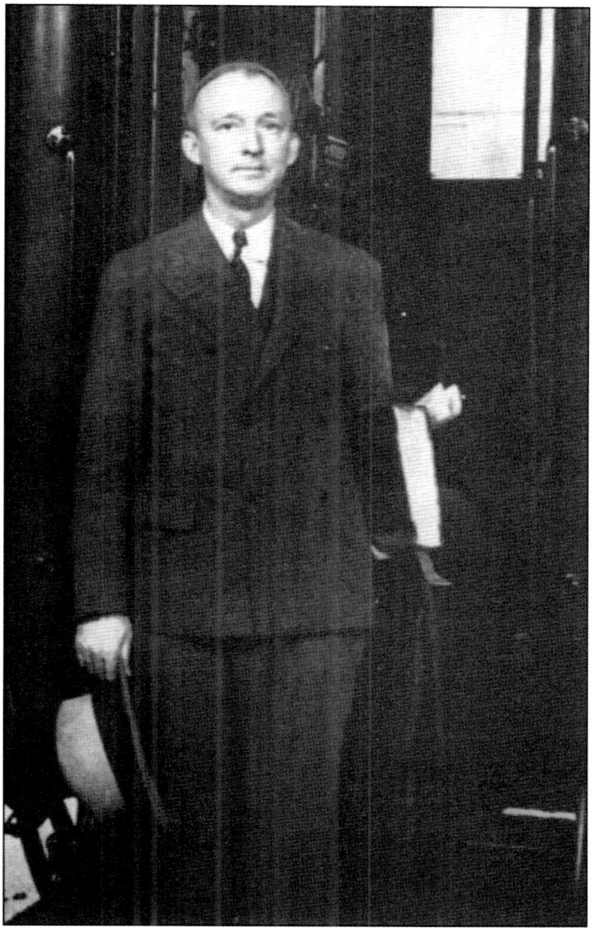

Busting Up the Ring. The Justice Department considered Mobile so corrupt that it sent in a special prosecutor, Hugo L. Black of Birmingham, a future US Supreme Court justice. Black said the area liquor distribution center was so "rotten" that the smell had reached all the way to Washington. (Courtesy of the *Birmingham News*.)

A Necktie Party. This Daphne gang prevented a group of black visitors from using the beach in their town close to Fairhope in the 1920s, when racist and pro-Prohibition forces often joined forces. Hugo Black, who was elected to the US Senate with Klan support he later repudiated, refused to allow Baldwin County residents on his jury for the big bootlegging trial in Mobile. (Courtesy of George DuBrock collection.)

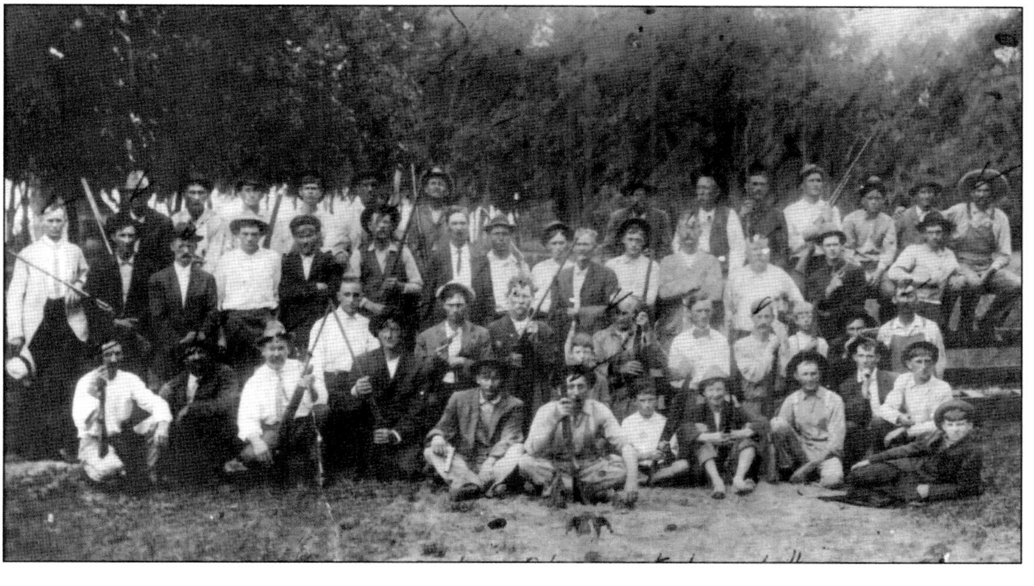

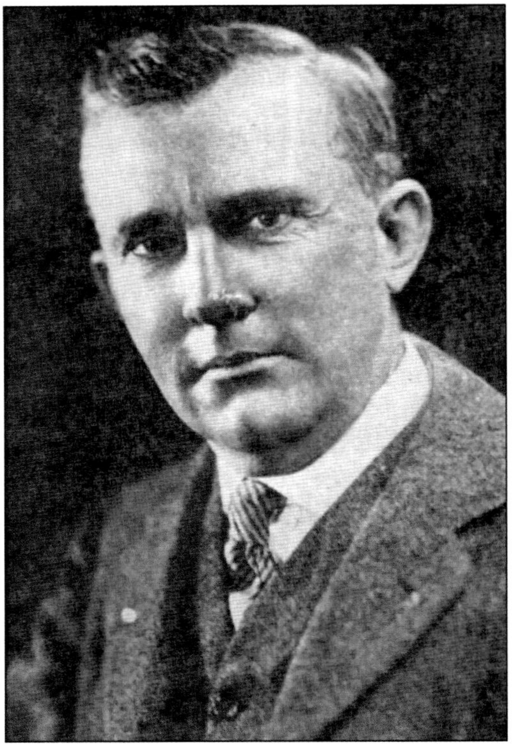

ANOTHER KLAN POLITICIAN. Bibb Graves, who succeeded "Plain Bill" as governor of Alabama, was elected in 1926 with KKK support but later cracked down on the organization after it turned violent with floggings. The *Fairhope Courier* editorialized against the violence, urging the governor to take a stand, while the county seat, Bay Minette, hosted a Klan picnic and fair. (Courtesy of Marie Bankhead Owen collection.)

MONKEY TRIAL CAPTIVATES COUNTRY. After Clarence Darrow, left, and William Jennings Bryan clashed in the "trial of the century" over the teaching of evolution, Darrow came to Fairhope to rest in the winter of 1927. While in town, the longtime KKK opponent became a Klan target after giving a rousing speech on civil rights at the black Eastern Shore Industrial School. (Courtesy of Library of Congress.)

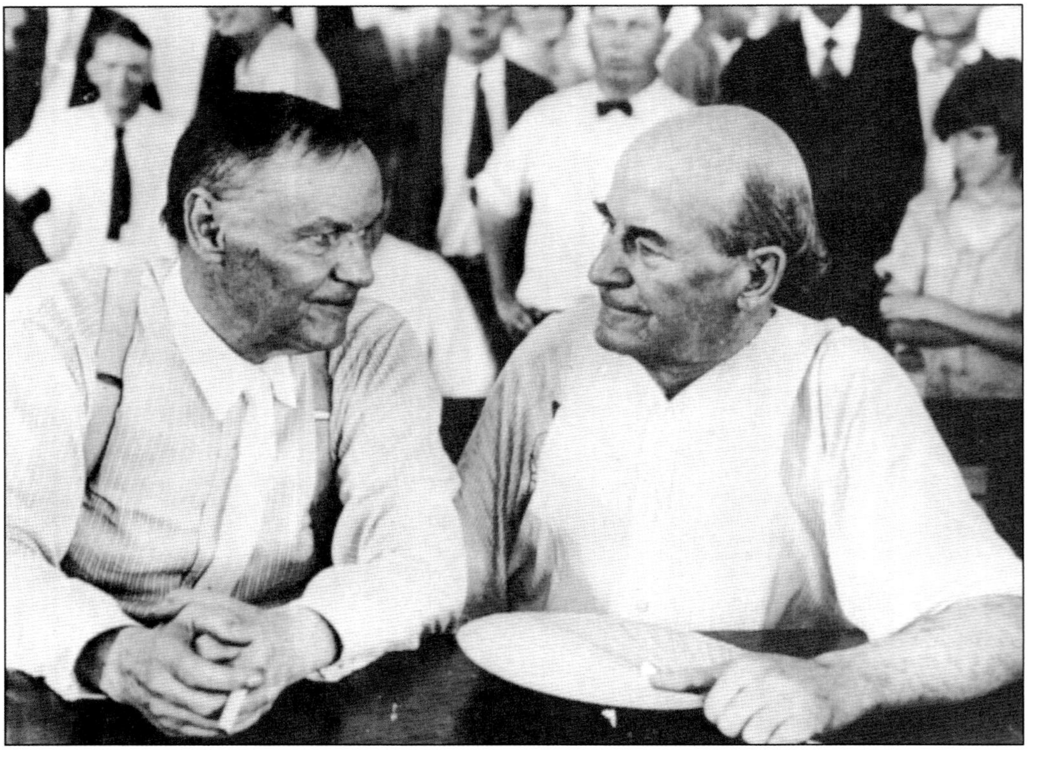

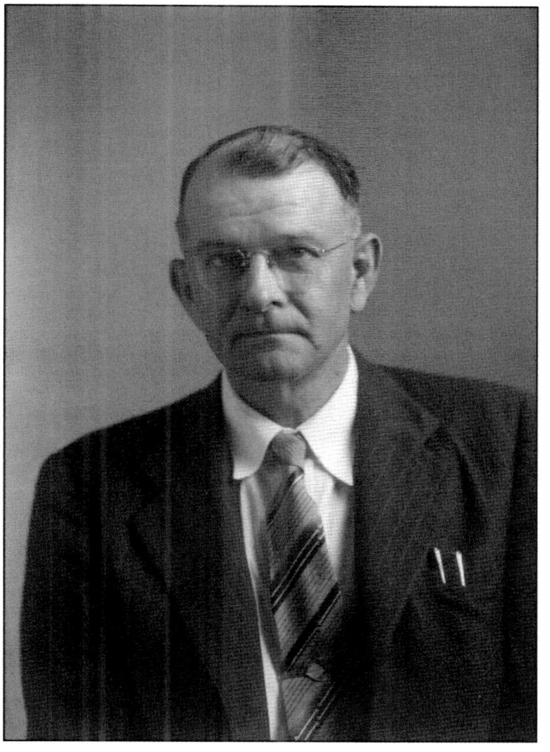

MONKEY ON HIS BACK. Jack H. Titus, the town marshal, was well known for carrying his pet monkey around on his back. While there was a lot of civic unrest following Darrow's controversial speech, with *Time* magazine reporting that the noted lawyer was run out of town, there is no record of Titus making any arrests. (Courtesy of Matt Green.)

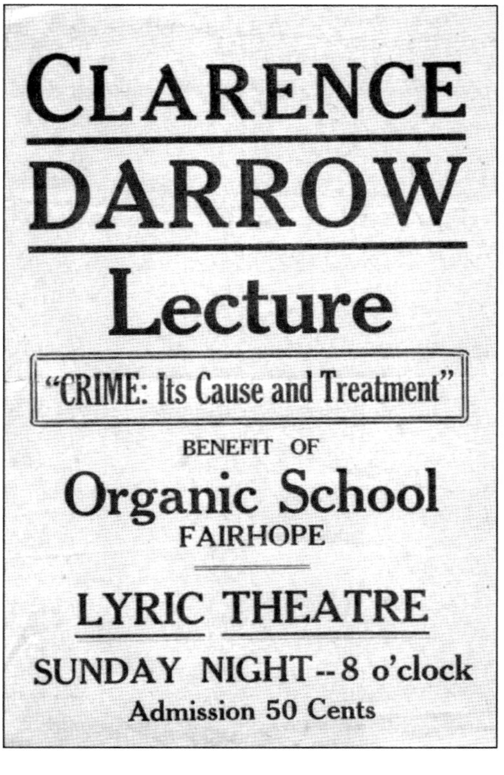

CLARENCE DARROW LECTURES. While in Fairhope, Darrow gave several lectures to benefit the town's progressive School of Organic Education. This poster is from his well-attended talk at the Lyric Theater in Mobile. He also spoke in Fairhope, lecturing on his favorite author, Leo Tolstoy. He frequently visited the school, reading Tolstoy to the students and posing for art classes. (Courtesy of Claire Gray.)

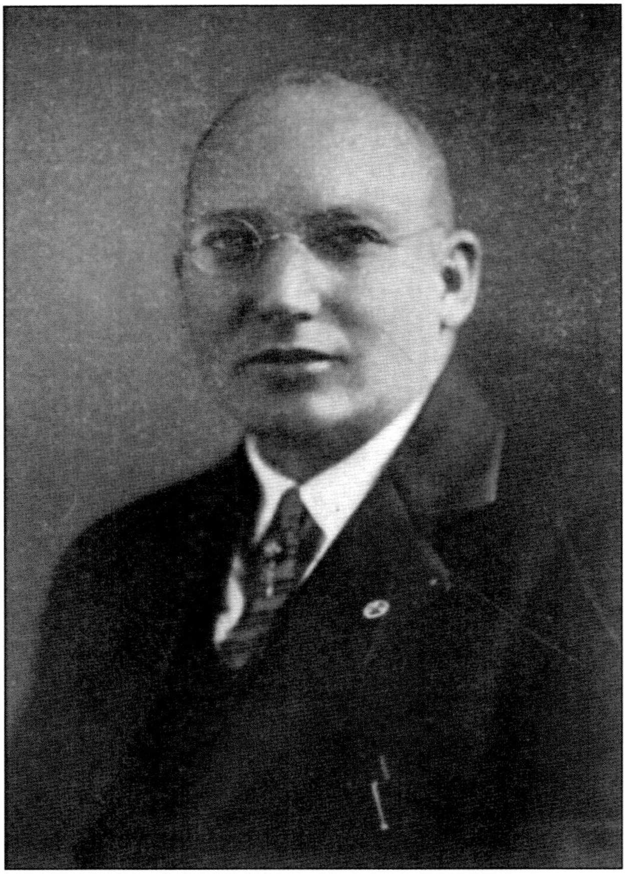

Fairhope Klan Leader. According to a relative who saved his KKK memorabilia, Dr. Claude G. Godard was the grand cyclops of the local Klan. During the 1920s, when the group had its second emergence, claiming several million white, Protestant members nationally, many prominent citizens such as doctors and preachers took leading roles. (Courtesy of Marie Bankhead Owen collection.)

Busy Fairhope Corner. The building that housed Dr. Godard's office and drugstore still stands at the southwest corner of Fairhope Avenue and Summit Street. Part of Godard's residence can be seen to the far right. It is located across the street from where Darrow lodged at a hotel run by his friend and fellow philosopher Capt. Jack Cross, an Englishman. (Courtesy of FMH.)

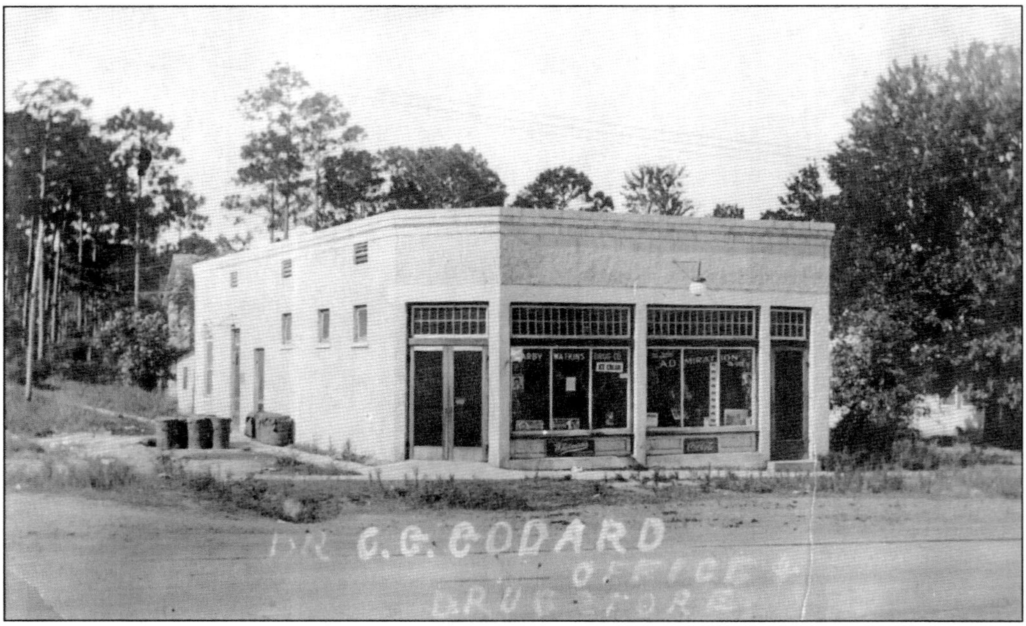

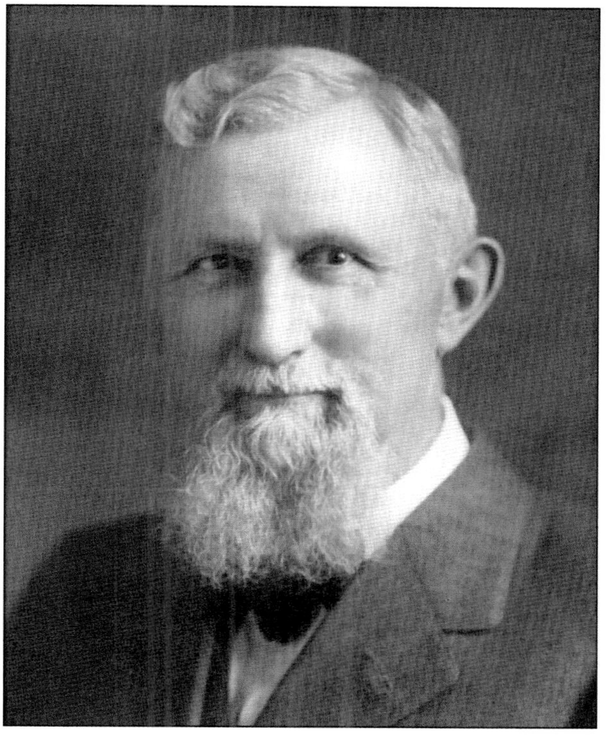

Opposing the Klan. Thomas Hunt Molton was a Birmingham millionaire and real estate baron who retired to Fairhope. When the Klan burned several crosses in Fairhope in the mid-1920s, Molton was vocal in his outrage. An avid horseman, he buried his favorite mount, Old Prince, with a large obelisk at his Lone Pine estate on the corner of Fairhope Avenue and Ingleside Street. (Courtesy of Birmingham Public Library.)

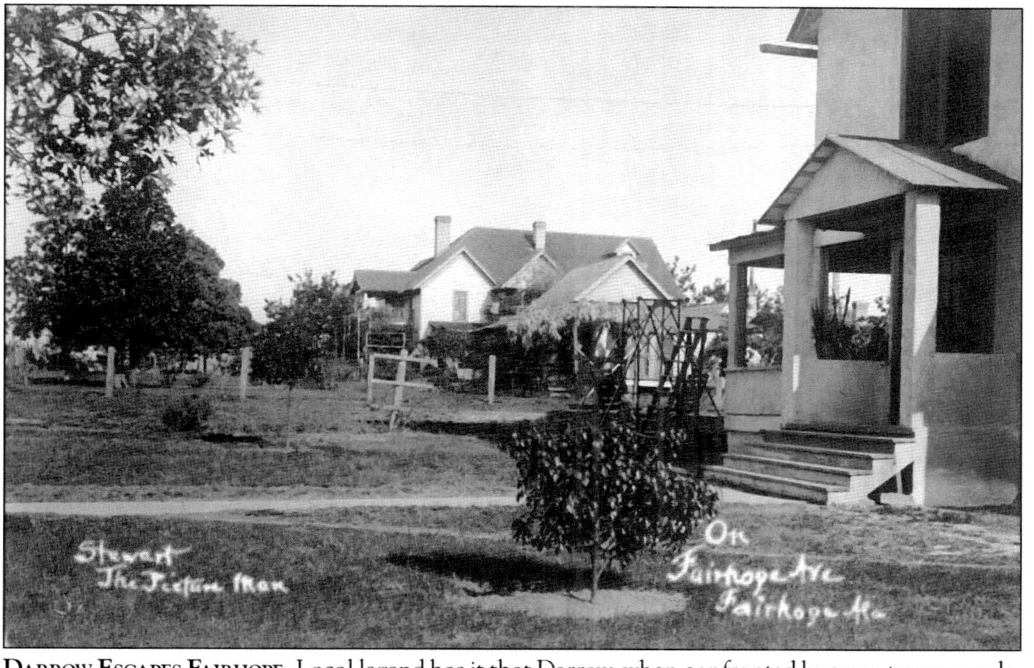

Darrow Escapes Fairhope. Local legend has it that Darrow, when confronted by some townspeople, left his hotel through the back entrance and made his escape up Fairhope Avenue. He arrived here at the home of Dr. Volney M. Schowalter (no longer standing) and was later spirited across Mobile Bay by friends, and left on a Louisville & Nashville Railroad train. (Courtesy of Reed Myers.)

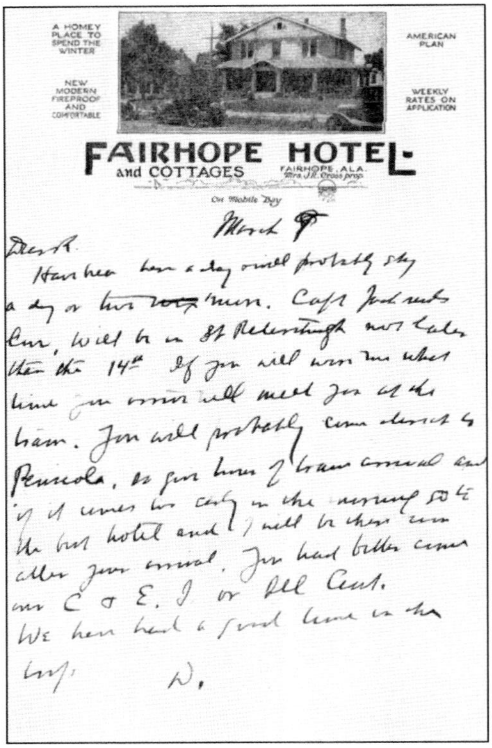

A HOMEY PLACE TO SPEND THE WINTER

NEW MODERN FIREPROOF AND COMFORTABLE

AMERICAN PLAN

WEEKLY RATES ON APPLICATION

FAIRHOPE HOTEL and COTTAGES

FAIRHOPE, ALA. Mrs. J.R. Cross prop.

On Mobile Bay

March 9

We have had a good time on this trip.

D.

LAWYER IS NOT DAUNTED. Despite his earlier misadventures, Darrow returned to Fairhope the next year. On this March 9, 1928, note on Fairhope Hotel stationery, he writes to his wife, Ruby, that Captain Jack sends his love. "We have had a good time on this trip," he wrote from Fairhope, where he had more supporters than detractors. The Fairhope Hotel still stands, now used as an office building. (Courtesy of University of Minnesota Law Library.)

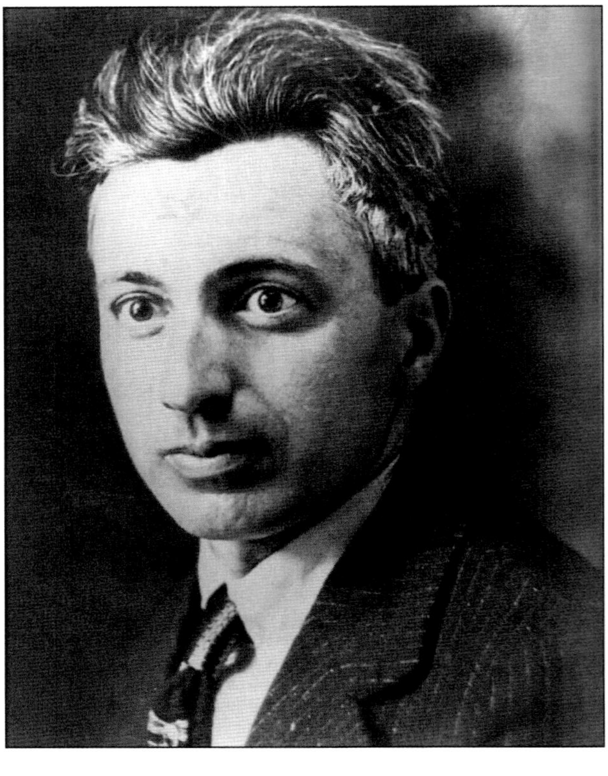

MONKEY TRIAL ENGINEERED. George Rappelyea, the Dayton, Tennessee, engineer who was responsible for creating the divisive so-called Monkey Trial for publicity, afterward moved to Mobile, where he was a boat designer. He visited often and addressed the Fairhope Forum in 1926, speaking on the trial and his belief in evolution. (Courtesy of University of Tennessee.)

Four

Ain't We Got Fun?

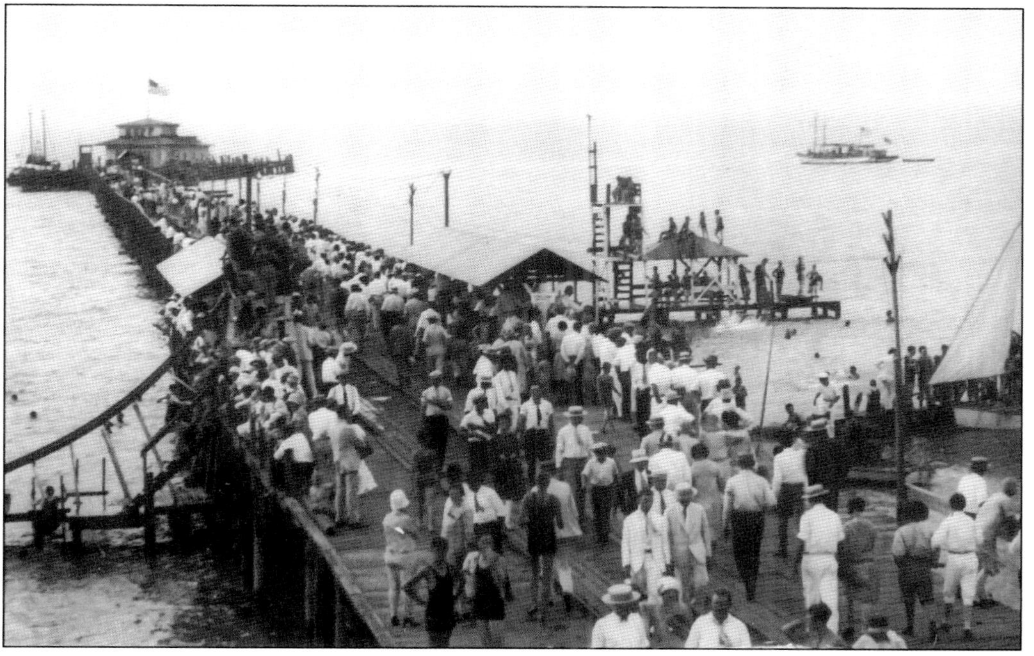

Crowds Congregate on Pier. Visitors flooded Fairhope's public wharf where the bay boats brought hundreds to enjoy dancing, swimming, and waterfront enjoyment, especially on holidays. Bathing attire, which would have been scandalous during the previous decade and remained so in many other places, was accepted in the tolerant resort town during the Rcaring Twenties. The pier remains the town's most popular promenade. (Courtesy of FMH.)

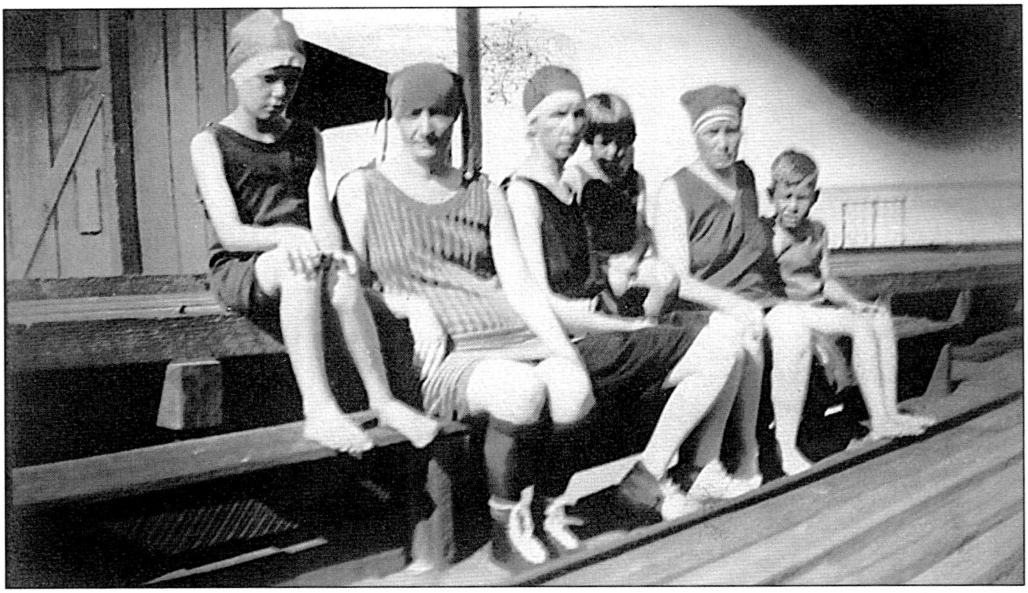

Watching the World Go By. Wearing vintage rubber swimming caps and bathing shoes, this group takes a break on the Fairhope pier. They are, from left to right, Frances Sundberg, a Mrs. McLaughlin, Nell Slosson (the children's aunt), Ruth Sundberg, Lois Sundberg (the children's mother), and Edwin Sundberg. The family had come to Fairhope from Mobile to visit the children's grandparents on the Slosson side. (Courtesy of Pinky Bass.)

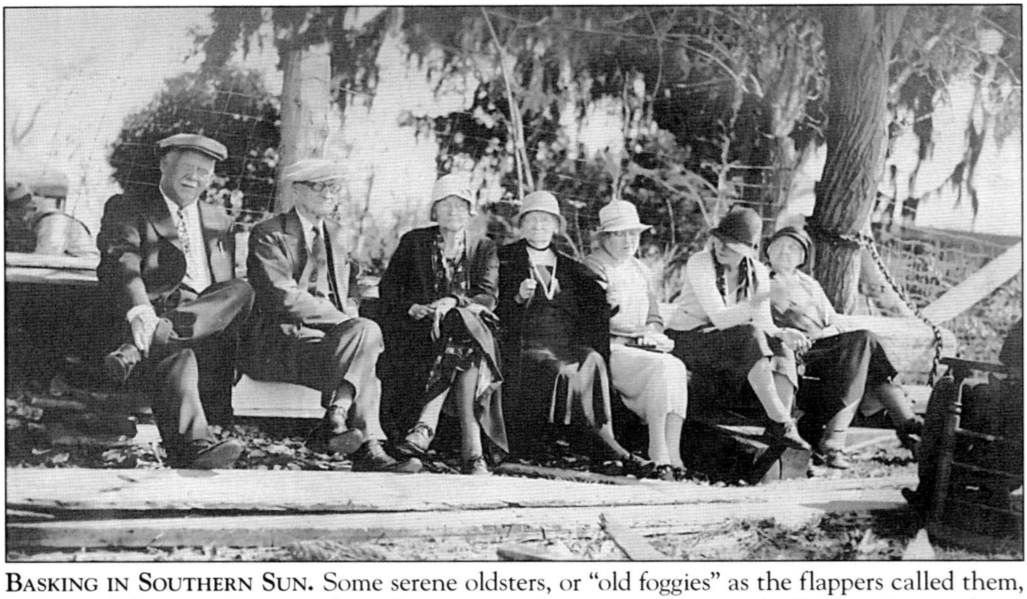

Basking in Southern Sun. Some serene oldsters, or "old foggies" as the flappers called them, gather in balmy weather to soak up the sun near the moss-strung trees by Fairhope's waterfront. Fairhope attracted an older crowd during the winter months and still has a snowbird season during which people from northern states flock to the Gulf area. (Courtesy of WOFC.)

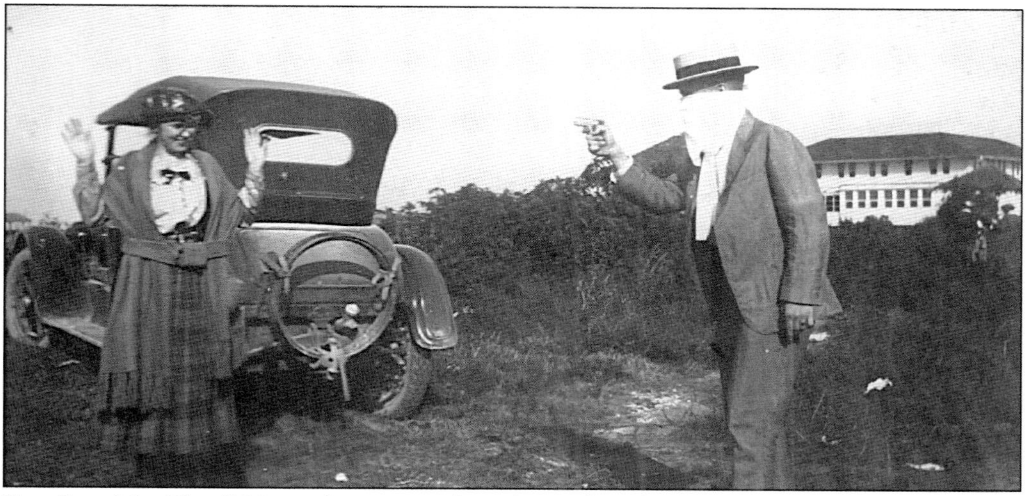

YOU SLAY ME. The 1920s, evolving around a culture of youth, developed its own new slang, due in part to the rising popularity of the gangster movies coming out of Hollywood. Here, a couple clowns for the camera, with the Fairhope Casino by the pier visible in the background. The pistol may or may not be real. (Courtesy of FMH.)

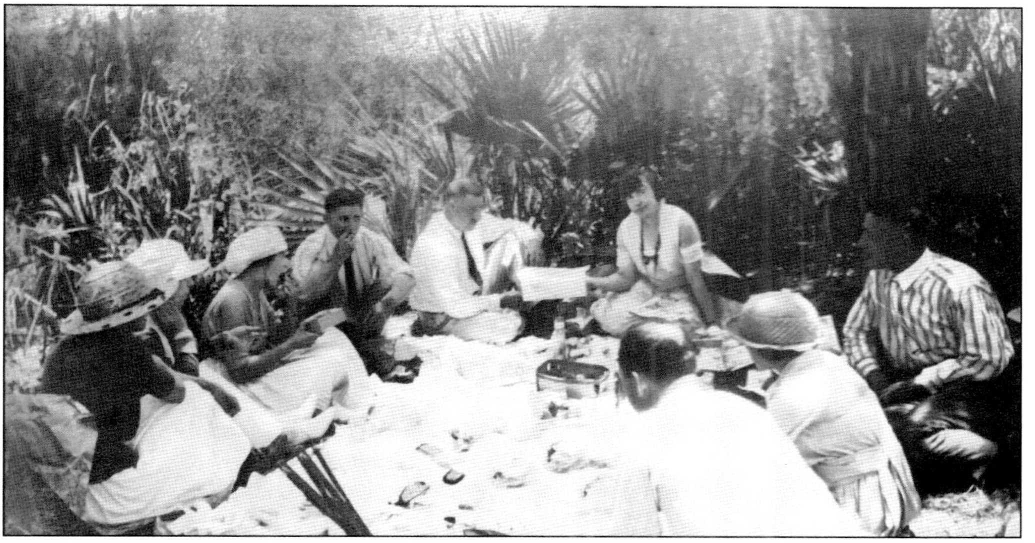

PICNIC IN THE PALMETTOS. This family having a relaxed beach picnic in the bay breezes, with the locally plentiful palmetto fronds framing their party, did not have to worry about sand blowing in their food. They may very well have driven in a "breezer," as many of the new convertibles of the period were called. (Courtesy of FMH.)

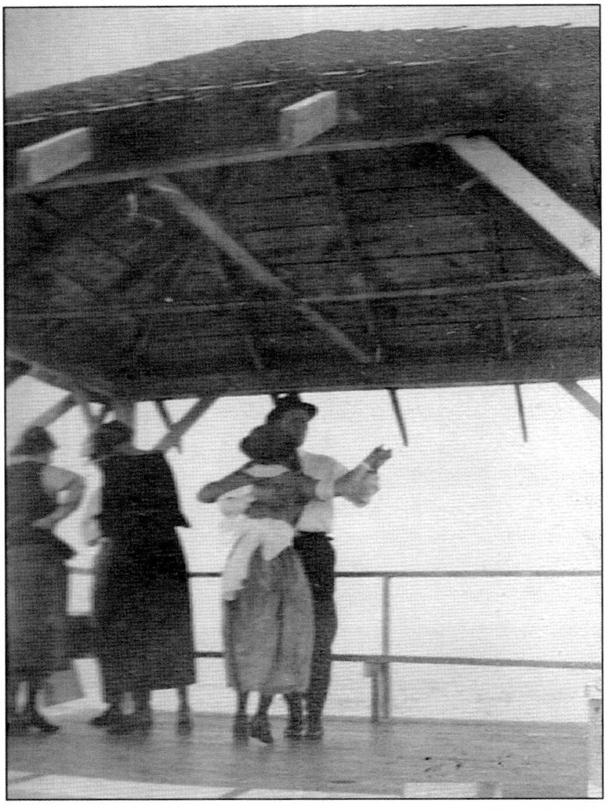

Just You, Just Me. An intimate pavilion provided a secluded spot for dancing on Fairhope's beach. The Roaring Twenties ushered in the Jazz Age, with new dances and music becoming the latest rage. Fairhope featured two large dance clubs with orchestras, but these dancers apparently prefer their private party. (Courtesy of FMH.)

Patent Medicine High Jinks. Fairhope's costume parties were often elaborate, as demonstrated at this patent medicine–themed gala at the Colonial Inn. The old so-called patent medicines were not regulated during the 1920s, and many contained drugs and opiates and alcohol, despite Prohibition. They did not cure any ailments, but probably did help people feel no pain. (Courtesy of WOFC.)

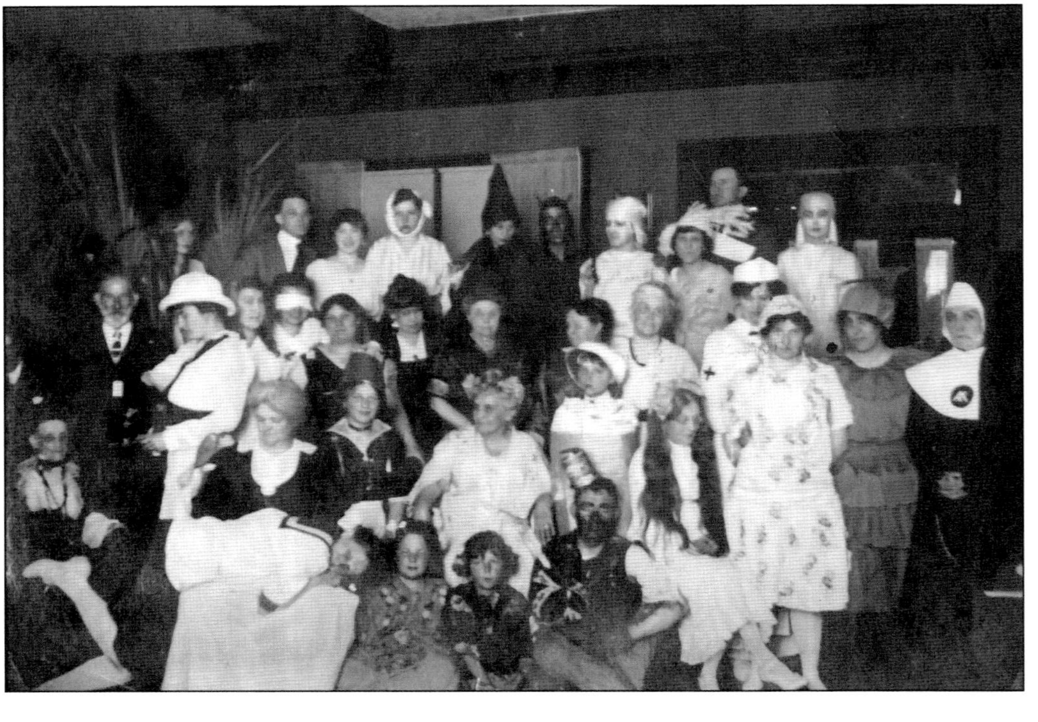

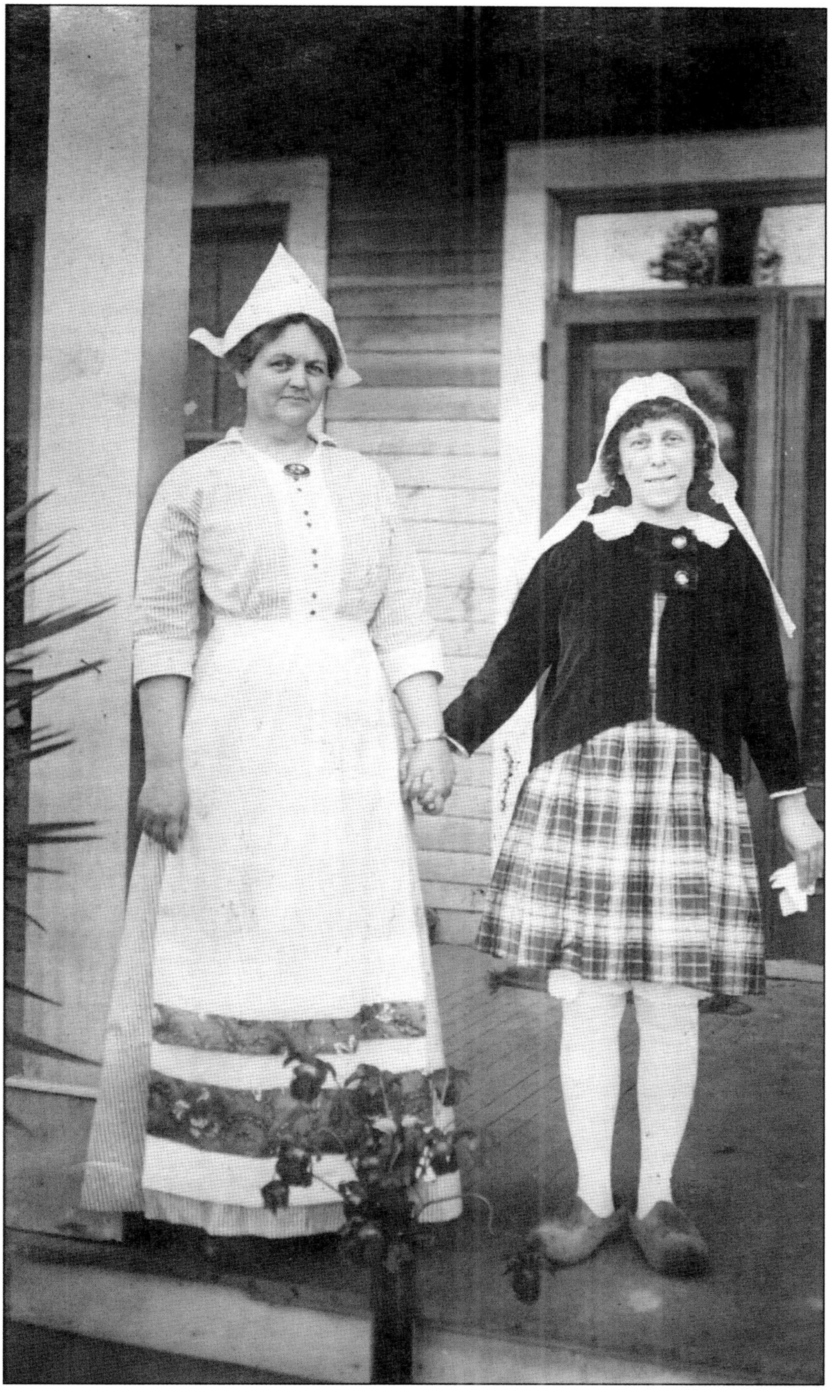

Going Dutch to Party. Fairhopers loved costume parties and looked for any occasion to have them. They often went all out, issuing specially printed invitations complete with a listing of the menu. Here, two partygoers get into the swing of things with their Dutch costumes. (Courtesy of WOFC.)

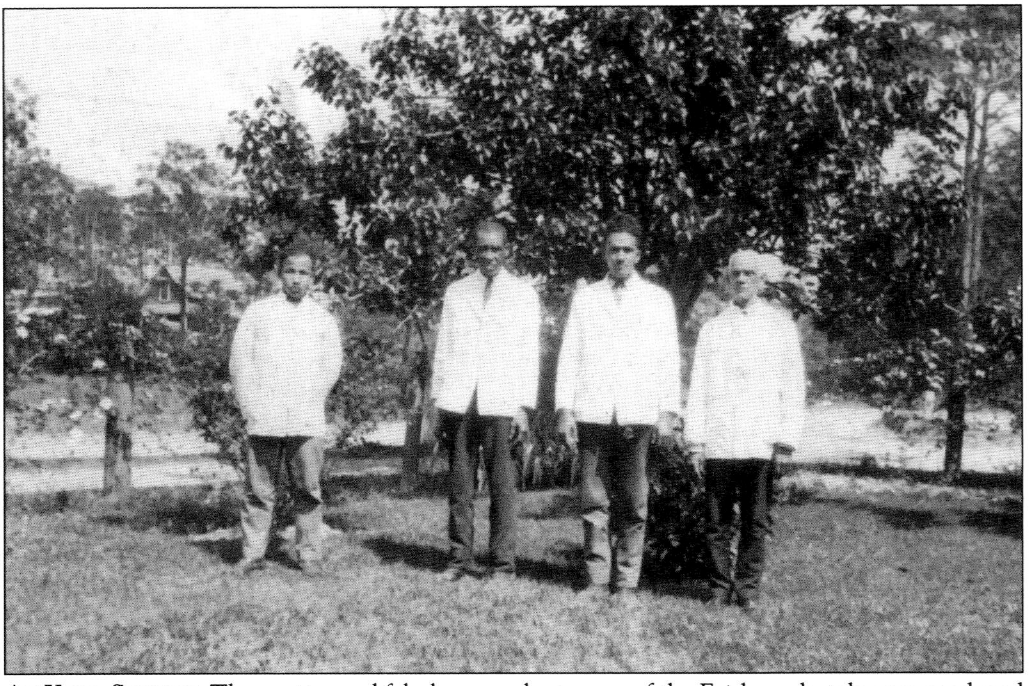

AT YOUR SERVICE. The parties and fabulous meals at some of the Fairhope hotels were produced by servants and waiters who lived in the area. They prepared the home-cooked dishes and served the iced drinks to guests on the shaded porches of local hotels. These uniformed servers worked at the Colonial Inn in the 1920s. (Courtesy of WOFC.)

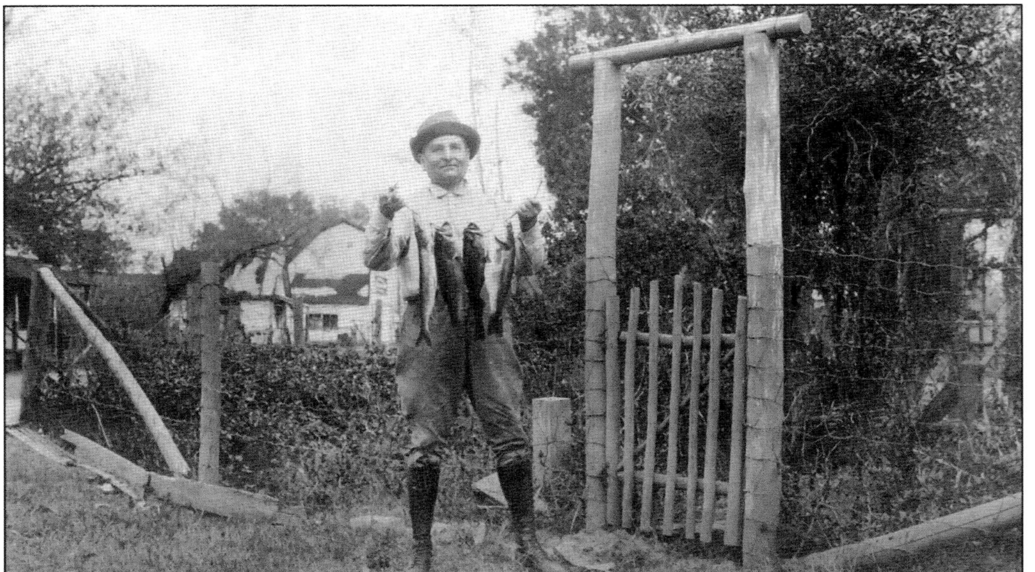

NICE STRING OF FISH. An angler proudly displays his catch of the day in Fairhope, where guided fishing expeditions were a cottage industry for many of the locals. Today, there is still good fishing off the public piers. Some town gift shops sell stickers saying, "Fairhope, a drinking town with a fishing problem." (Courtesy of WOFC.)

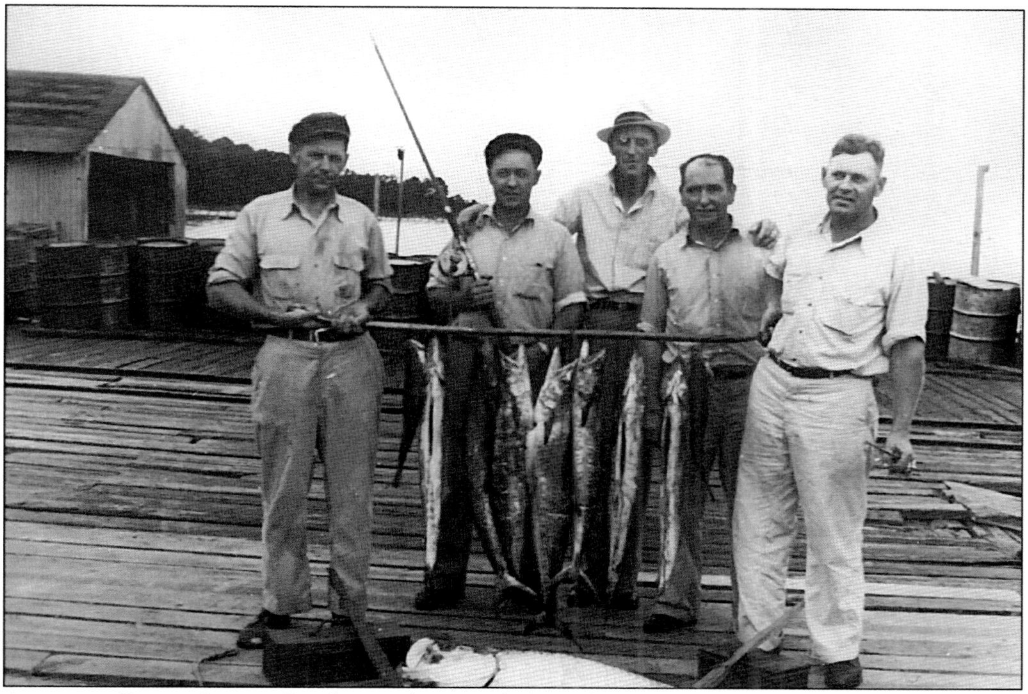

Another Great Catch. Displaying their catch from the old fuel dock at the end of Pier Street, these Fairhope fishermen are, from left to right, Walter and Herbert Forster, James Gaston, Clayton Baldwin, and Fred Forster. The Foster family initially handled all the gasoline brought over by boat. The area now features a public park, smaller pier, and boat-launch area. (Courtesy of Azille Forster Anderson.)

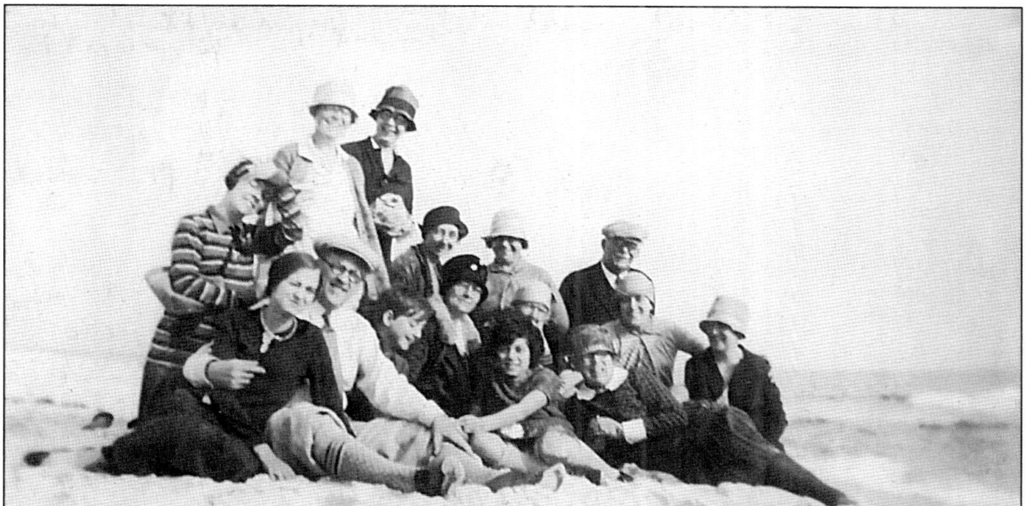

Gulf Beaches Beckoned. Many visitors to Fairhope took day trips farther south to the sandy white beaches of the Gulf of Mexico. Just over 20 miles away, the resort city of Gulf Shores now has beaches lined by high-rise condominiums, but in the 1920s the pristine dunes were the highest things standing along the seashore. (Courtesy of FMH.)

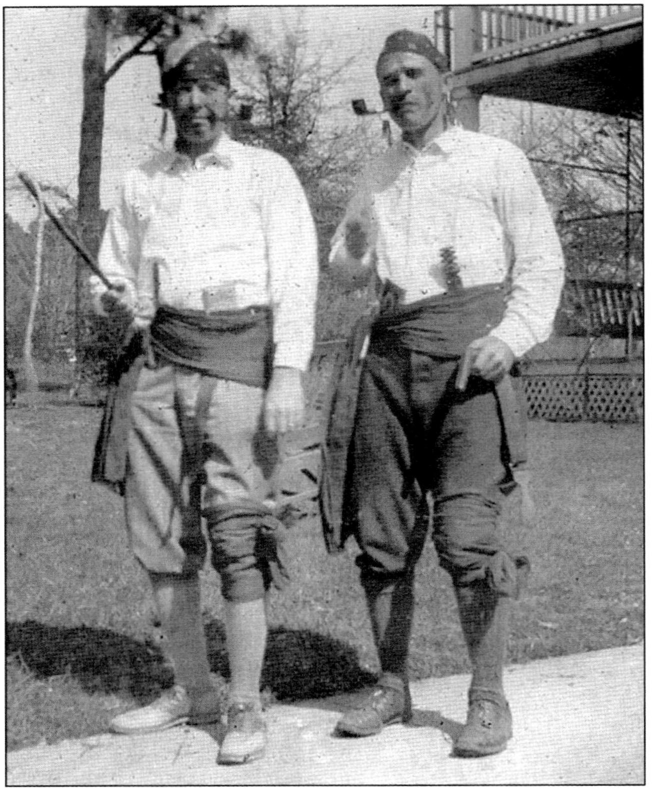

A Pair of Cutthroats. Real pirates roamed the Mobile Bay area in the early days, pilfering cargo going to and from Mobile, then the capital of King Louis XIV's French Louisiana colony. They hid in the many bays and inlets along the shore. Here, two pretend pirates are all dressed to kill for a 1920s Fairhope treasure-hunt party. (Courtesy of WOFC.)

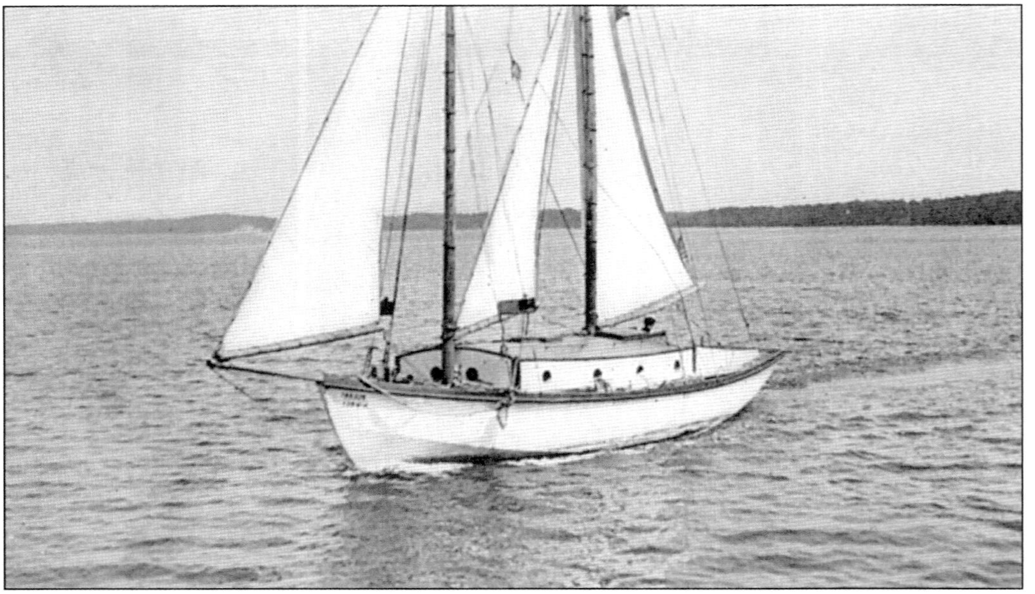

Fairhope Sailing the Best. Sailing was so much better along the Eastern Shore that the Mobile Yacht Club moved its headquarters to Fairhope in 1920, building its clubhouse on South Mobile Street by the bay. In later years, it became the La Carona dance club. The Fairhope Yacht Club was organized in 1942. (Courtesy of Cathy Donelson.)

Just Off the Tennis Court. James E. Hill celebrated his 84th birthday surrounded by ladies at the Fairhope Tennis Club. He always played in an immaculate white starched shirt. The Peoples Cooperative Store ran advertisements in May 1923, saying, "Now is the time to wear those white pants and tennis shoes." Fairhopers liked sporting the latest styles and bought their Keds there. (Courtesy of FMH.)

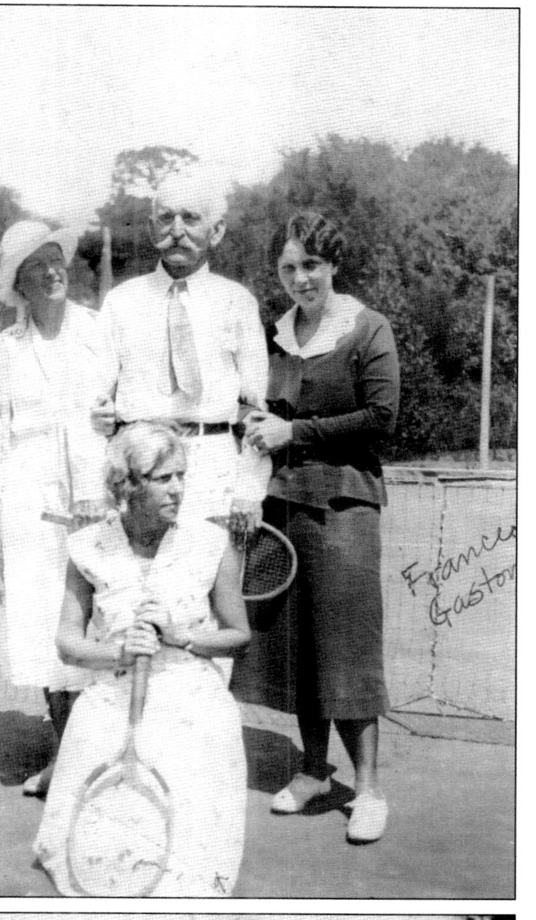

Par for the Course. Golfing became an appealing pastime on Fairhope's new nine-hole course, which opened in 1916. Golf and tennis were considered hobbies of the rich, but the course was a hit, with the newspaper opining, "While relatively few of our people are golf players," the links would attract visitors. (Courtesy of FMH.)

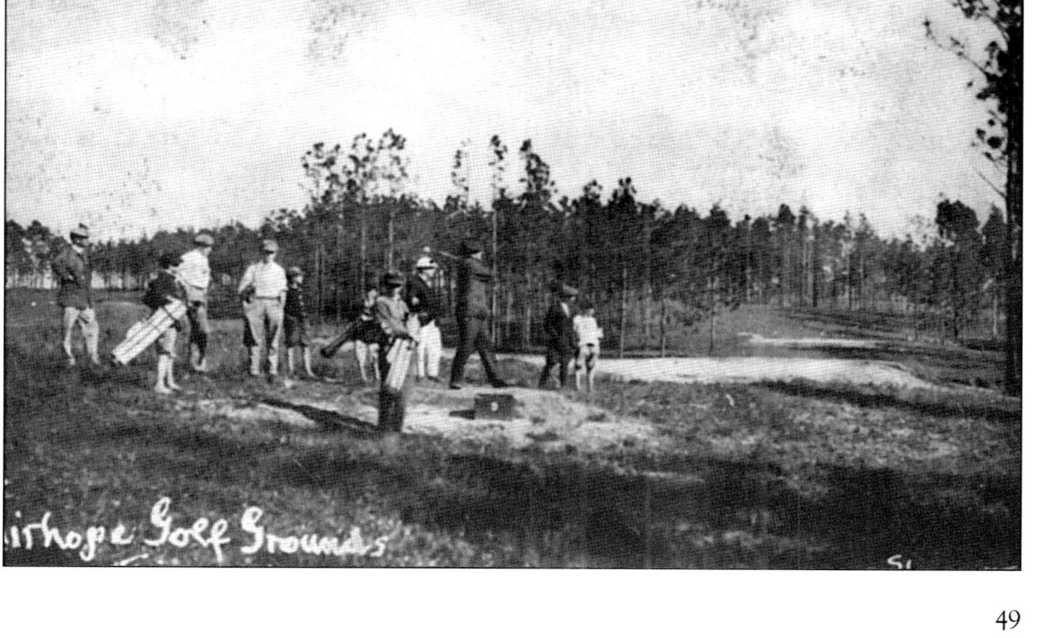

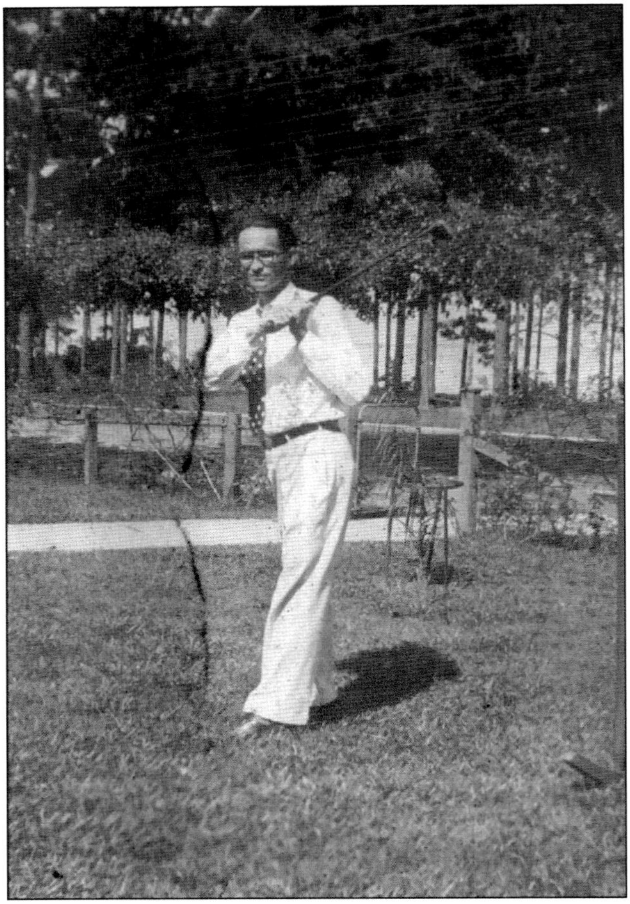

TAKING A PRACTICE SWING. A visitor practices for a golf match in Fairhope during the 1920s, when the game was coming into its own. Golf tours were being organized nationwide, and sports figures became heroes of the day. Fairhope's links were favored because they stayed green throughout the year. (Courtesy of WOFC.)

FAIRHOPE CHRISTENS CLUBHOUSE. The Fairhope Golf, Gun and Country Club opened its new clubhouse, which still stands as a residence, with a New Year's night dance in 1923. The club served as the social center at the challenging golf course, which was bounded by deep gullies on one side and a poultry farm on the other. (Courtesy of Edwin Skinner.)

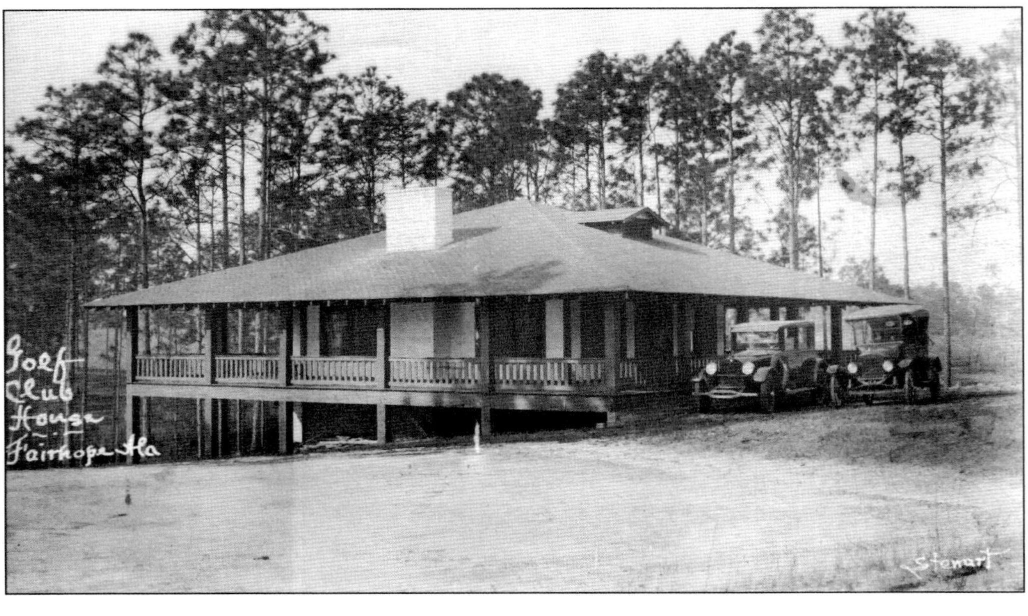

Five

Village Grows into a Town

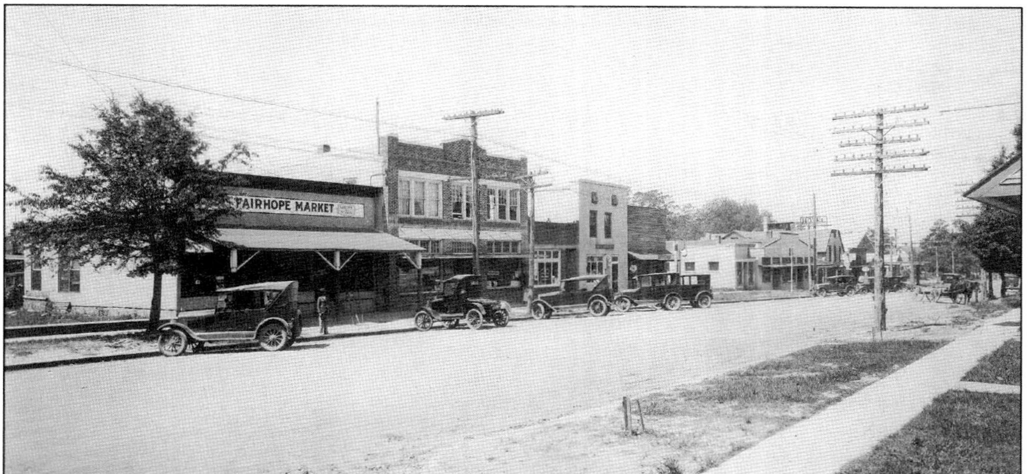

A Flourishing Uptown. Fairhopers came uptown—not downtown—to the growing commercial district to shop. This is the scene that would have greeted the Funk family when they arrived in 1921. That year, Fairhope Avenue featured a new brick-faced FSTC building in the center of what remains the main city block. (Courtesy of FMH.)

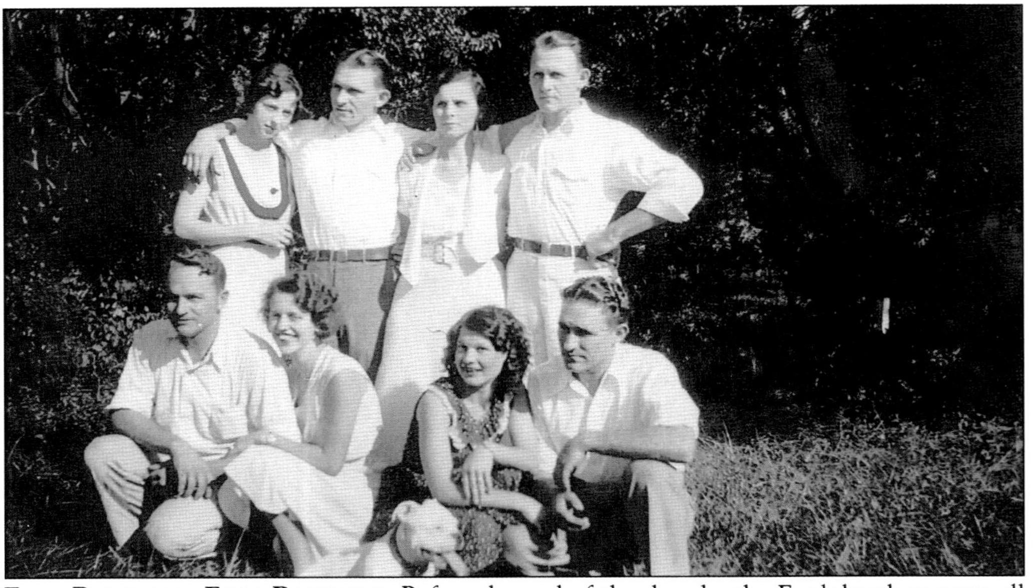

Four Brides for Four Brothers. Before the end of the decade, the Funk brothers were all settled into careers and family life in Fairhope. During the 1920s, people from small towns headed to the growing cities, and those from rural areas moved to town. Starting the decade with only 853 souls, Fairhope had a population of more than 1,500 by 1930. (Courtesy of Flora Maye Simmons collection.)

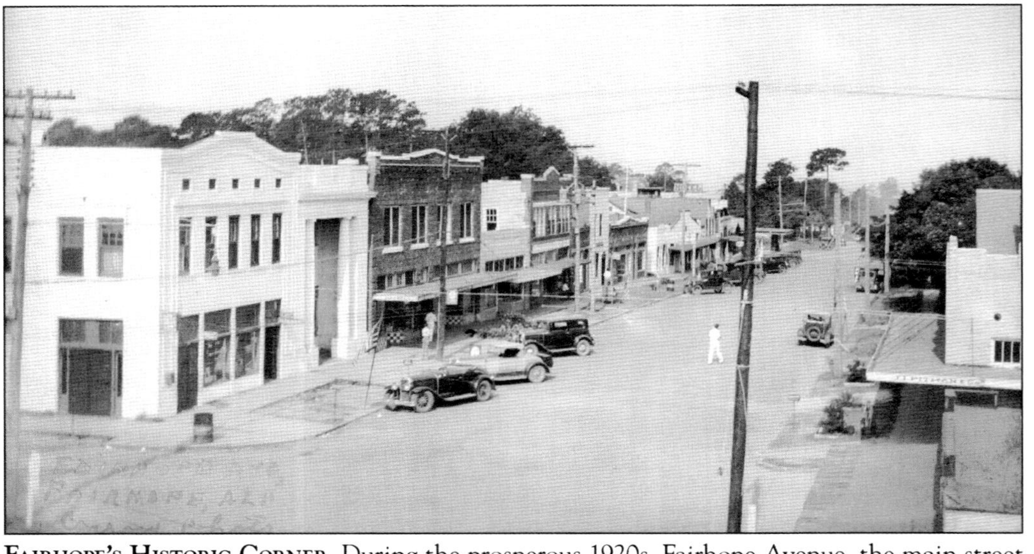

Fairhope's Historic Corner. During the prosperous 1920s, Fairhope Avenue, the main street leading to the bay, gained a new look thanks to a construction rally. Nearly all of the buildings on the left are still standing, including the 1916 Fairhope Pharmacy on the corner, the oldest drugstore in Alabama still operating on its original site. All are part of Fairhope's commercial National Historic District. (Courtesy of Helen Dyson collection.)

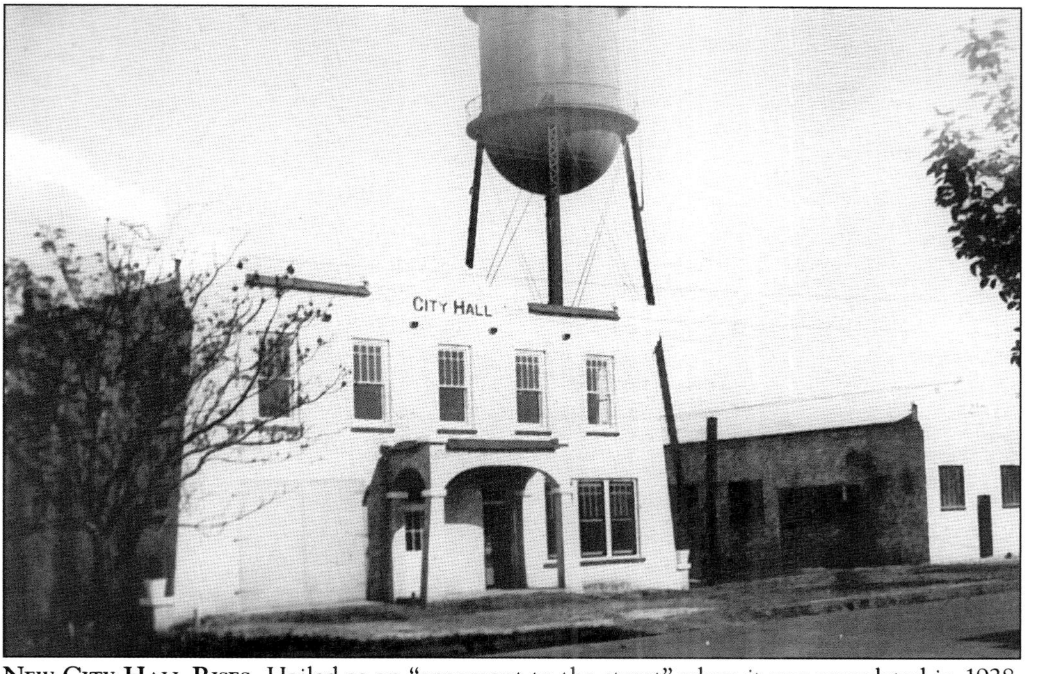

New City Hall Rises. Hailed as an "ornament to the street" when it was completed in 1928, the new city hall was flanked by the power and utility building on the right. Called "first-class" construction by the newspaper, the landmark at 24 North Section Street is now the Fairhope Museum of History. (Courtesy of Azille Forster Anderson.)

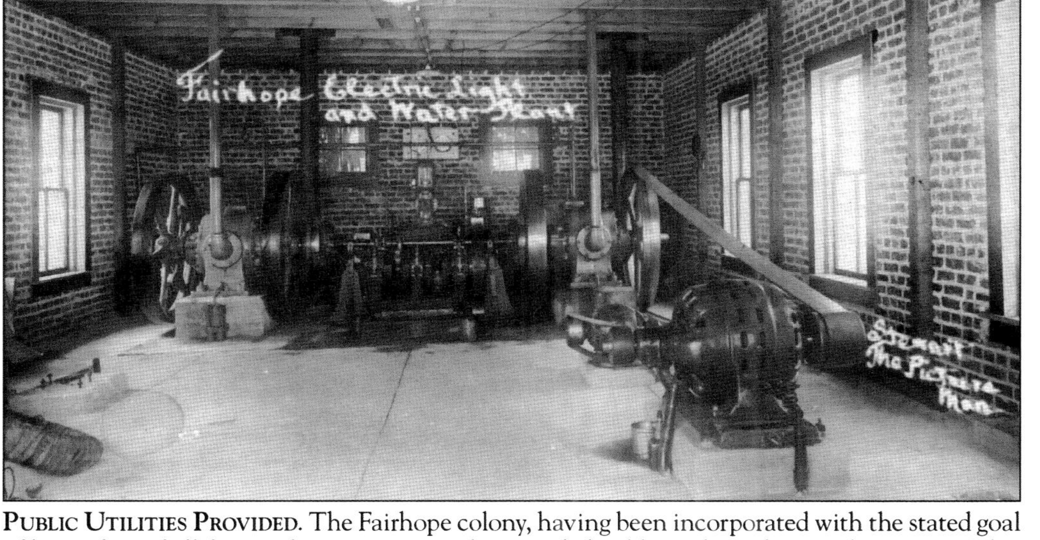

Public Utilities Provided. The Fairhope colony, having been incorporated with the stated goal of being free of all forms of private monopoly, provided public utilities from its beginning. This is the interior of an early power and water plant. Today, the City of Fairhope still provides water, electricity, and natural gas to city and area residents. (Courtesy of the FSTC.)

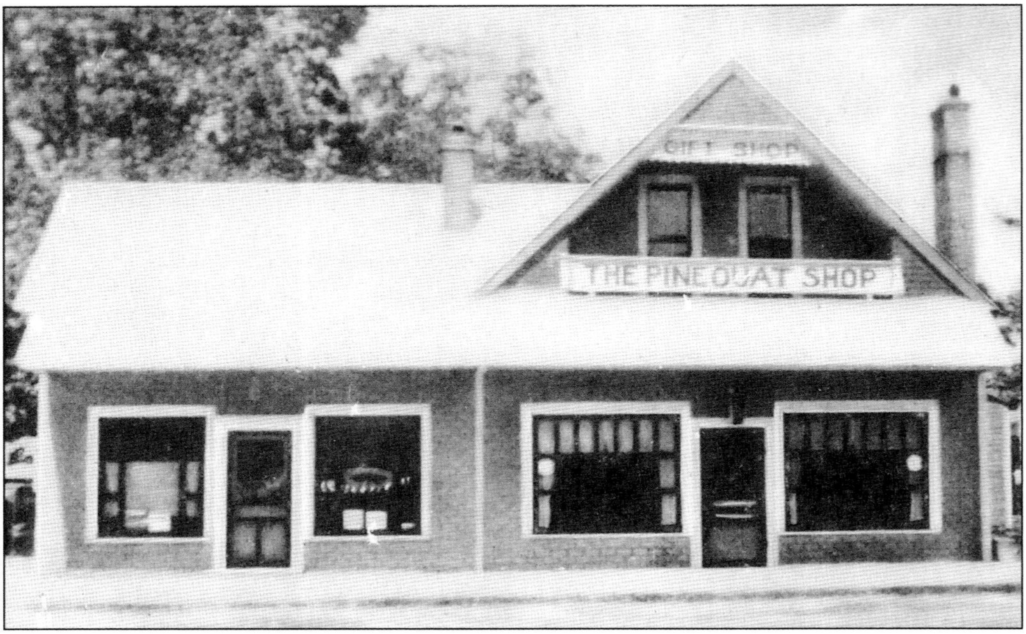

Town Landmarks Remembered. The Pinequat Shop on Fairhope Avenue was a souvenir shop where visitors bought locally made crafts and delicacies. In 1920, it was featured nationally in a full-page color illustration in the *Ladies' Home Journal* for its "unique and artistic pine needle baskets." The publication featured it again in 1924. When it was torn down in 1957, the shop was the town's oldest business. (Courtesy of FMH.)

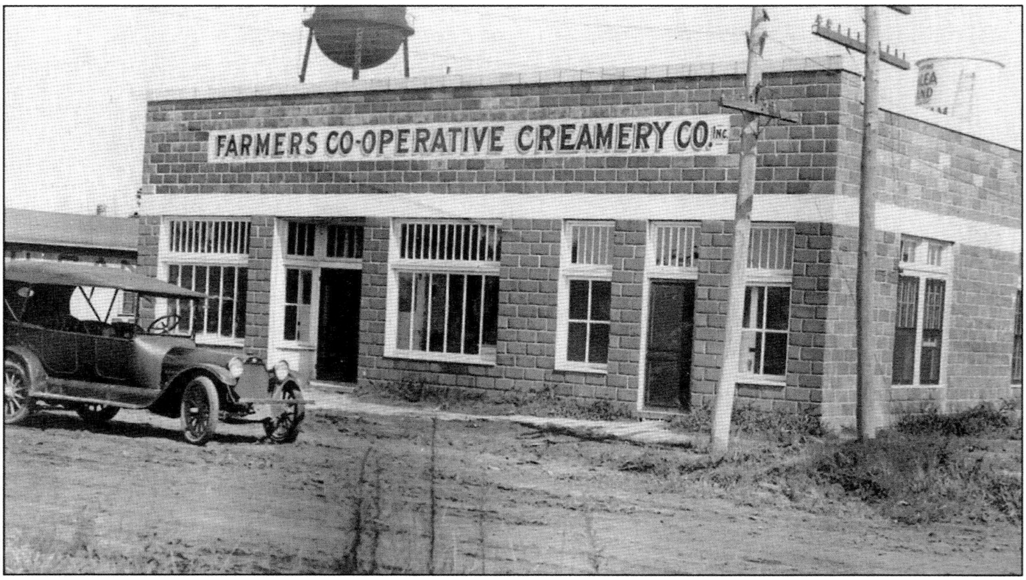

Fairhope's Own Ice Cream. The popular Azalea Brand ice cream sold for 10¢ a pint as a promotion when it was churned out by the new Farmers Cooperative Creamery Company, built in 1922. The creamery site at the west corner of North Bancroft Street and Fairhope Avenue now features a shady picnic area with a fountain. (Courtesy of FMH.)

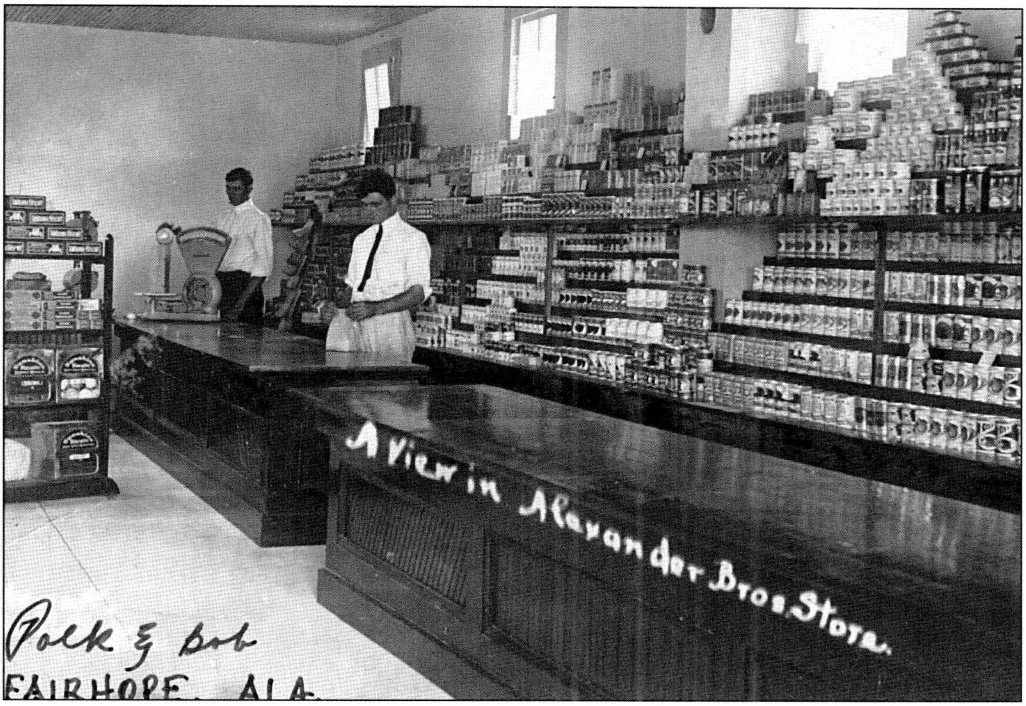

Easy Grocery Shopping. For many years, Fairhope grocery shoppers did not have to wander the aisles of big stores looking for items on their lists. All they had to do was go to the counter and get what they needed from the clerk, like one of the Alexander brothers, either Polk or Bob, and tell him to "put it on the ticket." (Courtesy of Ben Lucassen.)

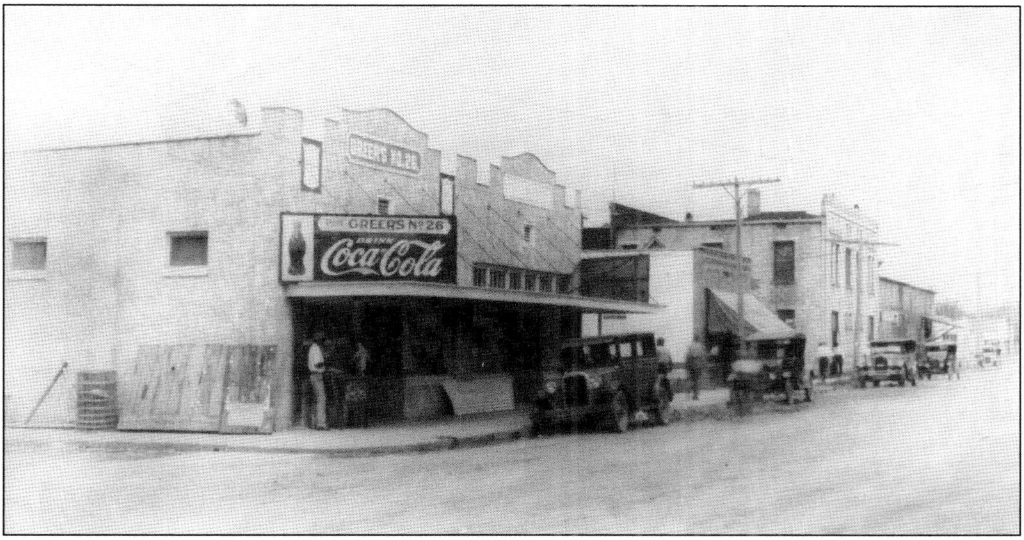

First Chain Store Opens. The Mobile-based Greer's grocery chain, founded in 1916, established the first cash-and-carry markets in the region and later developed self-service stores. It opened a grocery in Fairhope in 1928, becoming the first chain store in a town that still supports mostly local business. This building at 24 South Section Street is now an antique store. (Courtesy of Flora Maye Simmons collection.)

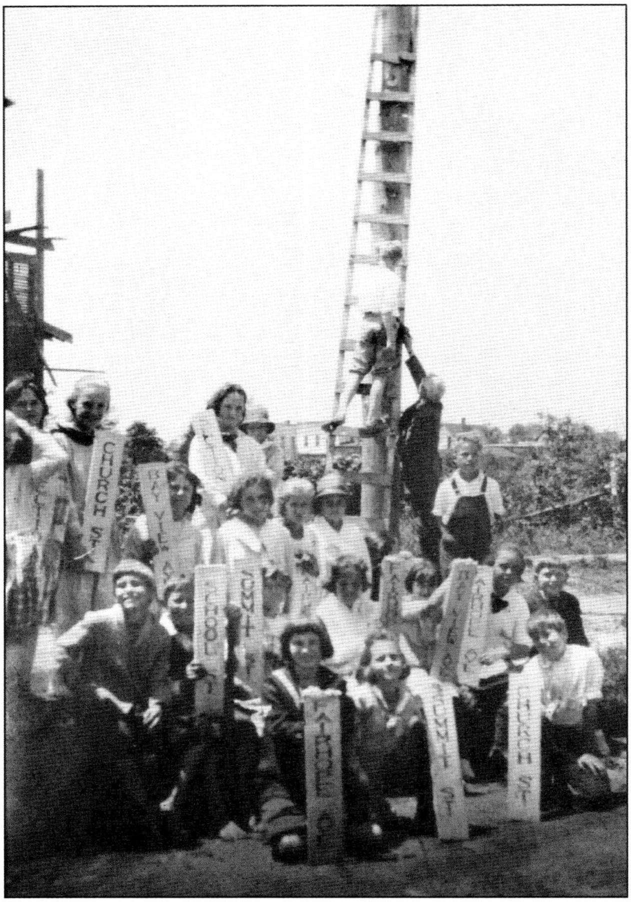

Street Signs Go Up. Students at Fairhope's Organic School made hand-lettered street signs in shop classes that both boys and girls took. As the town grew during the 1920s, they climbed ladders to hang the signs marking the town's main streets. That decade saw major growth in the business district and the construction of many of its extant buildings. (Courtesy of FSTC.)

The Uptown Post Office. Fairhope began as a one-horse town, literally. Ernest B. Gaston owned the lone horse, named Dolly. Soon, the sandy streets were lined with horseless carriages, as shown in this view of the former post office at 66 North Section Street. Until the mid-1930s, Fairhope's post office was located in this Greeno Masonic Lodge, built in 1911. (Courtesy of Flora Maye Simmons collection.)

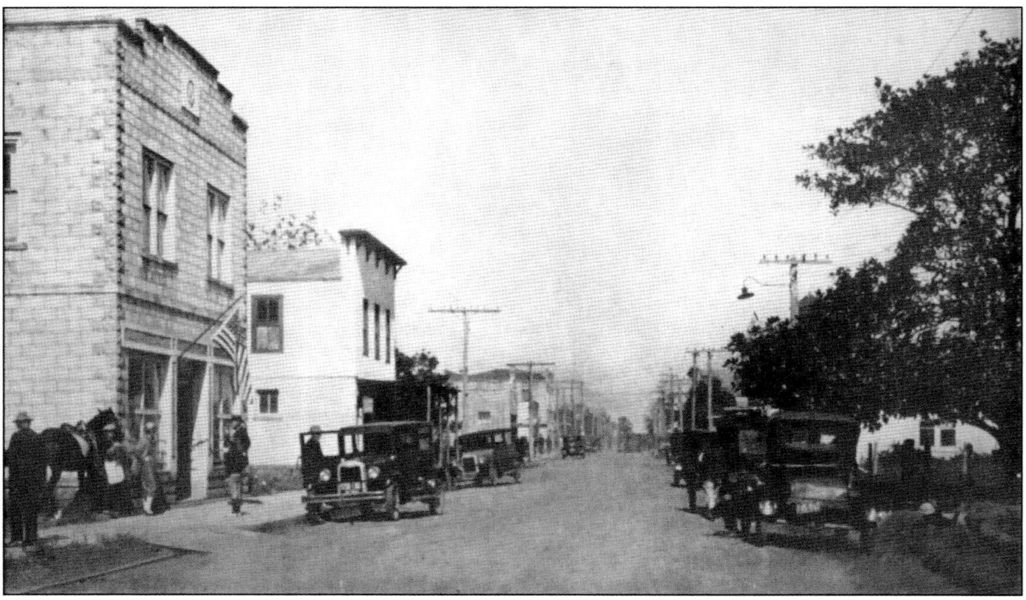

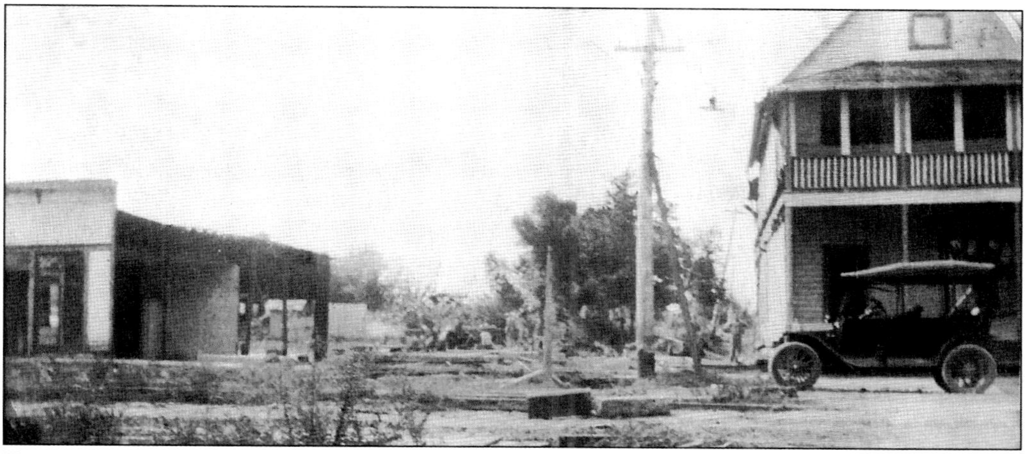

Town on the Move. With the growth along Fairhope Avenue, the Adolph O. Berglin home was moved around the corner to Church Street. Berglin, a Wisconsin native who served as Fairhope's mayor from 1914 to 1916, established one of the first creameries in Alabama. Ice, milk, and ice cream were sold at his bay-front creamery, and people also bought milk at his house. (Courtesy of Robert Berglin.)

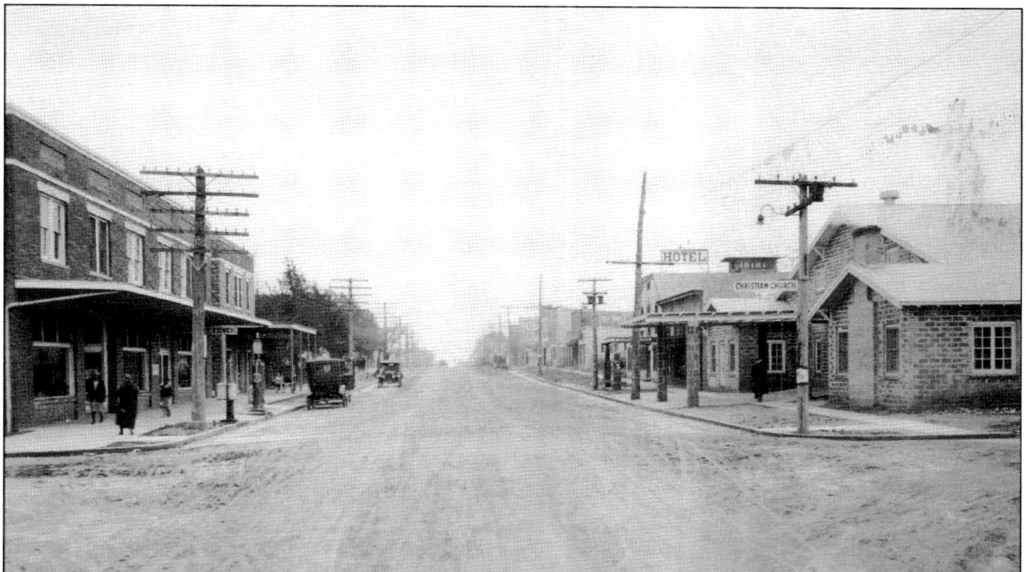

Corner Church and Fairhope. In 1921, this Fairhope Avenue corner did not hold any commercial structures. The next year, the brick Peoples' Cooperative Store with upstairs Civic Club Hall, left, was built. Today, it is still the corner Fairhope Hardware store. The movie theater on the right was built in 1924 on the original Berglin homesite. (Courtesy of Flora Maye Simmons collection.)

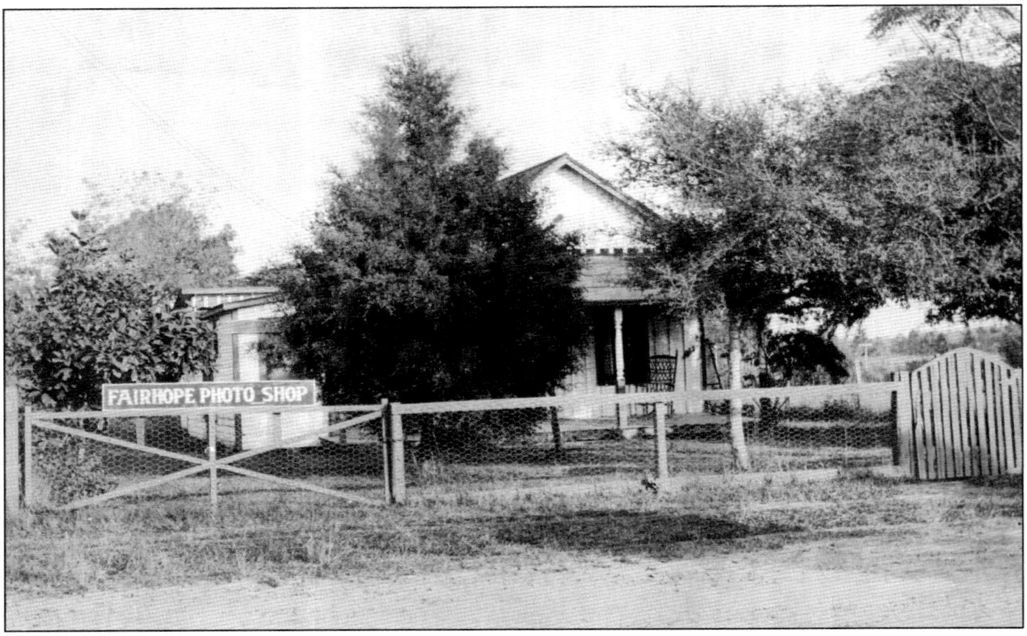

THE PICTURE MAN'S HOME. Fairhope's premier photographer, Frank Stewart, lived in this modest board-and-batten home and studio once located on Johnson Avenue. Documenting Fairhope's growth from its founding until his death in 1942, Stewart "The Picture Man" left behind an invaluable legacy of vintage photographs that provide a visual record of the community and its citizens. (Courtesy of FMH.)

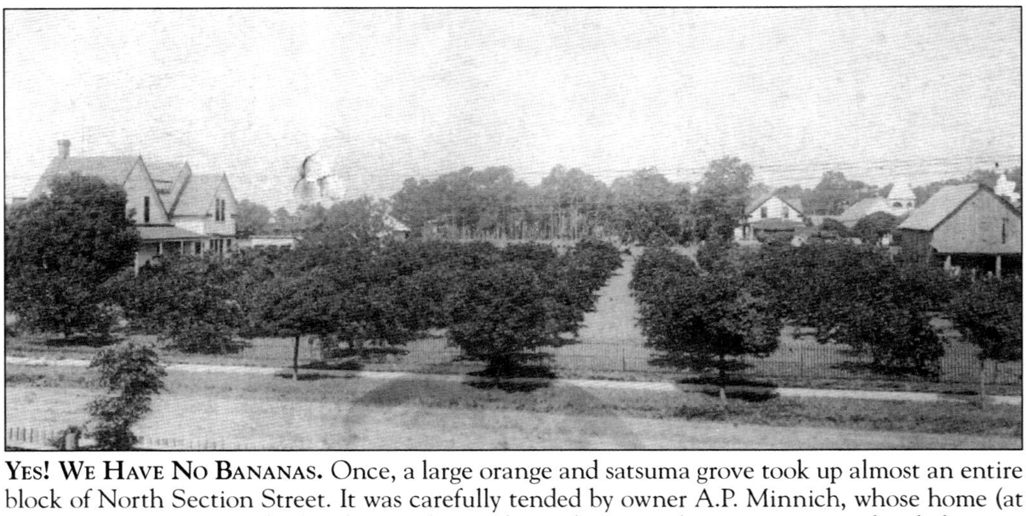

YES! WE HAVE NO BANANAS. Once, a large orange and satsuma grove took up almost an entire block of North Section Street. It was carefully tended by owner A.P. Minnich, whose home (at left) still stands. After the big freeze of 1924, he and many other area growers decided not to replant their citrus trees, and the industry waned. (Courtesy of FMH.)

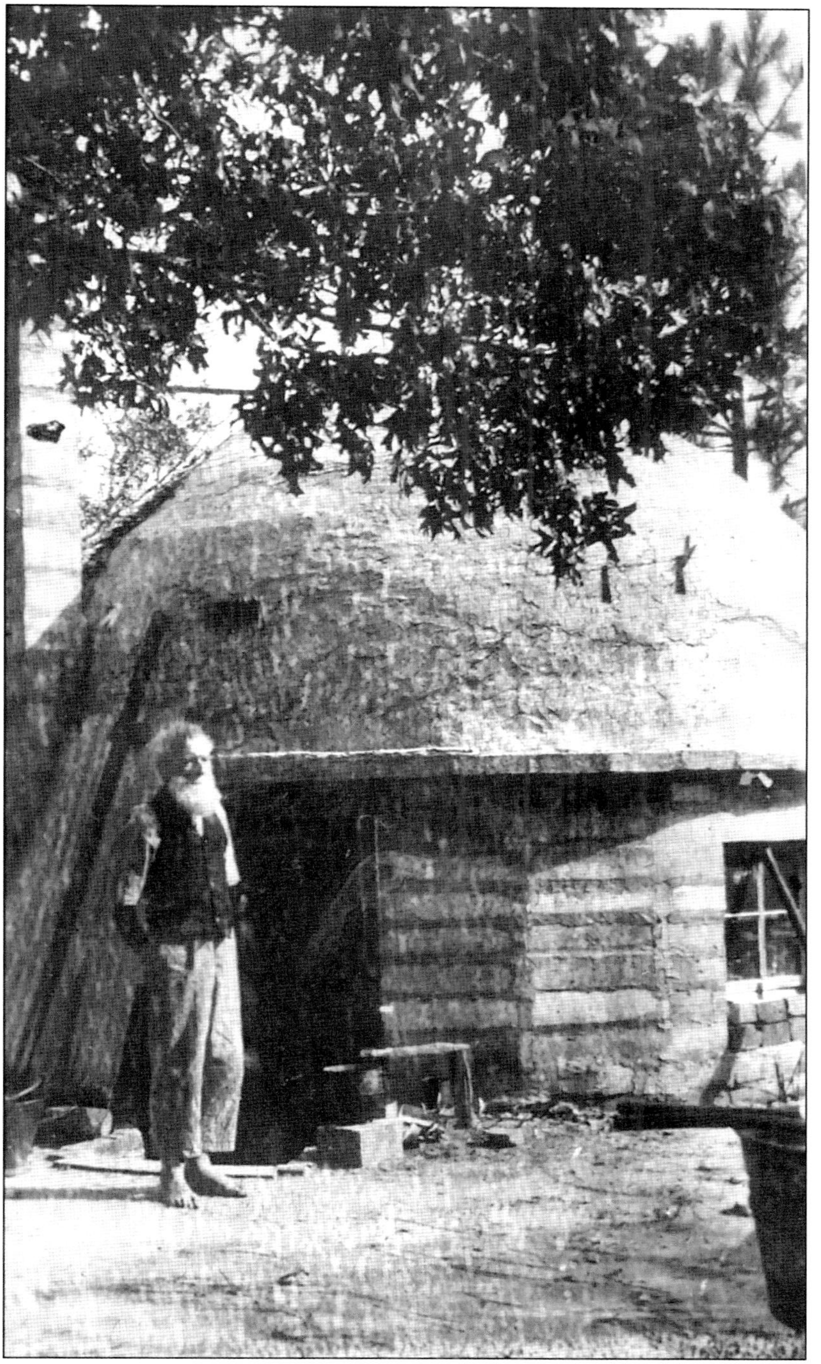

THE HERMIT'S HIDEAWAY. Henry James Stuart, a philosopher also called "the Hermit" and "the Weaver," built his distinctive masonry-dome home in the Montrose area of Fairhope that he called Tolstoy Park. He marched to the beat of his own drum and usually carried a handsaw to ward off snakes when he walked into town barefoot. His quaint dwelling is now a National Register of Historic Places landmark. (Courtesy of FMH.)

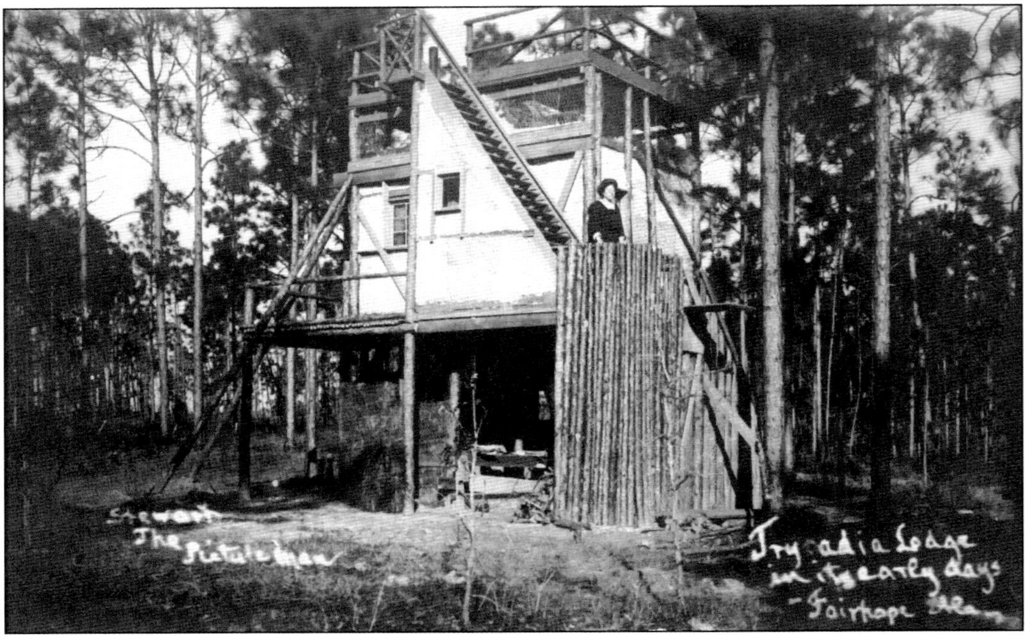

LADY LIVED IN TREE. "Bird Lady" Emma Schramm, another colorful Fairhope freedom lover, built her whimsical home, which she named Trycadia Lodge, up in the trees. The Organic School teacher performed all of the construction by herself, and by the 1920s this makeshift structure had become a comfortable two-story dwelling. (Courtesy of Bill Payne.)

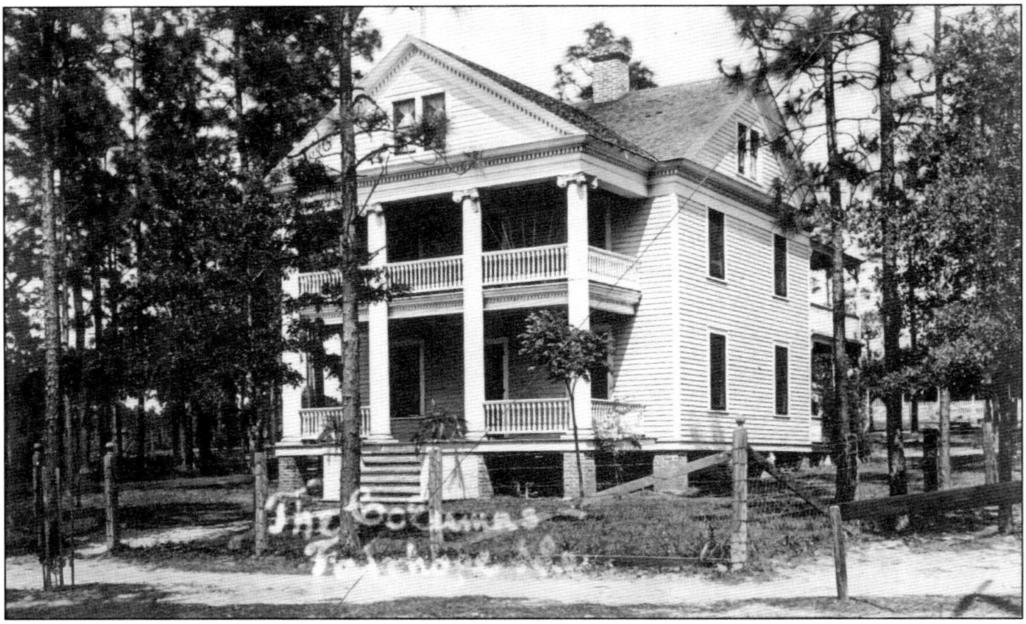

TOWN'S FINEST RESIDENCE. While single-taxers avoided ostentation, Aaron Moog, a merchant at nearby Battles Wharf who did not favor colony ideals, built this mansion called The Columns, perhaps to thumb his nose at them. Later, the house at the corner of Bayview and Magnolia Avenues was purchased by Dr. E.C. Slosson. (Courtesy of Pinky Bass.)

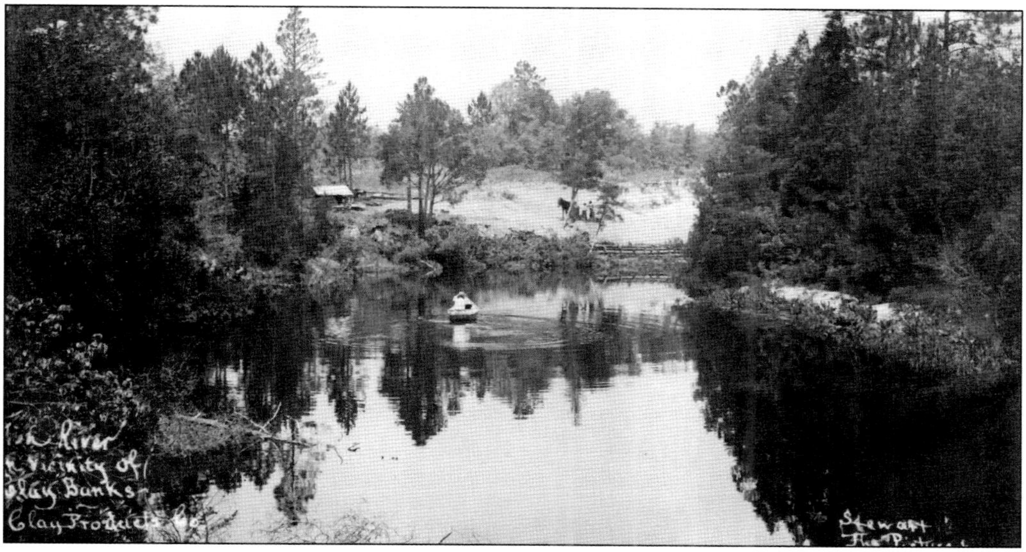

New Tile Builds Town. Abundant clay deposits on the Fish River, which had provided bricks for more than a century, were raw materials for the Clay Products Company. Operated by the Brown family for generations under a variety of names, the company produced the new hollow structural clay tiles that would become the building blocks of Fairhope, which gained 39 new buildings in 1921. (Courtesy of Pinky Bass.)

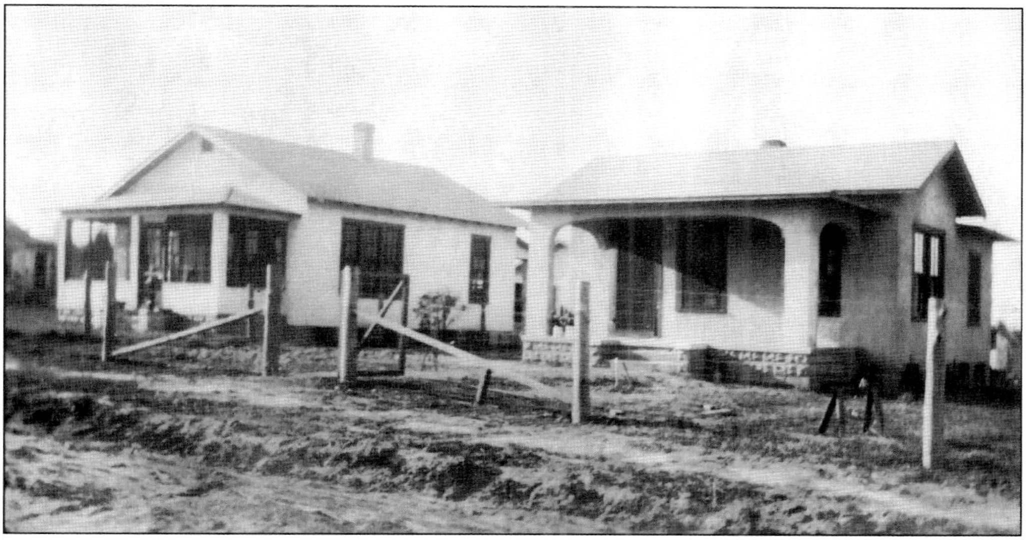

Modern New Home. Termed "modern" in the postwar building boom, many Fairhope houses rested on ornamental concrete block foundations, constructed of the orange so-called Clay City tile and coated with stucco. The European new urbanism planner Cebria de Montoliu drew up a plan for the town in 1922, encouraging the Spanish style "of such charming appearance." (Courtesy of FSTC.)

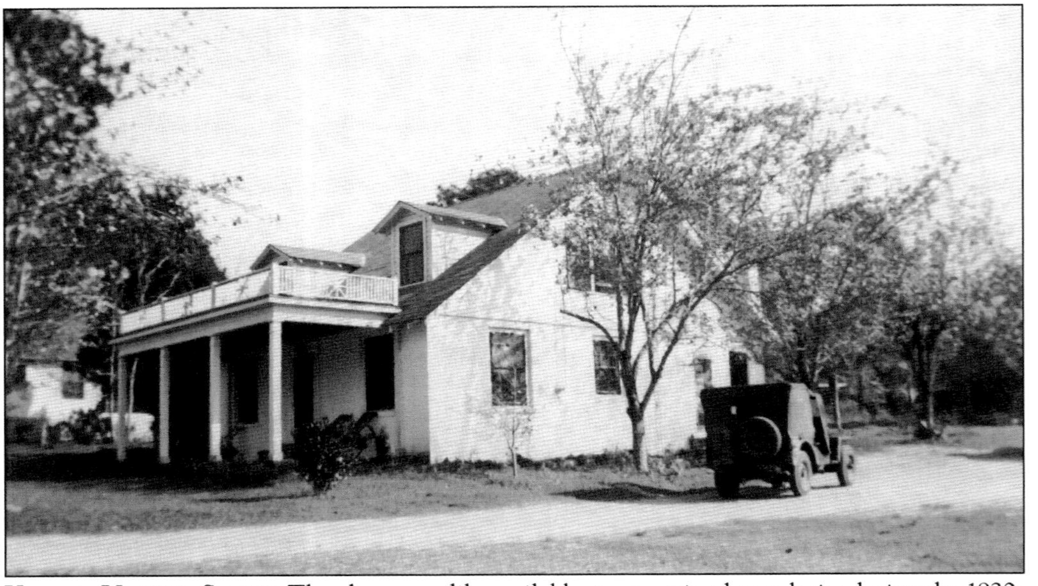

Keeping Up with Styles. The cheap, readily available stucco gained popularity during the 1920s and was used extensively for remodeling in Fairhope. This original frame home on White Avenue was brought up to date with a stucco coating. Many Spanish Mission–style homes, which were coming into vogue on the West Coast and in Miami, were also built in town during this period. (Courtesy Florence Lowell Kellogg.)

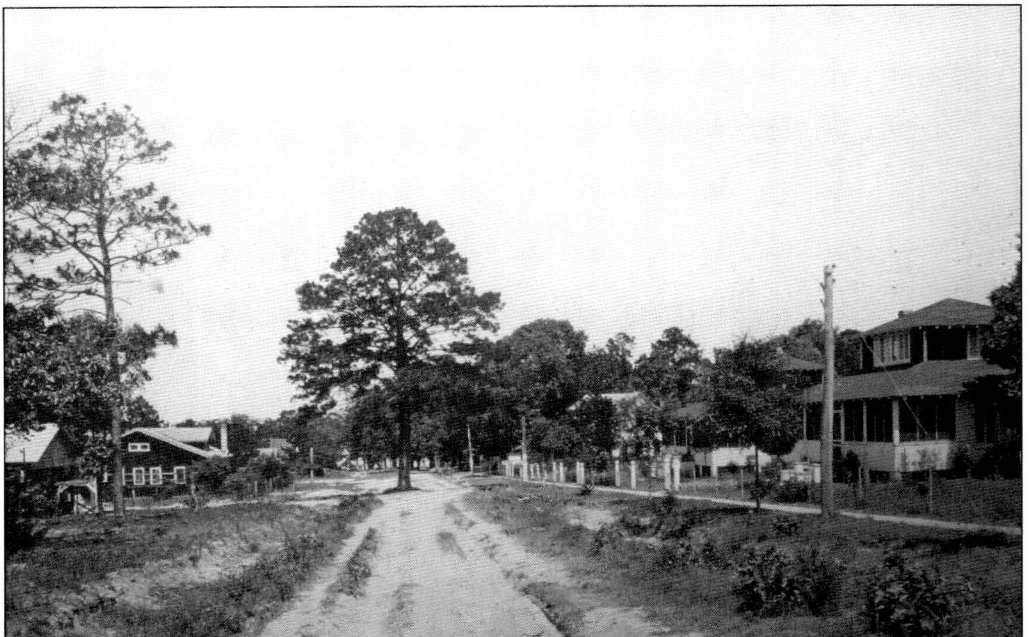

White Avenue Historic District. Most of these homes lining White Avenue as it leads to the bay are still standing. Fairhope has numerous structures and districts listed in the National Register of Historic Places, but many of the landmark cottages have fallen to the bulldozers to make way for bigger homes to accommodate an influx of affluent newcomers. (Courtesy of Earl Irwin.)

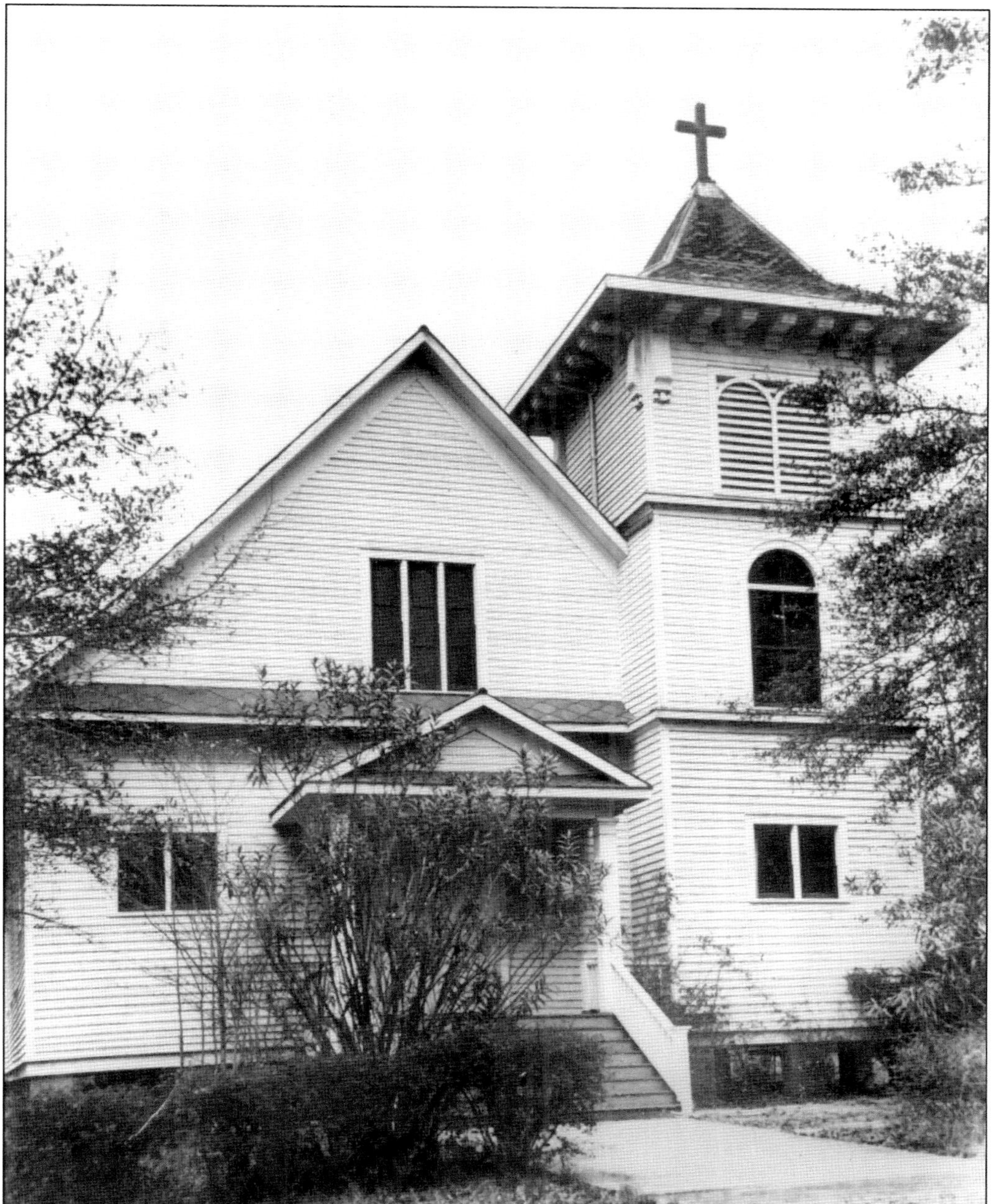

Spiritual Growth in Fairhope. The St. Lawrence Catholic Church was built in 1922 on South Bayview Avenue at the end of Gaston Avenue. After contractor George Lucassen completed the church, his son Bernard Lawrence Lucassen was the first baby baptized here. The structure was torn down after a new church was built on South Section Street in 1953. (Courtesy of Bernie and Ann Lucassen.)

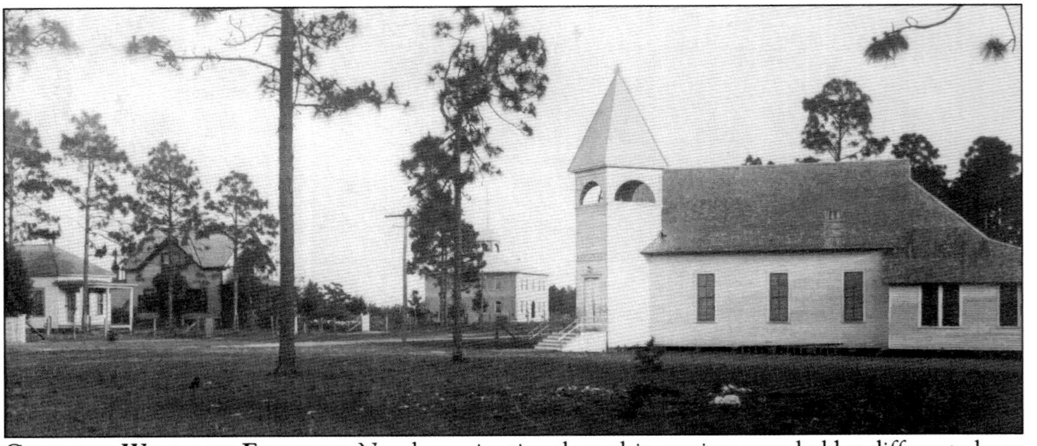

Churches Welcomed Everyone. Nondenominational worship services were held at different places around town until the Christian Church was built in 1901. The church and the public school in the background are both gone, but the Church Street homes on the left still stand, now housing businesses. The Rosicrucian and Theosophical Society also met here with lectures on subjects like Buddha, mental telepathy, and the popular Ouija board. (Courtesy of Reed Myers.)

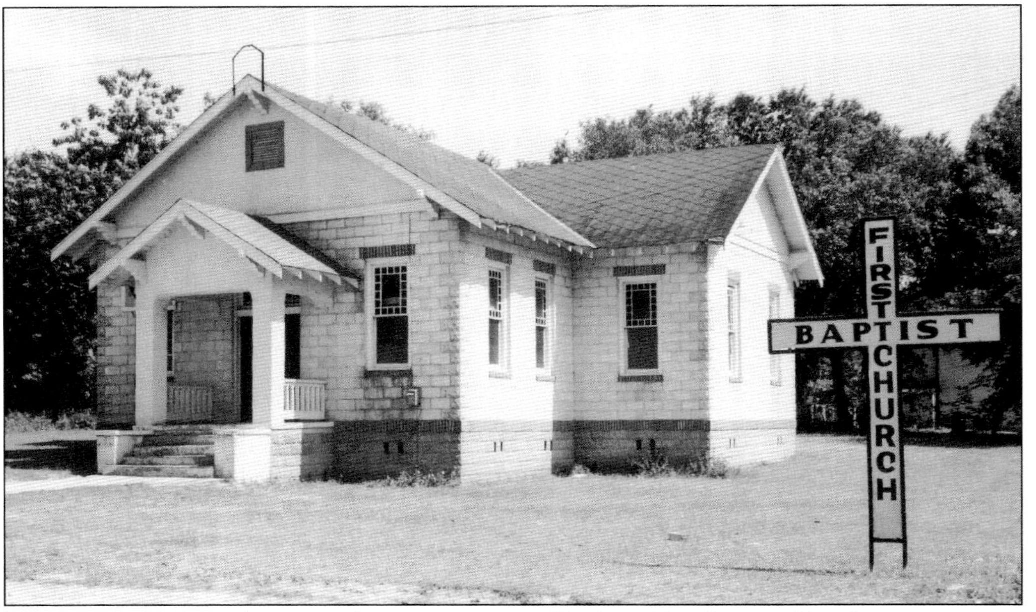

Theater on Morphy Avenue. The congregation of Fairhope First Baptist Church met in various homes and churches until it gained its own sanctuary in 1924. The building would later be used as a county satellite courthouse, and today it serves as Theater 98, the outgrowth of community theater acting groups that had their beginnings in the early 1900s. (Courtesy of Palmer Hamilton.)

Six

OUT FOR A JOYRIDE

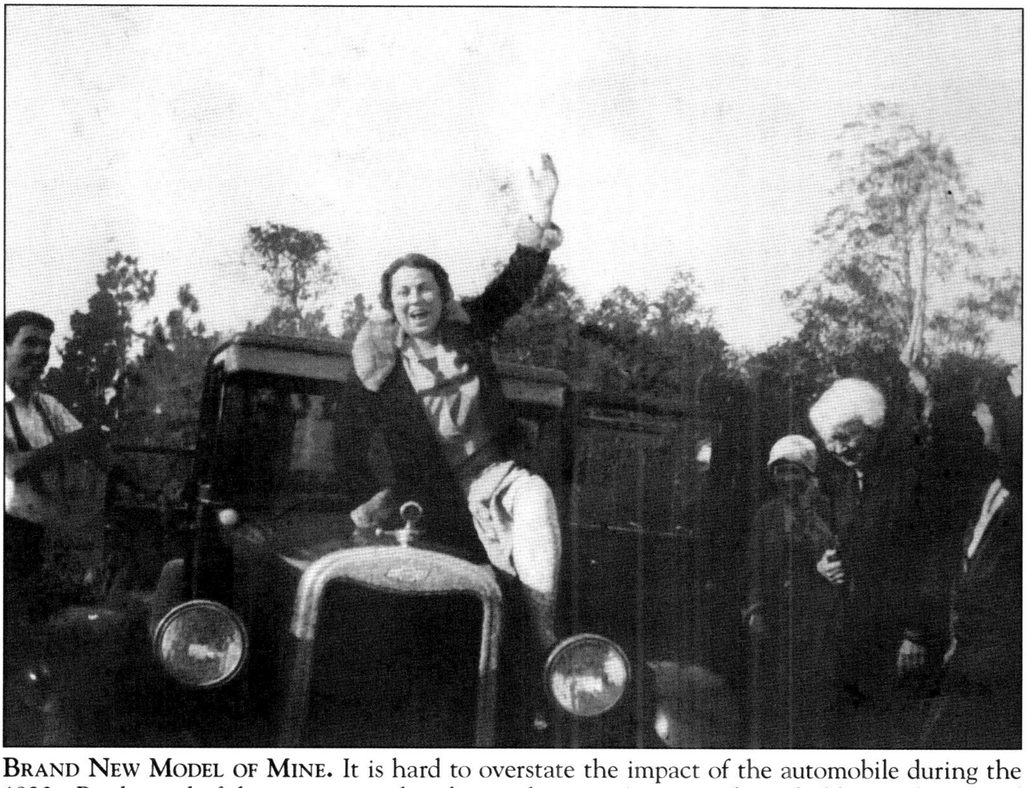

BRAND NEW MODEL OF MINE. It is hard to overstate the impact of the automobile during the 1920s. By the end of the prosperous decade, nearly every American household owned one, and mass production had made them available in different colors and styles. This Chevrolet seems to have made one Fairhope woman quite joyful. (Courtesy of WOFC.)

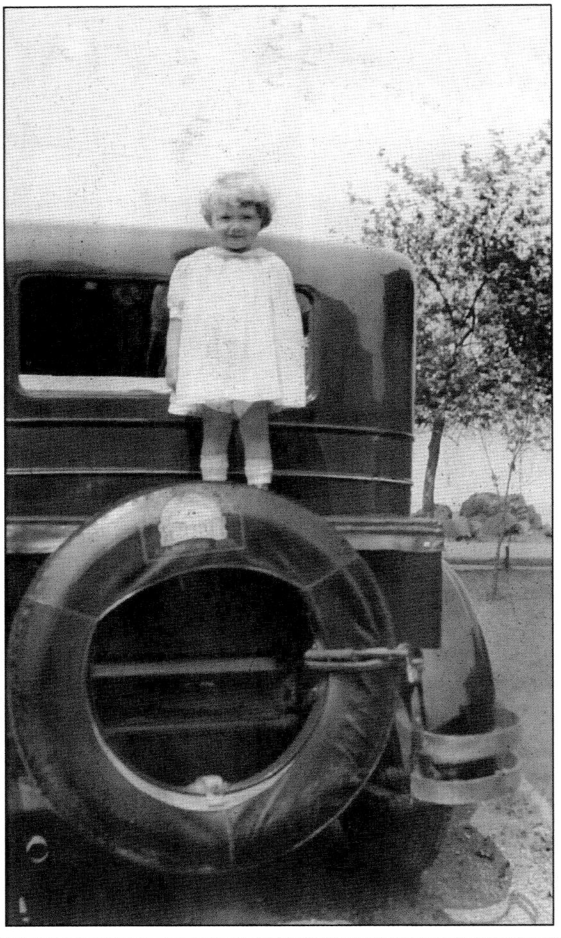

The Little Chauffeur. An entire new generation grew up viewing the automobile as a part of everyday life, rather than as a novelty. Every owner was justifiably proud of his new wheels, which were a status symbol. This baby's parents were doubtless pleased at the sight of their little one standing on the back of their motorcar. (Courtesy of WOFC.)

Fairhope Joins Motor Age. The Fairhope Wharf was served by horsepower until 1920, when the newspaper reported it had become motorized, retiring the "faithful little Jack mule." The paper says, "Cars from all parts of the country pass through Fairhope, eastward and westward, even to the limits of the continent." (Courtesy of Earl Irwin.)

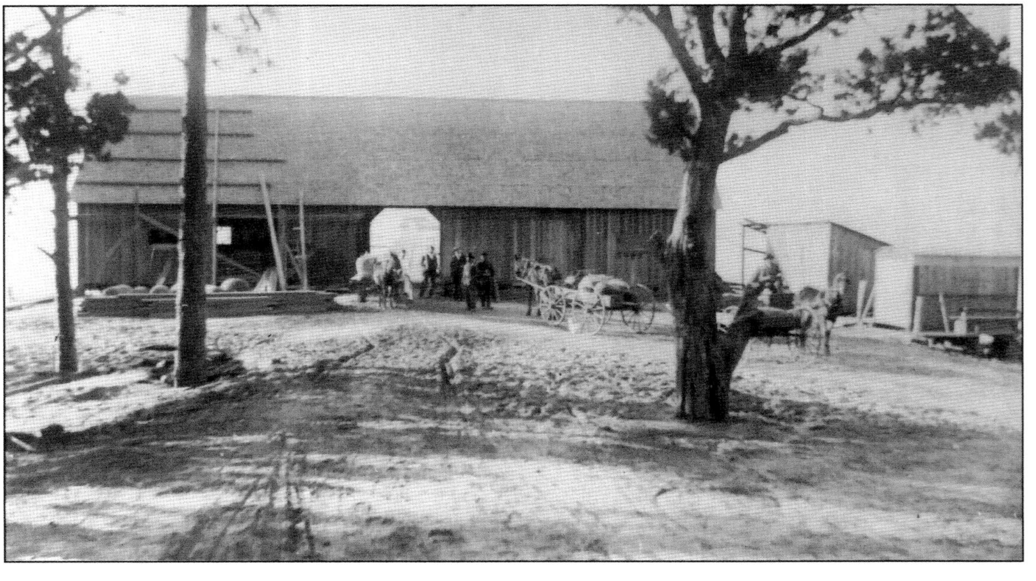

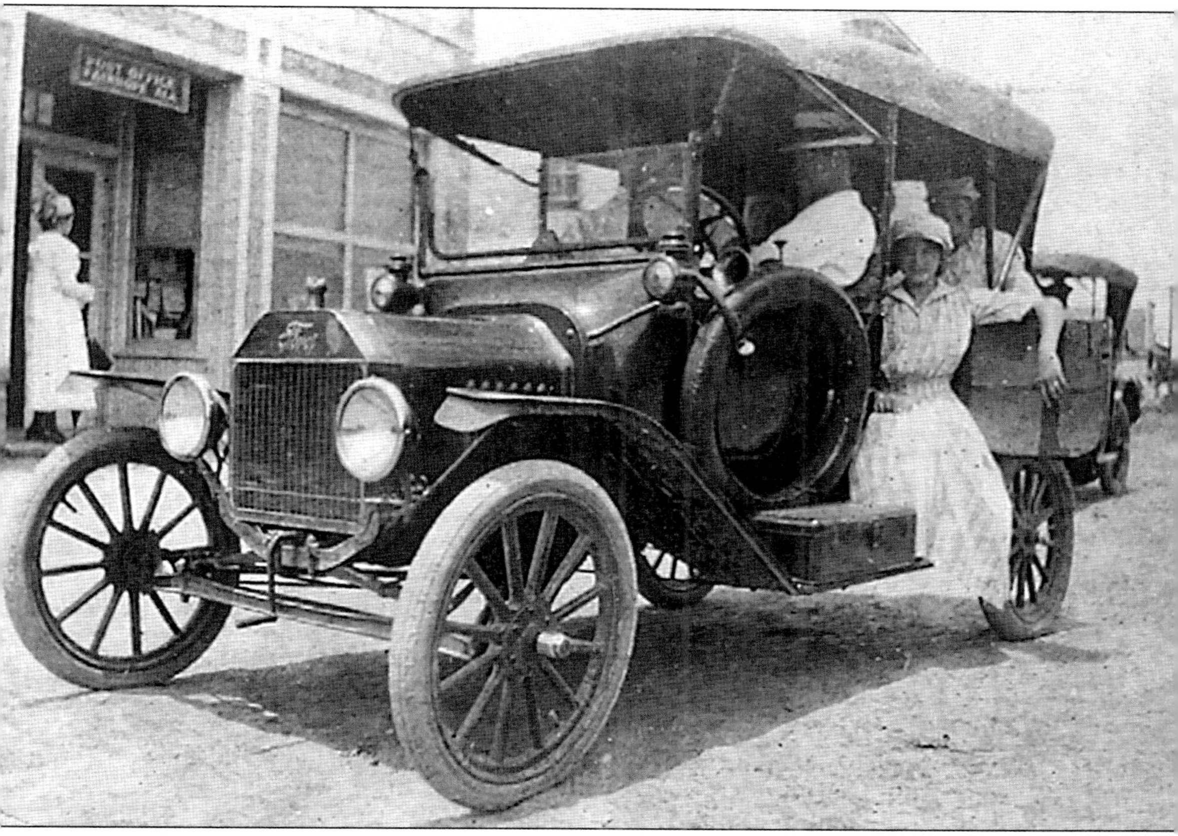

Madcaps Ride Uptown. The so-called "Flaming Youth" of the generation, such as the Sandbergs, immediately embraced the automobile, which provided a different mode of transportation, socialization, and courtship. Morals changed in the 1920s, as younger people began dating and riding together in automobiles without chaperones. Fairhope still had horses, but they were mostly advertised for trail rides as the livery stables closed. (Courtesy of FMH.)

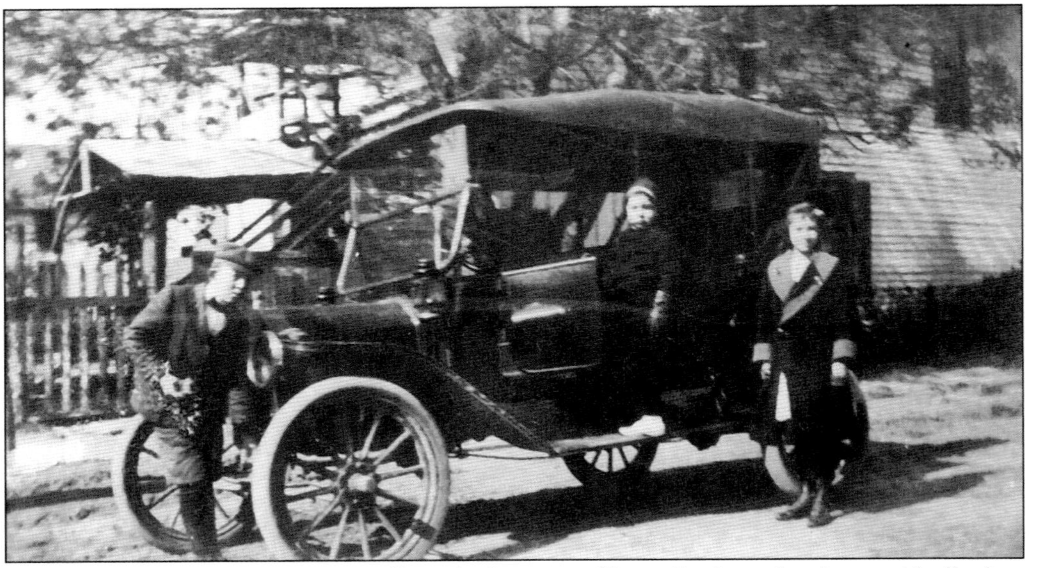

We're the Sunday Drivers. Initially, only the more affluent Fairhope families could afford an automobile. Adolph Berglin, for instance, was a mayor who owned the ice plant and creamery. Here, his oldest son, Lavigne, cranks the car for an outing as younger brother Marvin and sister Myrtle pose for the camera. Their Ford Model T was the country's leading motorcar, often called the "Tin Lizzie." (Courtesy of Robert Berglin.)

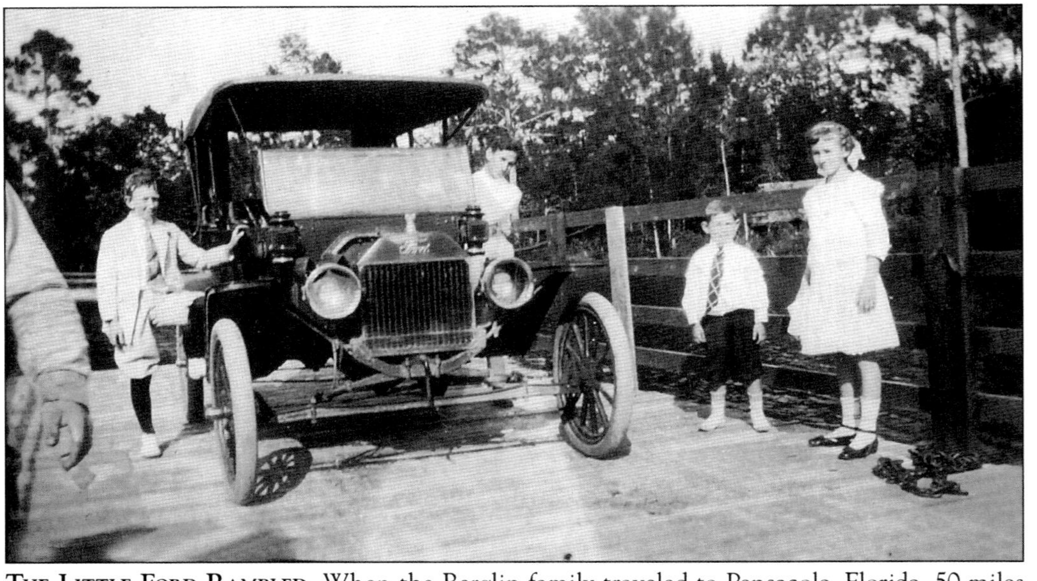

The Little Ford Rambled. When the Berglin family traveled to Pensacola, Florida, 50 miles west by bad road, they had to cross the Fish River on the old horse-drawn Marlow Ferry. By March 1920, a new bridge crossed the river, opening an easier route for motorists who mostly drove Ford's flivvers. There were eight million on the roads by the beginning of the decade. (Courtesy of Robert Berglin.)

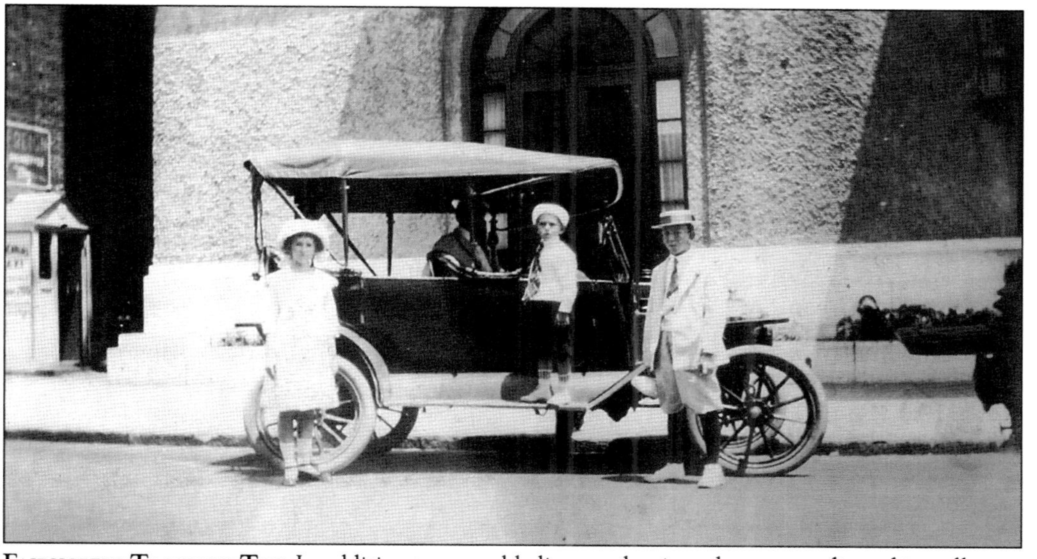

FAIRHOPERS TRAVELED TOO. In addition to assembly line production, the new credit and installment plans brought the automobile within financial reach of most families. As ownership became commonplace, more people were able to take weekend trips. Motoring excursions just for the sake of touring were in vogue. Here, the Berglin family has reached the Pensacola Hotel. (Courtesy of Robert Berglin.)

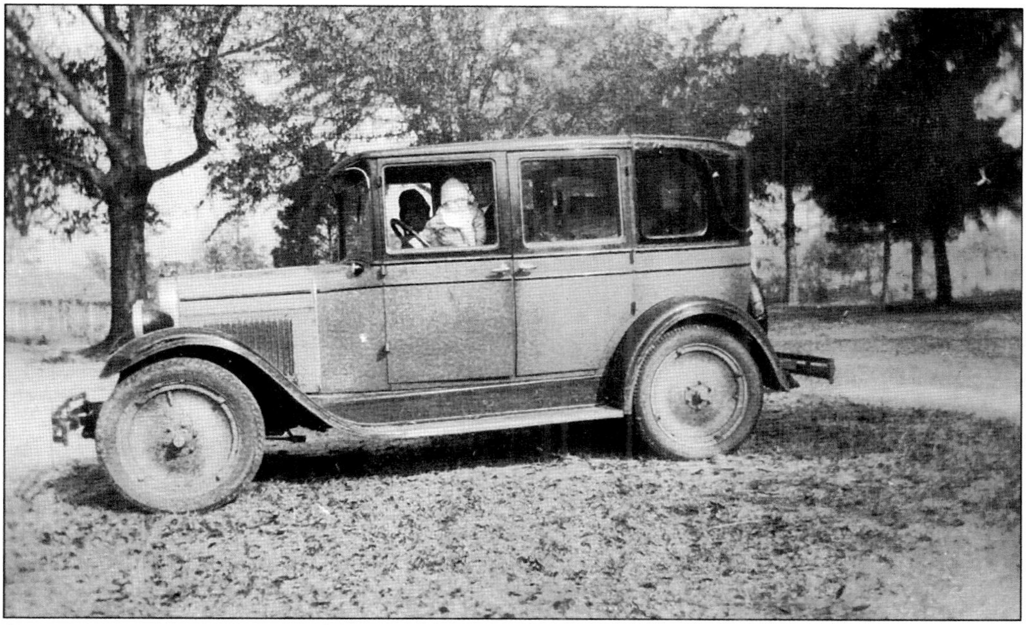

OUT IN AN AUTOMOBILE. Just like today, everyone wanted new designs as they came out. In this image, the Berglin family displays a new six-passenger sedan as well another new arrival: baby Evelyn. In Fairhope, a 1920 advertisement for a "Big Allen Four" boasted that the car took the north county hills with ease on high without a gearshift. (Courtesy of Robert Berglin.)

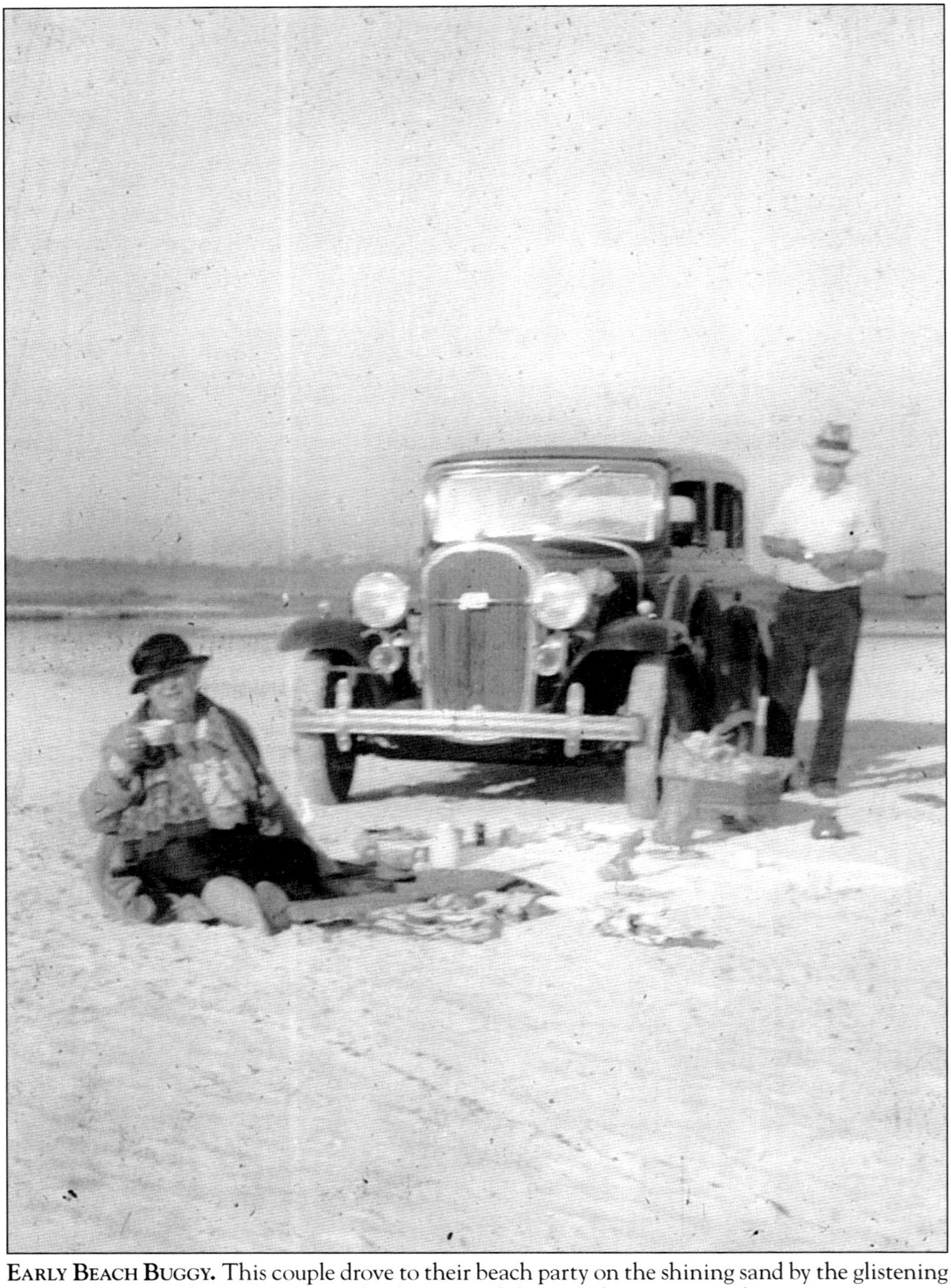

Early Beach Buggy. This couple drove to their beach party on the shining sand by the glistening water and waves. The national craze for the automobile came during an era of economic expansion when vehicles were no longer just a luxury for the wealthy. As touring became commonplace, Alabama's semitropical coast was an attraction. The state has banned beach driving since the early 1980s in order to preserve the dunes and sea oats. (Courtesy of FMH.)

Riding on the Trunk. A delighted William Simmons, age 10 in 1925, rides on the back of an automobile advertising Gaston Motor Company. The company was the first business in Fairhope to handle the new vehicles that would lead to a burgeoning motor trade. Many local young men also went to Detroit to work in the automobile industry during the 1920s. (Courtesy of FMH.)

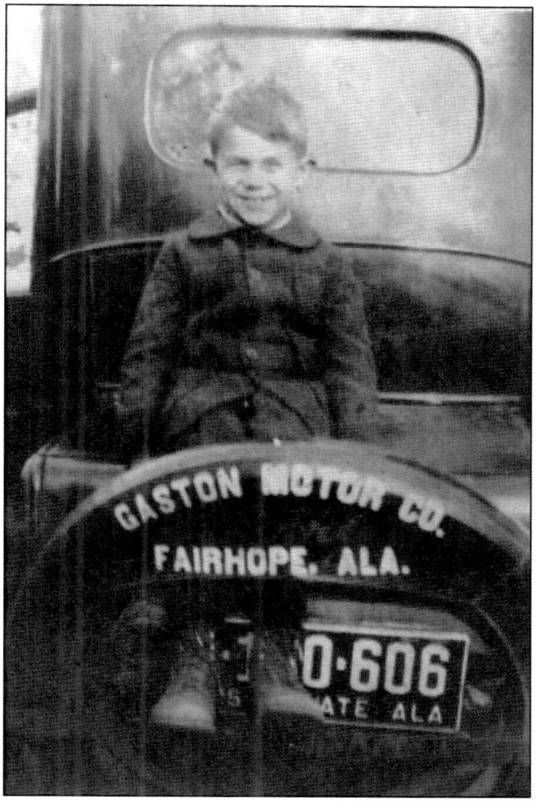

Thanks for the Buggy Ride. The staff at Gaston Motor Company gathers outside the garage started by James E. Gaston, a longtime city councilman. His company became an authorized Ford dealer in 1923 when it sold 64 vehicles, including trucks and tractors. Now remodeled as a Fairhope Avenue restaurant, it also was a stop for early coastal bus service. (Courtesy of FMH.)

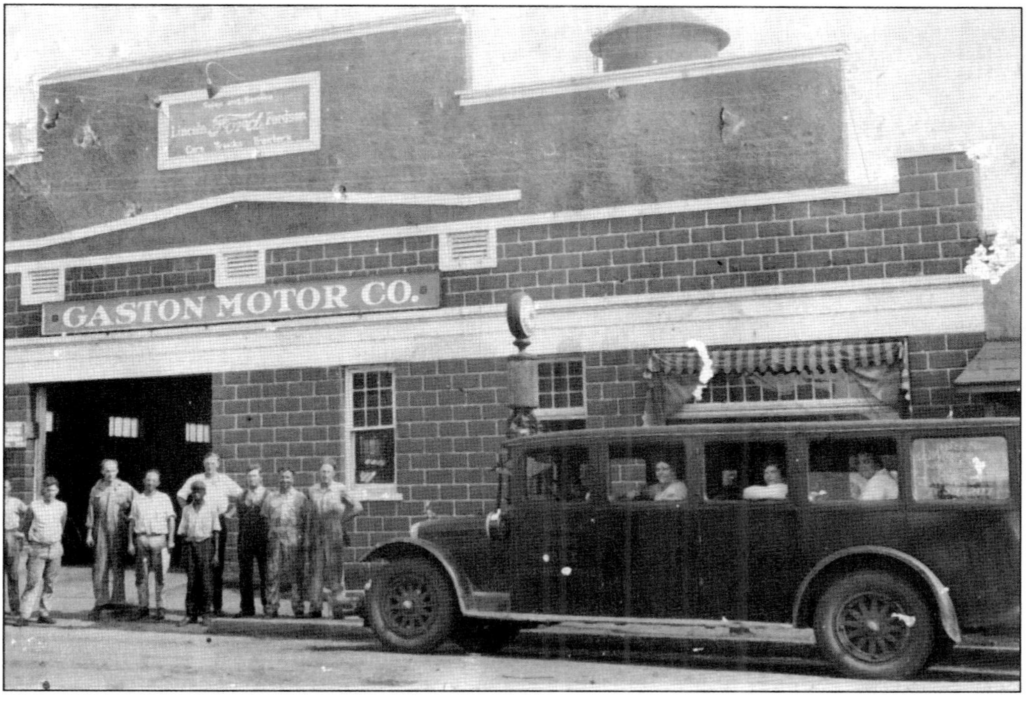

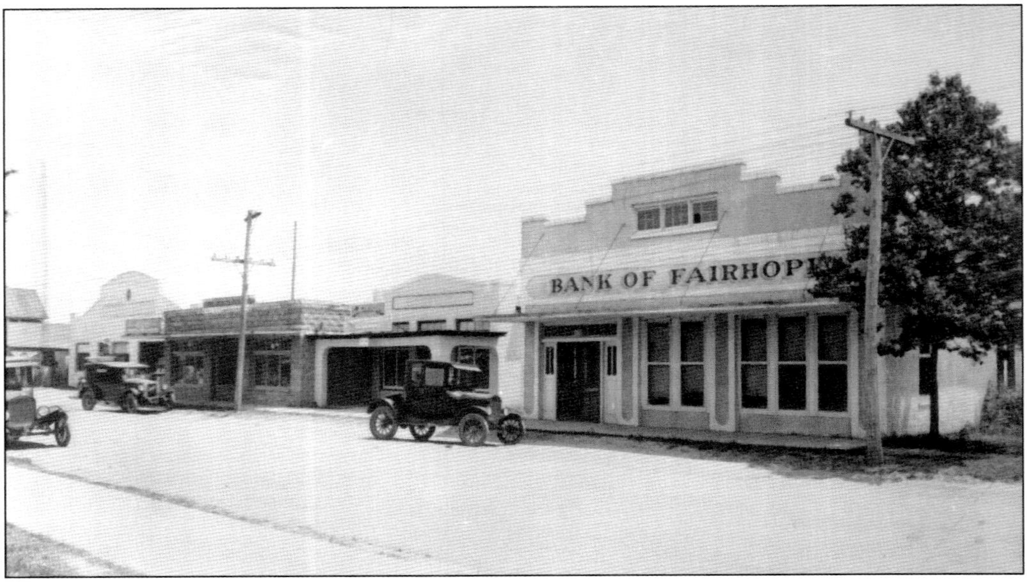

FAIRHOPE FENDER BENDER. This is the scene of a 1921 mishap that made the newspaper. "Mrs. Ruge backed her Mitchell into a telephone pole near the bank Thursday denting the body and the fender," reports the *Courier*, which kept track of all the local happenings. The former bank building still stands, along with a new light pole, on Section Street at the corner of Johnson Avenue. (Courtesy of Earl Irwin.)

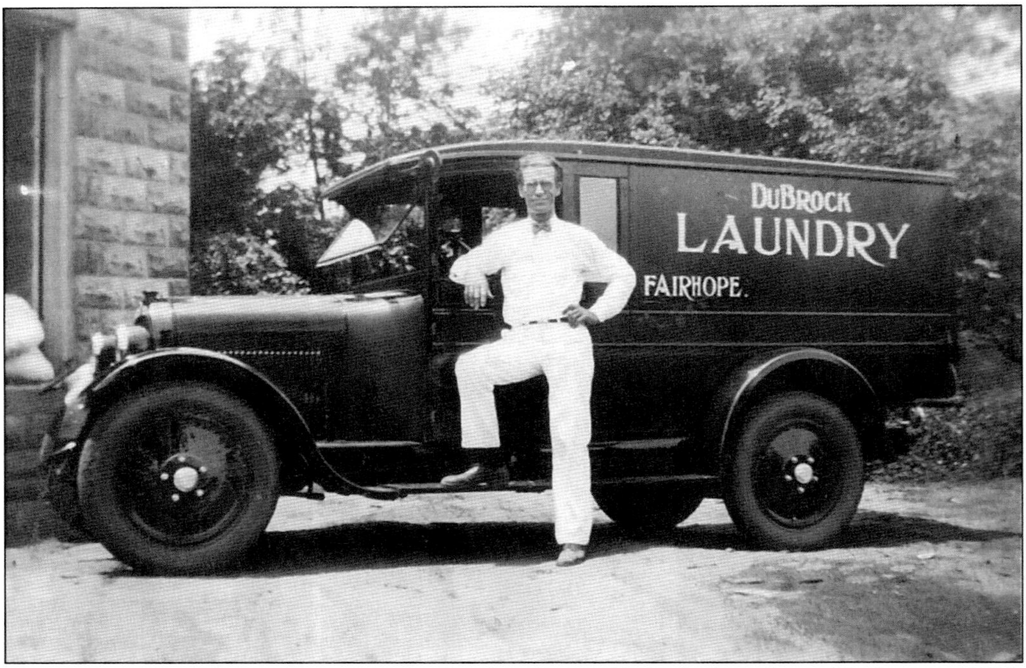

HOME DELIVERY AVAILABLE. Norvin DuBrock, who established a laundry in Fairhope in 1923, soon acquired a new delivery truck to bring fresh wash door to door. His steam-powered laundry, which operated for many years, still stands on the west side of the first block of North Church Street, now converted to shops. (Courtesy of George DuBrock collection.)

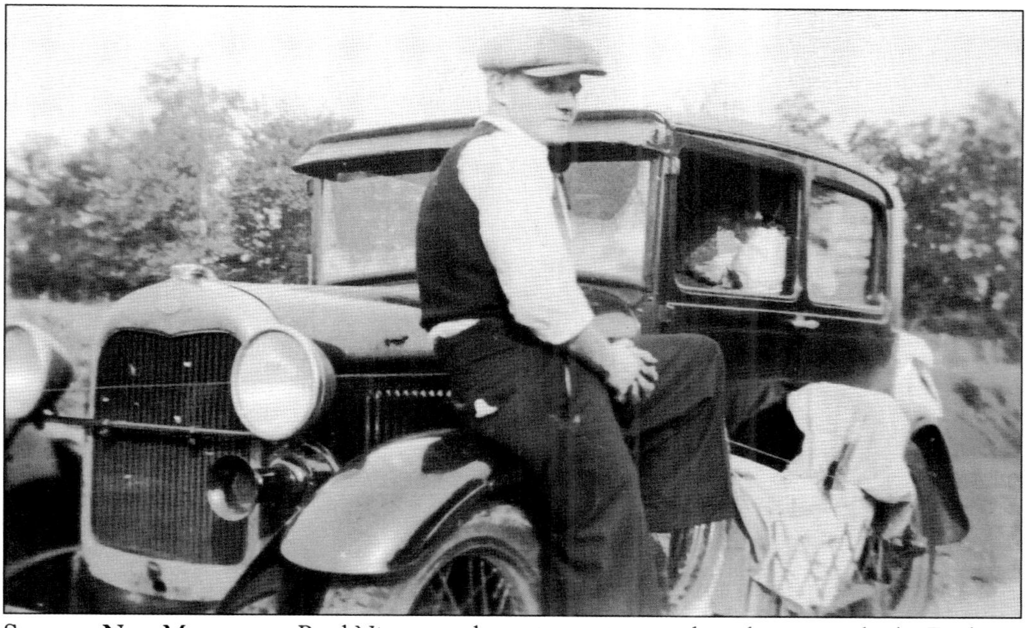

SHINING NEW MOTORCAR. Brad Niemeyer shows insouciant pride in his new vehicle. Fairhope never was much of a horse-and-buggy town because of its relatively late development in the 1890s and the worldliness of its residents, who quickly embraced the new mechanical age. By the early 1920s, there were dozens of automobile models to choose from in a range of colors beyond the old basic black. (Courtesy of Ken Niemeyer.)

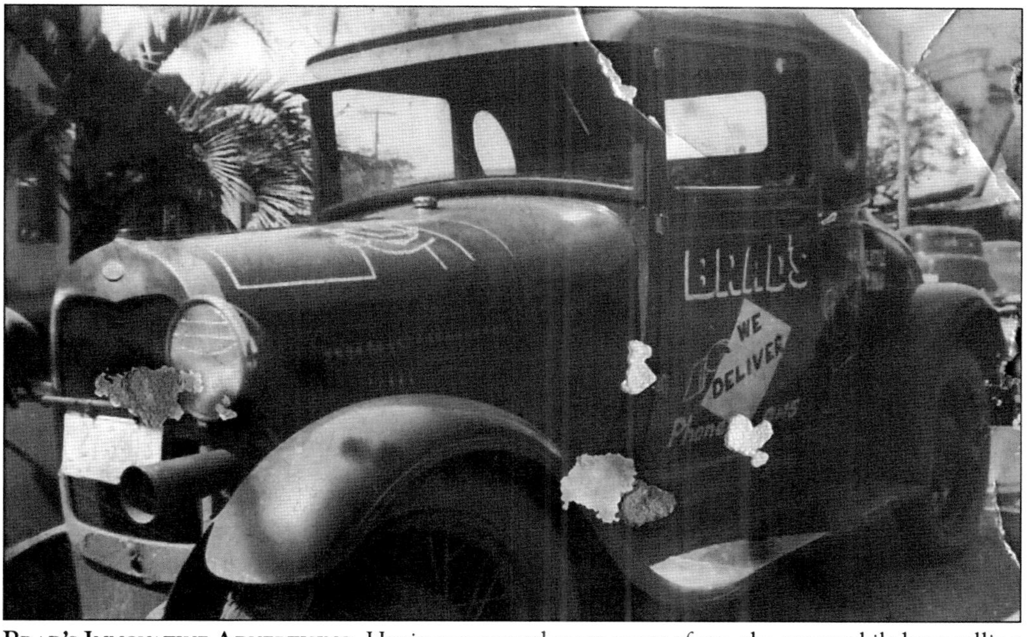

BRAD'S INNOVATIVE ADVERTISING. Having apparently seen years of use, the automobile kept rolling after it was converted from a sedan to delivery vehicle with customized painting for Brad's business. His café in the Walker Building on the south side of Fairhope Avenue had a soda fountain and offered dine-in, take-out, and delivery for call-in orders. (Courtesy of Ken Niemeyer.)

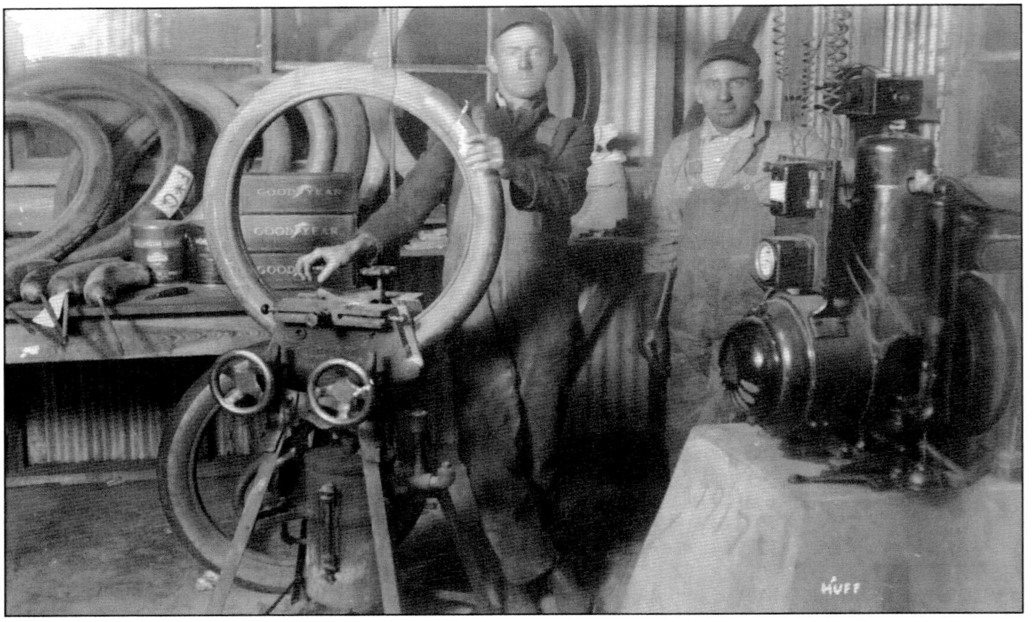

I OUGHTN'T AUTO ANYMORE. Rudolph Tuveson, left, and Howard Ruge fix a flat tire in the automotive repair shop they opened at 25 North Section Street in 1923 after returning from a driving tour of the West. The newspaper reported they had installed a pneumatic machine, probably for the new balloon tires that made riding much smoother. Ruge later served as Fairhope mayor from 1934 to 1948. (Courtesy of FMH.)

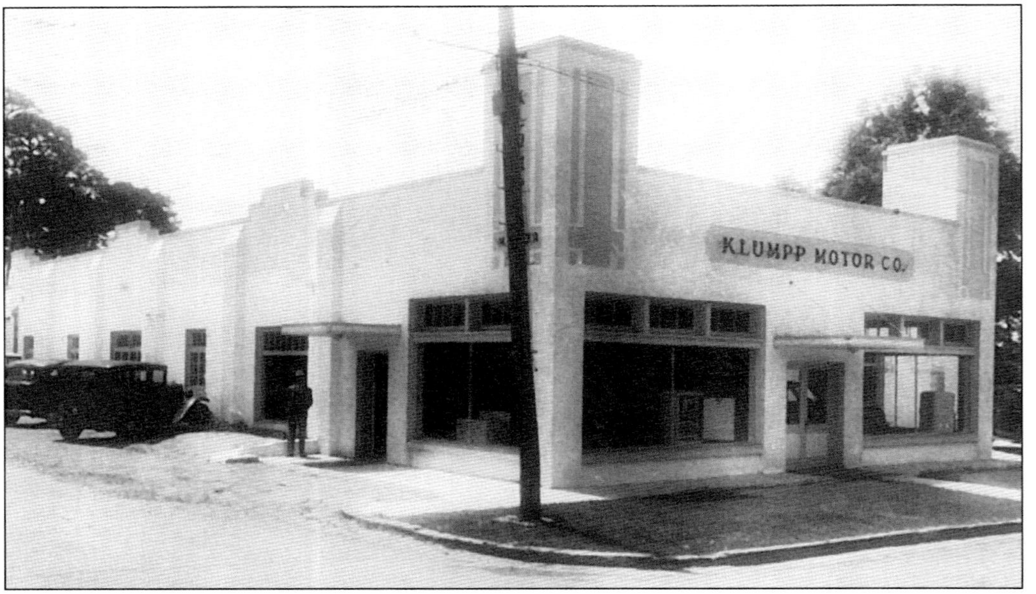

DECORATIVE ART DECO. Anthony J. Klumpp's new Chevrolet dealership was termed a "splendid fire-proof garage" when the distinctive Art Deco building opened on Fairhope Avenue. Klumpp, who later was mayor from 1948 to 1954, disposed of the old automobiles in the kudzu-covered gully behind his business, and for generations Fairhope youngsters explored the area trying to find vintage cars. (Courtesy of Reed Myers.)

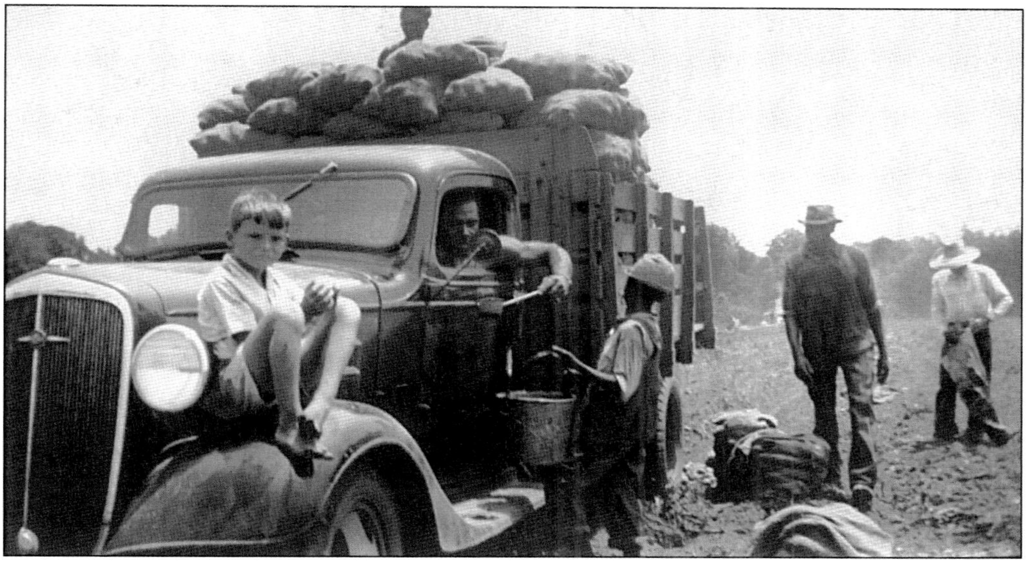

Potato Head Blues. With the coming of the automobile, trucks were not far behind. Heavier trucks appeared in the 1920s and were a boon to farmers, especially those near Fairhope who planted corn, watermelon, and Irish potato crops, such as the one shown here, to ship north. Trucks made hauling to the nearest railroad branch at Robertsdale, 15 miles to the east, much easier. (Courtesy of FMH.)

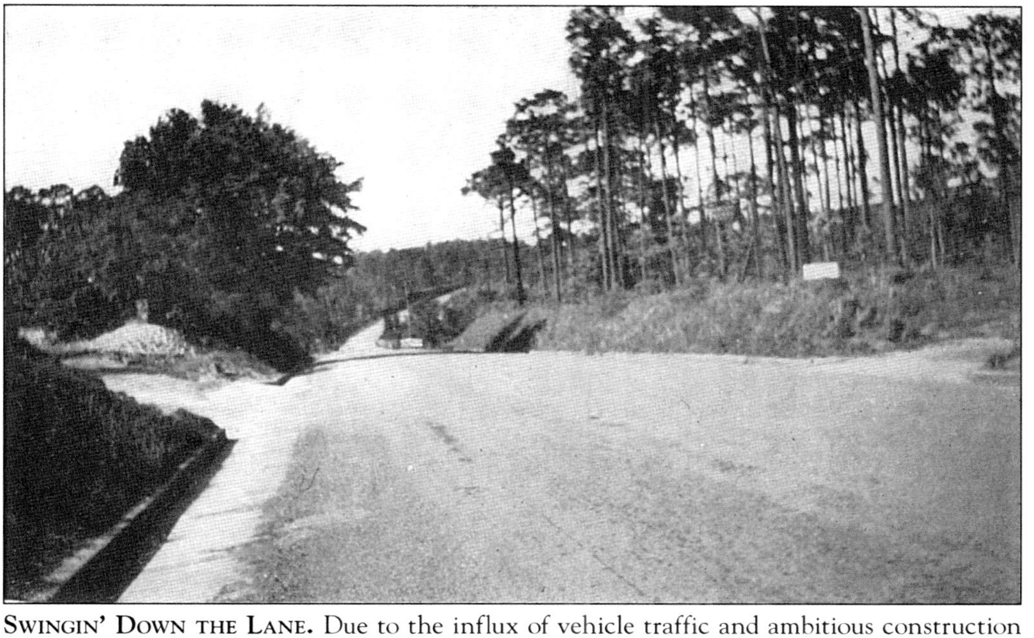

Swingin' Down the Lane. Due to the influx of vehicle traffic and ambitious construction programs, Alabama's hard-surfaced roads increased from 5,000 miles to more than 20,000 miles during the 1920s. North Section Street, later part of US Highway 98, became a main artery into Fairhope. Today, the Eastern Shore Art Center is located at the corner of Oak Street on the right. (Courtesy of FMH.)

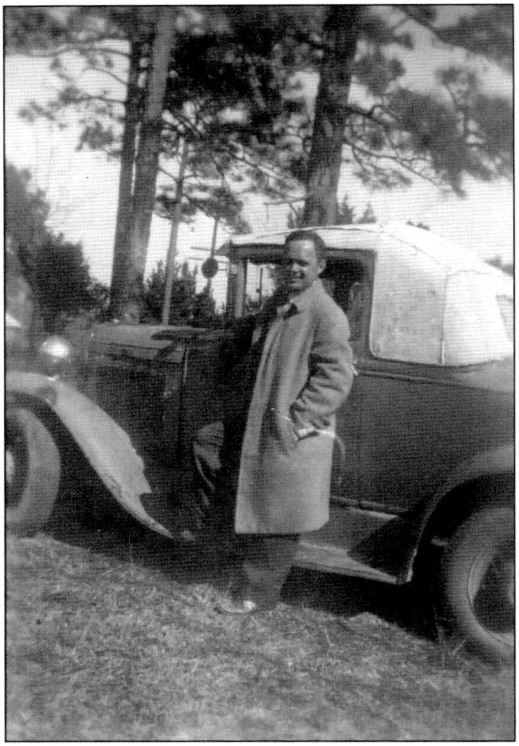

The Jazz Singer. Debonair local musician James "Jimmy" Lowell grew up in a large musical family and started out singing in a quartet with his brothers. When the Jazz Age and automotive age converged, he embraced both, acquiring a motorcar and playing in a band that entertained with the latest dance songs in the waterfront pavilions on Saturday nights. (Courtesy of Gladys Lowell Kellogg.)

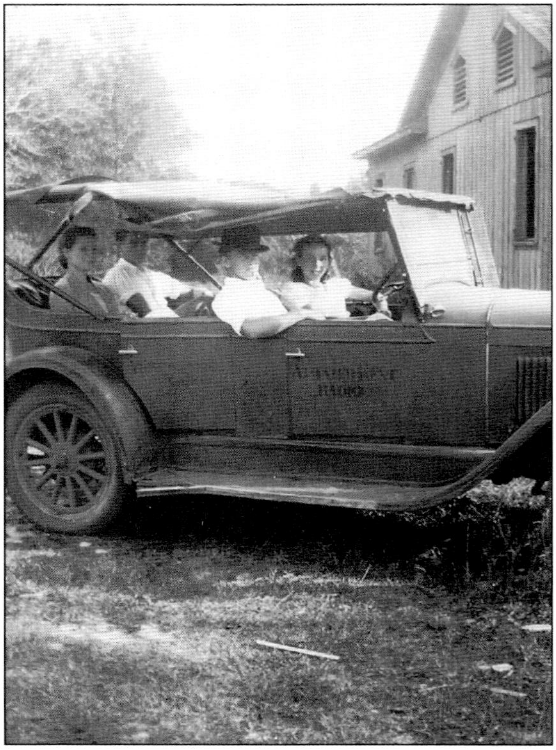

Up-to-Date Invention in Demand. The only thing more sought after than an automobile in the 1920s was a radio. The radio became the greatest craze of the decade, for the first time bringing live news, music, and sports broadcasts into homes. This unidentified, sporty young group of radio and roadster fans apparently enjoyed both inventions. (Courtesy of MJM.)

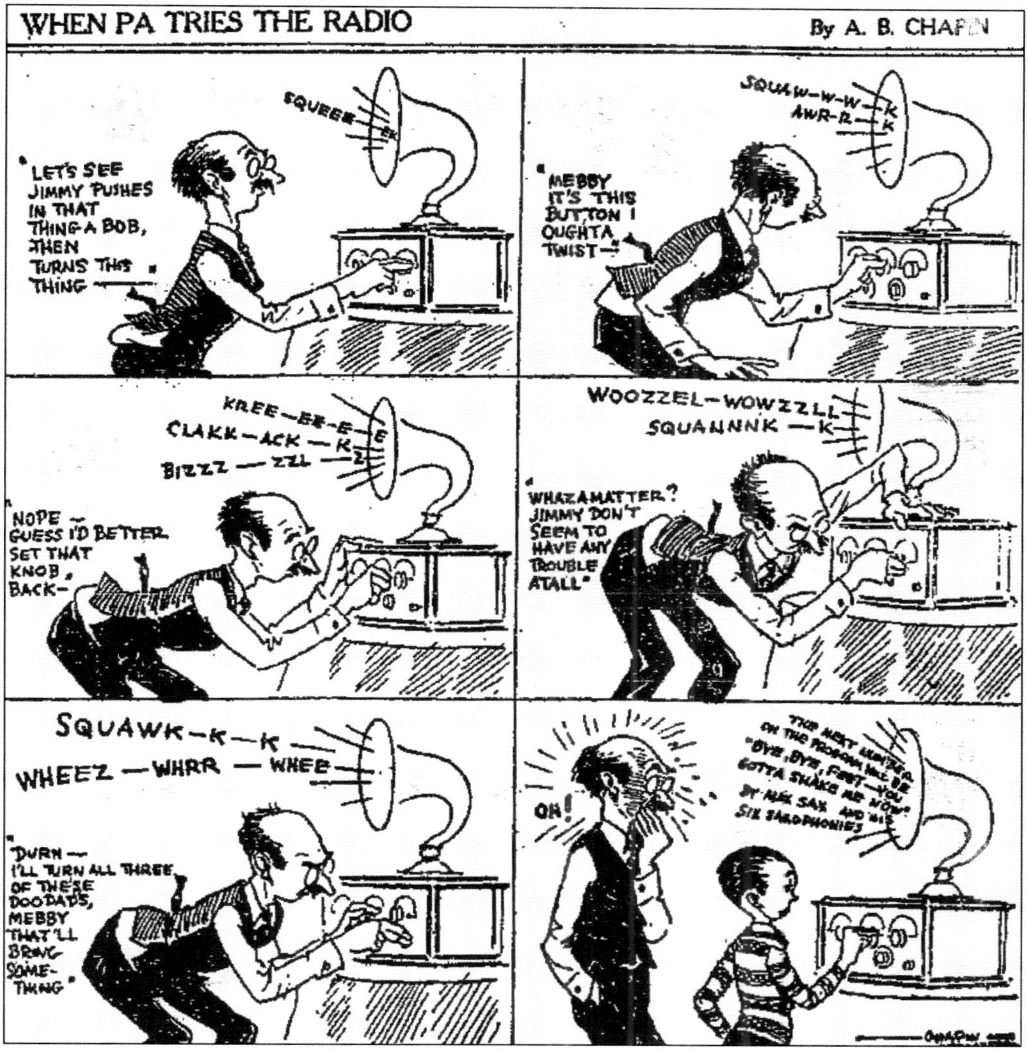

Radio Revolutionized the 1920s. A 1923 cartoon in the Fairhope newspaper shows there is not much difference between the radios of yesteryear and the new computers of today in some households. The Fairhope Electric Company ran advertisements saying, "The radio is past the experimental stage," while one Fairhope listener reported picking up a Los Angeles station. (Courtesy of the *Fairhope Courier*.)

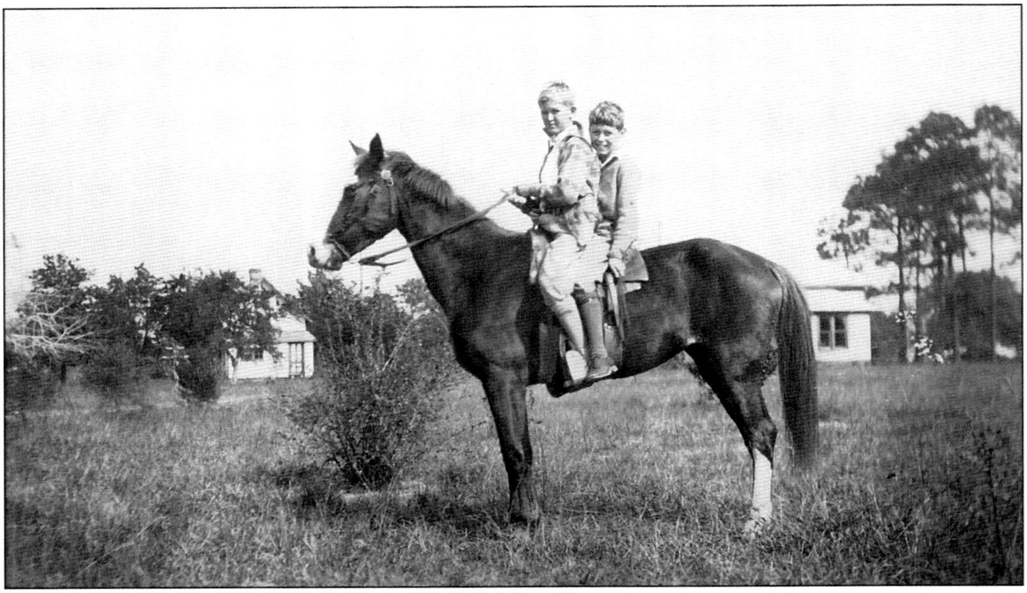

Git A Horse! Not everyone in Fairhope drove an automobile. Francis Albers, shown here with a fellow student behind, liked to ride his horse from his home on Summit Street to the Organic School a few blocks away. As late as 1921, the town passed an ordinance that "no person may ride or drive any animal recklessly." (Courtesy of MJM.)

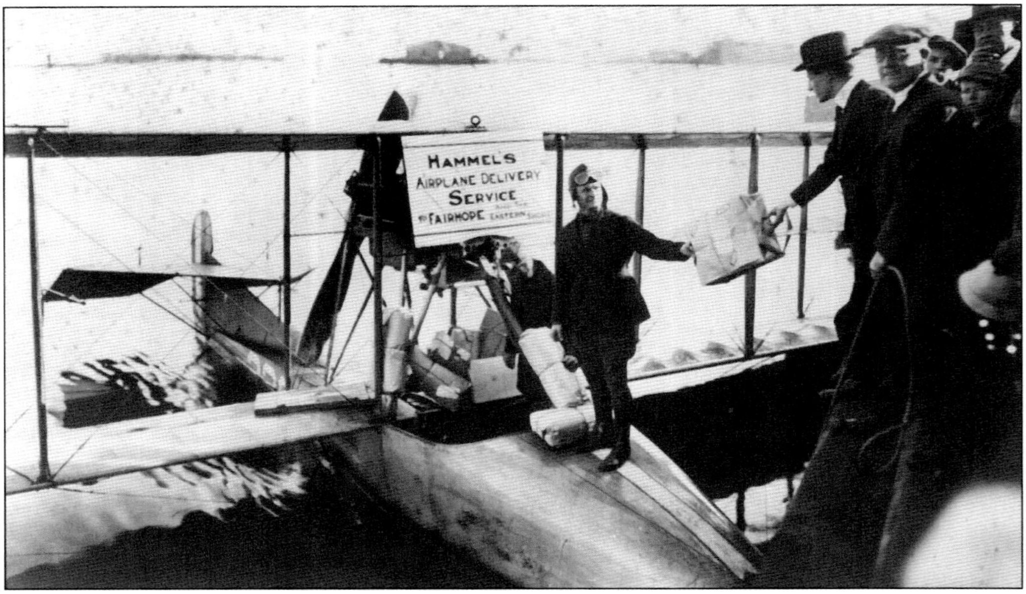

Young Man in the Flying Machine. World War I brought aviation to the fore, and the airplane became a new mode of transportation as pilots made record-setting flights. Here, an aviator delivers packages from Hammel's department store in Mobile across the bay to the Fairhope waterfront in the new craft. (Courtesy of Doy Leale McCall Library.)

Seven
BRIGHT YOUNG THINGS

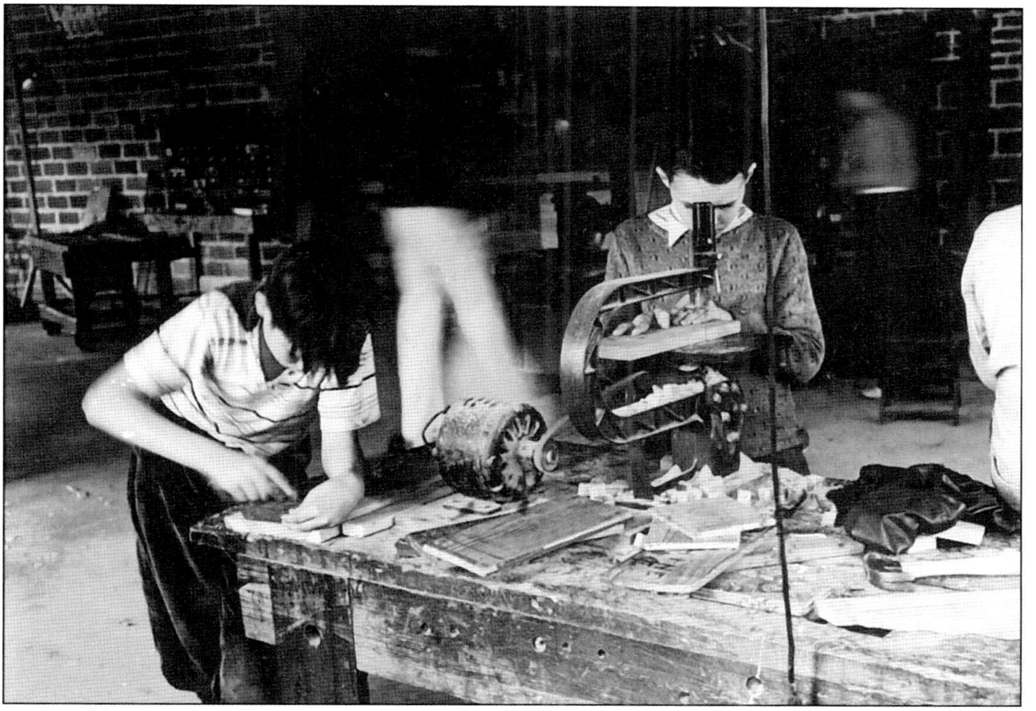

LEARNING BY DOING. Students at the Marietta Johnson School of Organic Education do woodworking projects in the school's Manual Arts Building, where both boys and girls took the required course. "Our shop is the most important place on campus," Johnson, the founder of Fairhope's famous progressive school, often said. (Courtesy of FSTC.)

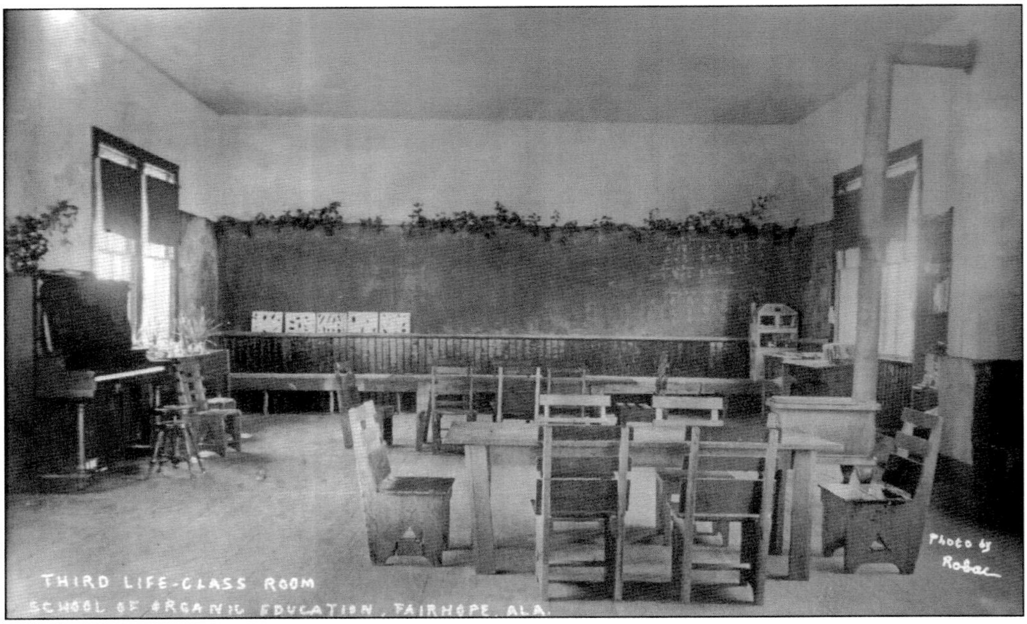

CHILD-CENTERED EDUCATION. The Organic School that drew national attention to Fairhope was based on the philosophy that the education of young children should be a natural development. It recognized the child as a complete organism in mind, body, and spirit. This early classroom in the school, founded in 1907, features furniture made by students. (Courtesy of Helen Dyson collection.)

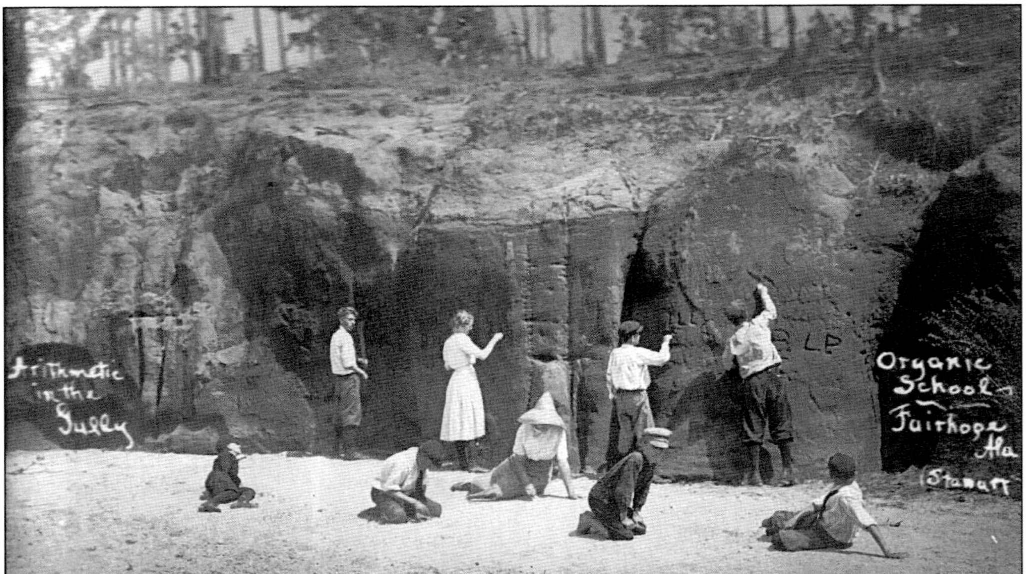

OUTDOORS A CLASSROOM. The experimental school held as many classes as possible out of doors, leaving behind shoes, textbooks, and grade ledgers in favor of informal settings. Groups of scholars often worked out arithmetic problems using the red-clay banks of one of Fairhope's gullies by the bay as their blackboard. (Courtesy of Pinky Bass.)

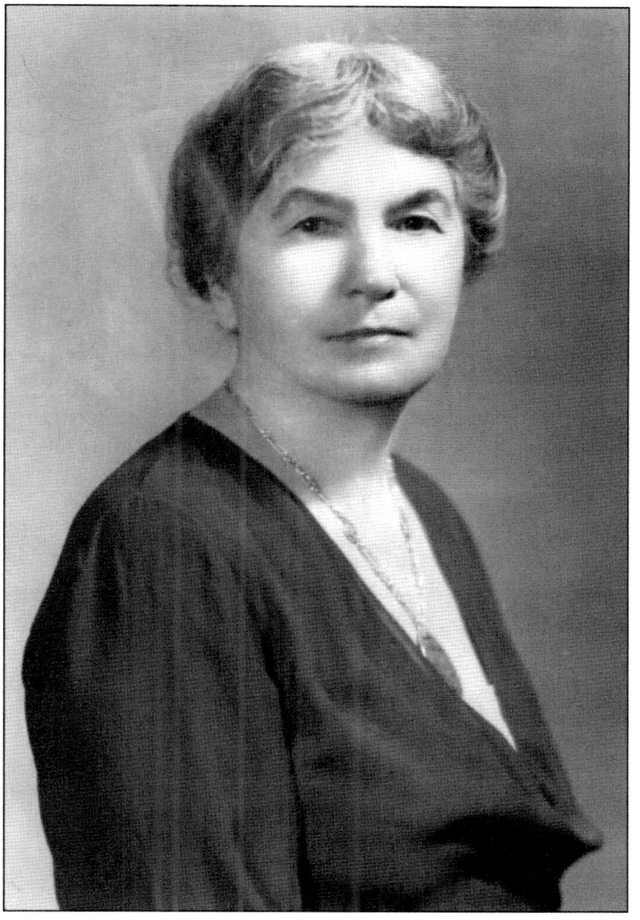

PREMIER PROGRESSIVE EDUCATOR. Educational reformer Marietta Johnson conducted her school on the belief that children love learning. Her ideas attracted the world's attention, and in 1922 she was invited by Clara Bryant Ford (the wife of Henry Ford) to speak about the Organic School in Detroit. The next year, Johnson was off to London to lecture. (Courtesy of MJM.)

CHILDREN OF THE EXPERIMENT. The unique school departed from the strictures of the traditional classroom curriculum, and promoted group work and social skills. The nationally known educator Dr. John Dewey visited the progressive school and features it in his 1915 book *Schools of To-Morrow*, pronouncing it a "decided success." (Courtesy of Helen Dyson collection.)

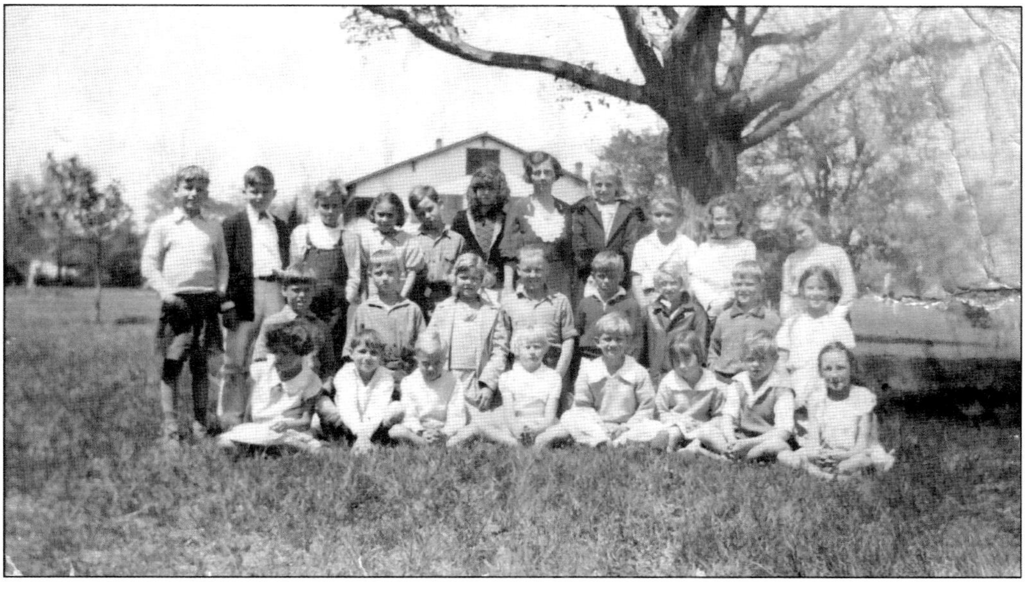

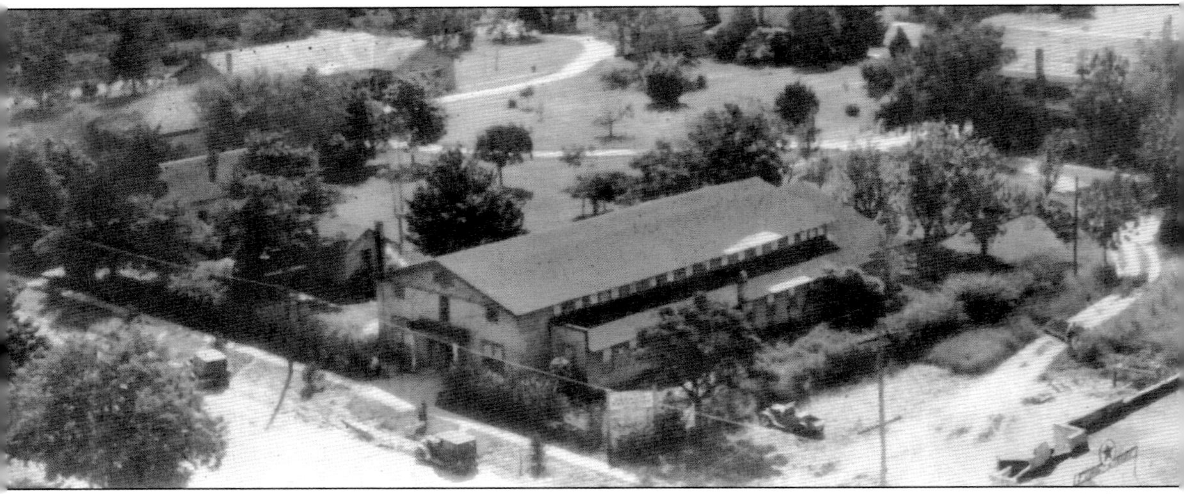

GROWING FAIRHOPE CAMPUS. By the early 1920s, the Organic School campus had grown to include the mostly student-built Comings Hall, in the foreground, facing Fairhope Avenue. The social center of Fairhope for many years, it was named for Lydia J.N. Comings, an author and educator who helped start the school and was considered "Fairhope's first lady." Comings Hall was used for plays, fairs, basketball games, dances, and community gatherings until it was razed in 1966. The school's other original campus buildings are listed in the National Register of Historic Places and are still in use as part of the Fairhope branch of the Faulkner State Community College. (Courtesy of FMH.)

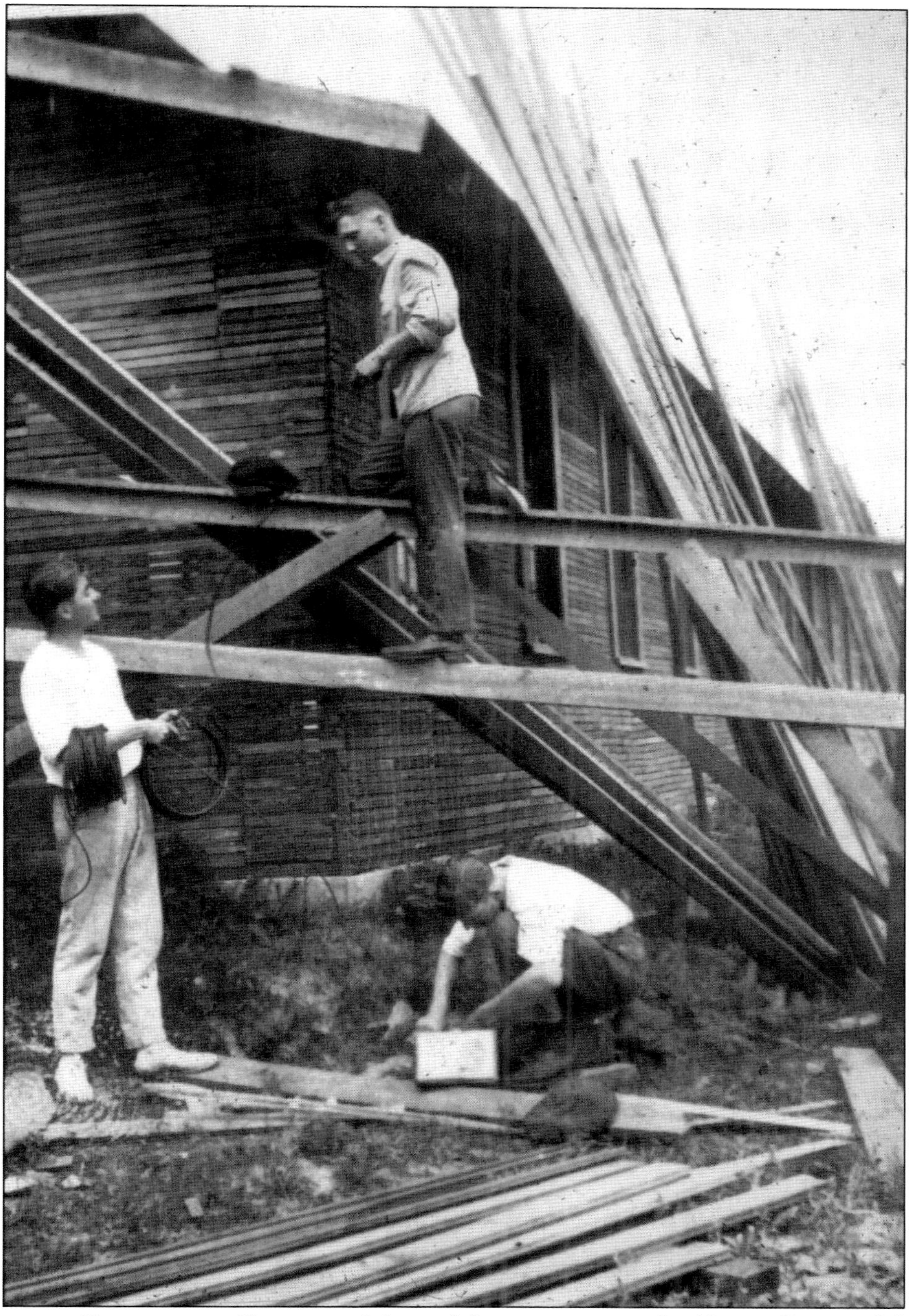

Students Constructed Buildings. Many of the structures on the 10-acre Organic School campus in the middle of town were built by the students, as shown by some older boys working on wiring. The original Bell Building at 10 South School Street is now the Marietta Johnson Museum, while the private Organic School still continues operation on another, smaller campus off Pecan Avenue in Fairhope. (Courtesy of FMH.)

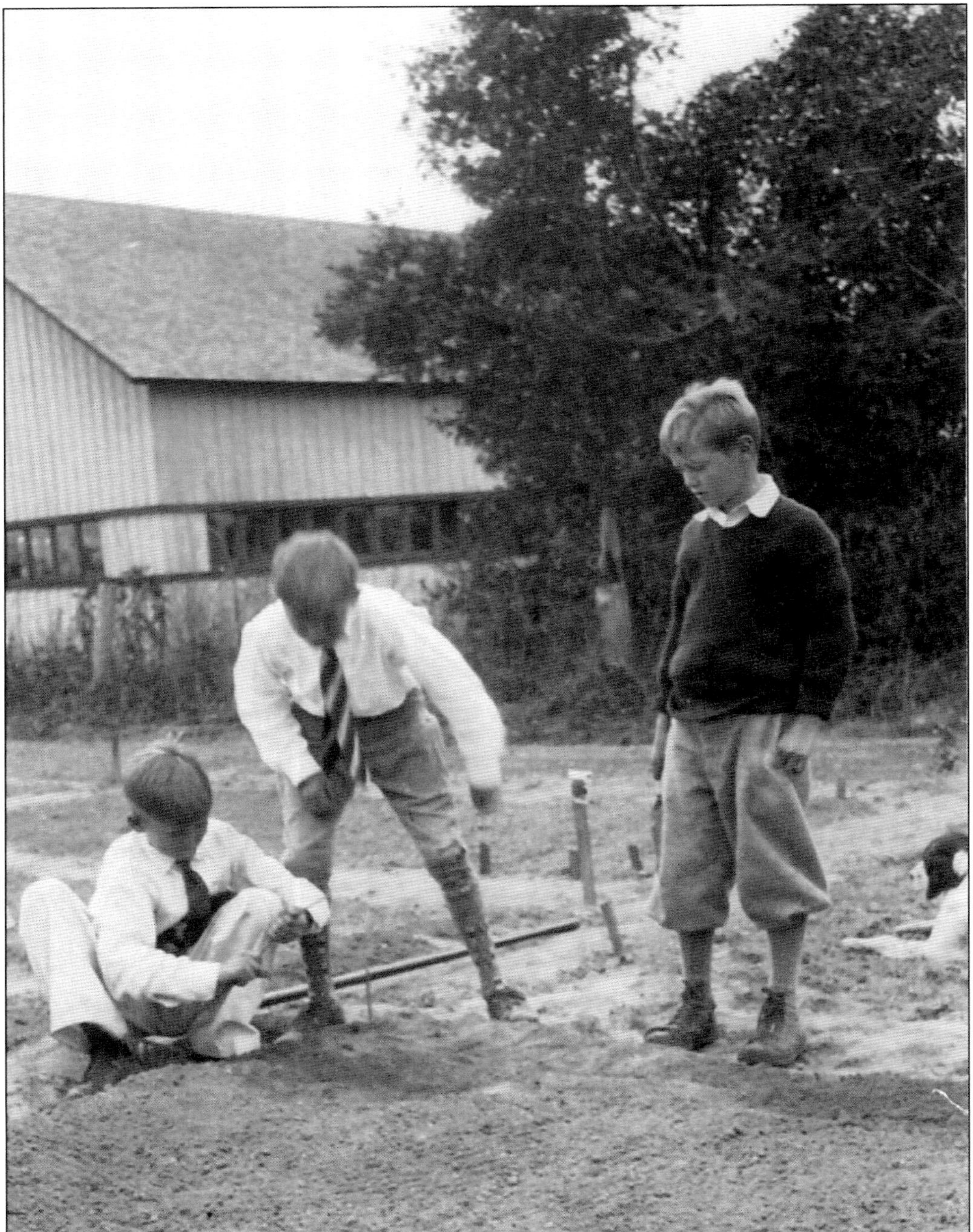

Organic Gardeners Too. Independent thinking was encouraged at the Organic School, where there were no tests, grades, or homework assignments. Here, some younger boys stake out garden plots, which students planted and cultivated at the school where no pupil was allowed to fail. The school's progressive theories were revolutionary in educational circles during the 1920s, but its principles would be copied in many other places. (Courtesy of MJM.)

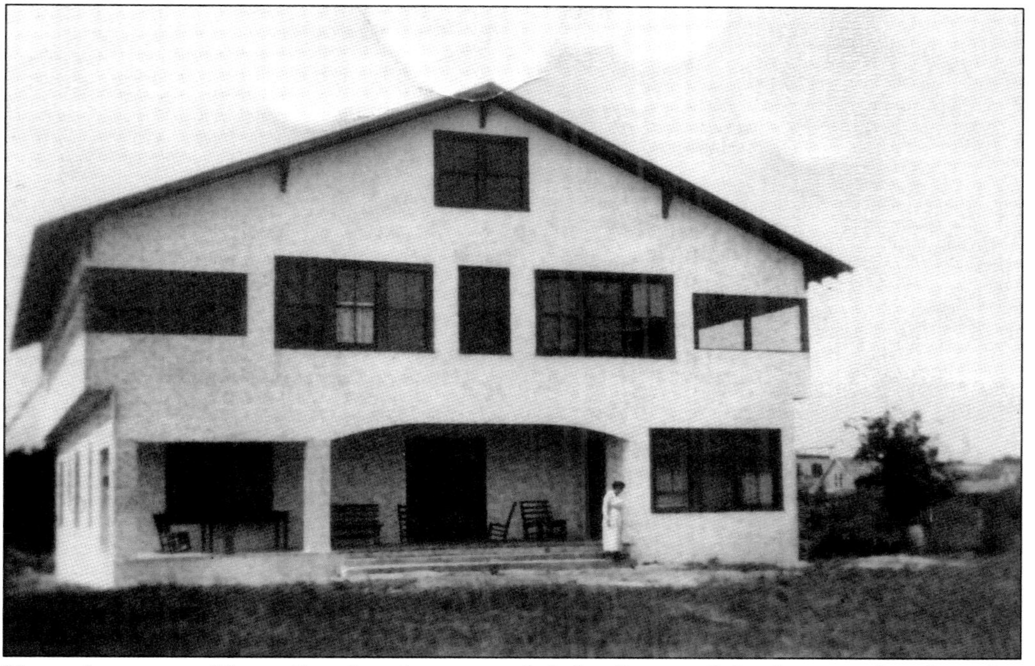

HOME AWAY FROM HOME. Local students attended the Organic School tuition free, but after this School Home was constructed in 1922, many liberal parents across the country sent their children to boarding school on the campus for $750 a year. Others enrolled for the winter term when families vacationed in Fairhope's mild coastal climate. (Courtesy of MJM.)

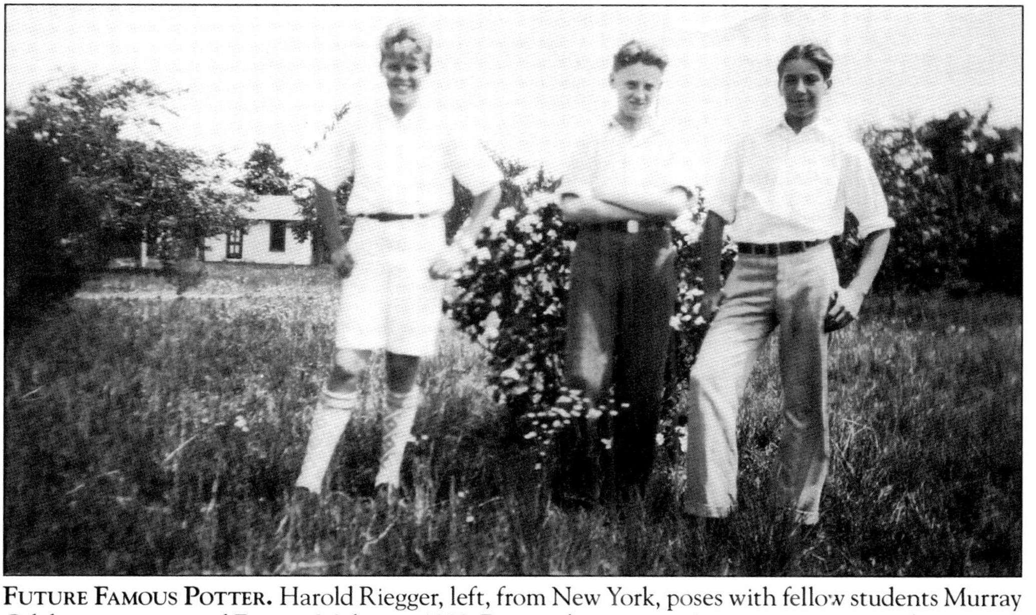

FUTURE FAMOUS POTTER. Harold Riegger, left, from New York, poses with fellow students Murray Gilchrist, center, and Francis Malito in 1929. Riegger became an American expert in the ancient raku pottery making and his work is displayed in several museums. He wrote he discovered his love of pottery—and other boys—at the Organic School in the 1920s, when alternative lifestyles gained acceptance. (Courtesy of MJM.)

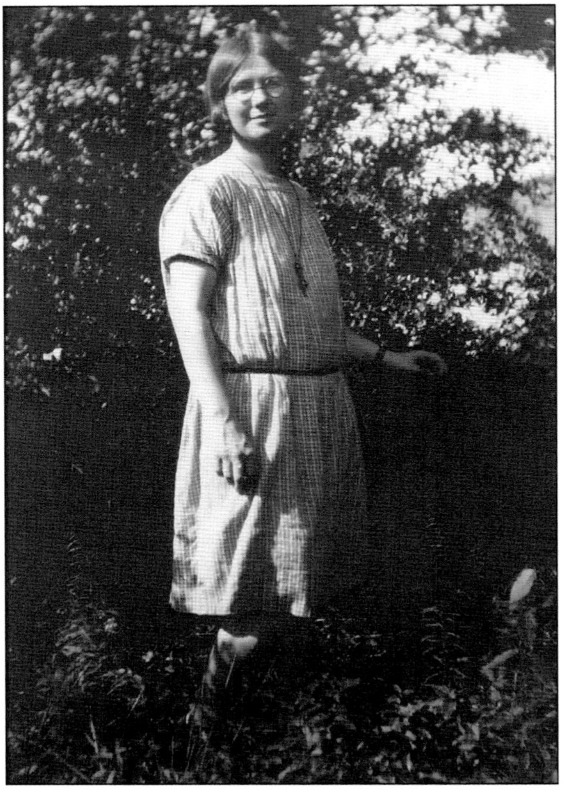

Mary Bobs Her Hair. Mary Chase, teacher at the Organic School, was a modern woman who in 1922 attempted to embrace the flapper style with bobbed hair, wristwatch, and the rising hemline of the new "tub frocks" being advertised as the latest fashion. She obviously had shed the restricting corset of the past too. That year, Gene Murray, who operated a ladies' shop in Fairhope, drove up east in her Oldsmobile to buy the latest styles in dresses for her store. (Courtesy of MJM.)

Just Monkeying Around. It is not known to whom this monkey belonged, as such pets were popular with several Fairhopers (including at least one teacher at the Organic School). The town marshal carried a monkey around, and students could bring their pets to school. They also were allowed to go barefoot, and to this day the phrase "Fairhope shoes" jokingly means bare feet. (Courtesy Flora Maye Simmons collection.)

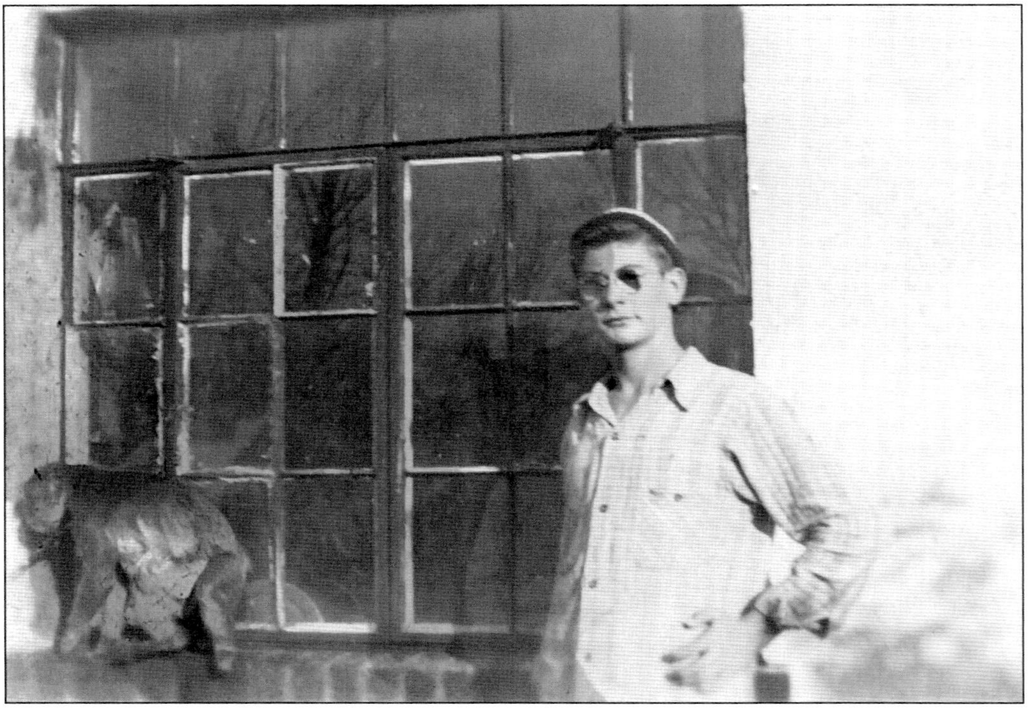

MASTER OF MORRIS DANCE. Charles Rabold left the music department at Yale University to teach at the Organic School, which became renowned for its folk dancing program. He was assistant director of the school, in line to succeed Marietta Johnson, when he was killed in a fiery monoplane crash returning from a California project in 1930. It was the world's worst air disaster at the time. (Courtesy of MJM.)

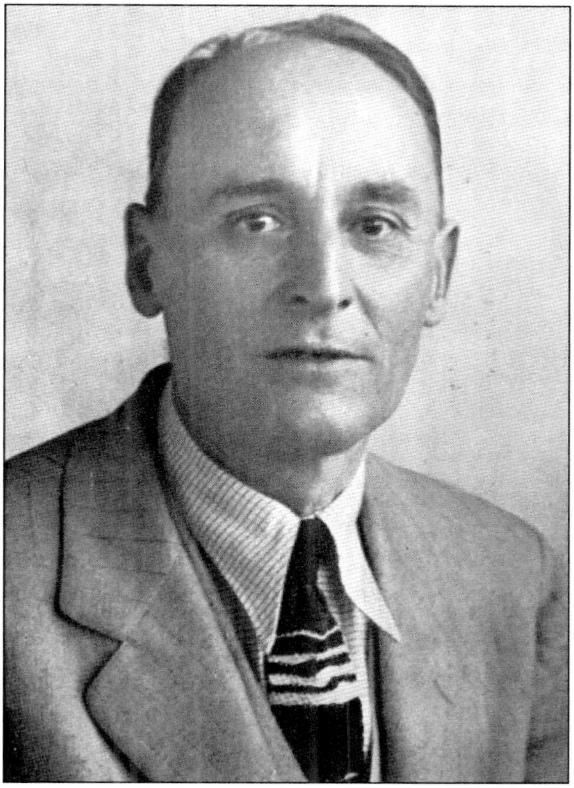

STUDENTS DANCED EVERY DAY. Folk dancing was a form of physical education and a required class at the school, where Rabold taught the dances he had studied under the noted English folklorist Cecil Sharp. Here, the boys demonstrate the handkerchief dance, a form of the traditional morris dance. The students performed at Fairhope functions and also across the country during the Jazz Age. (Courtesy of MJM.)

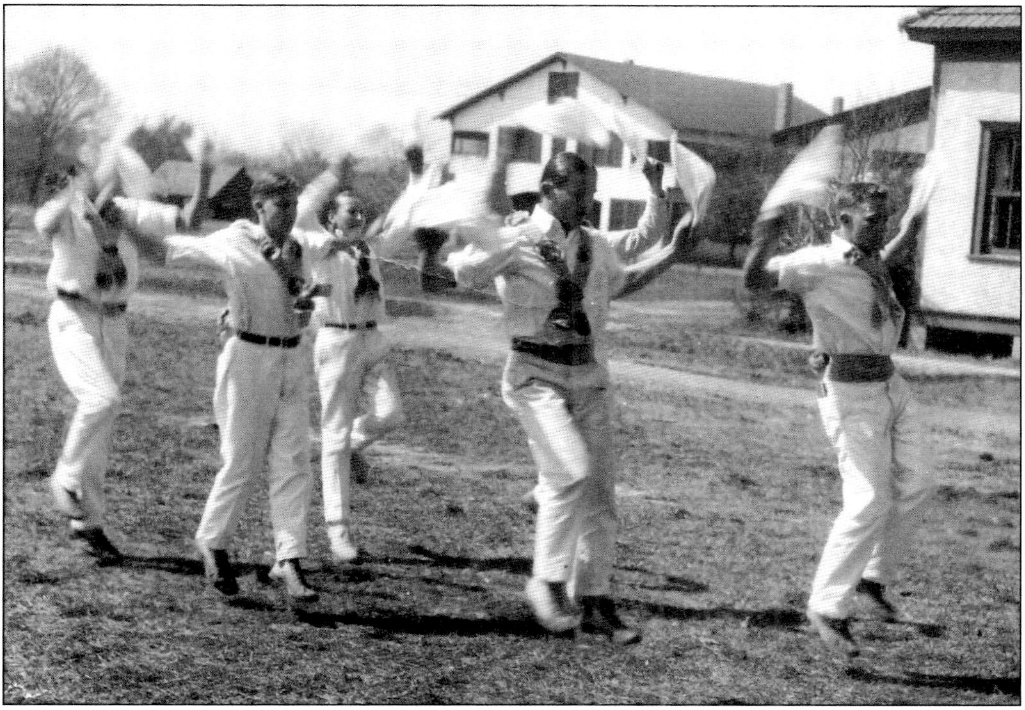

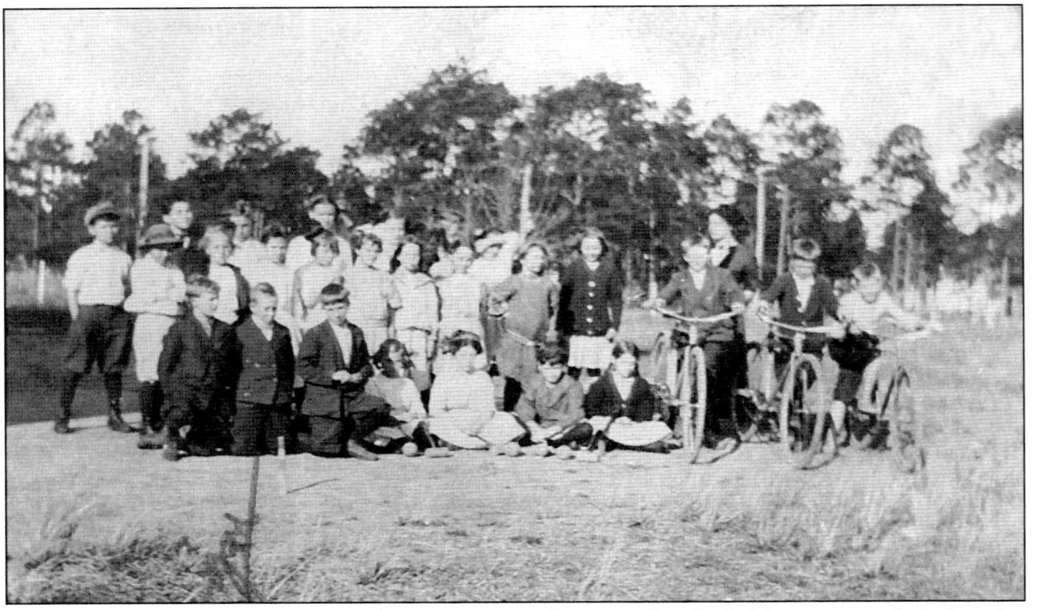

School Days for All. From the beginning, an education for all children was included in the FSTC constitution, which provided for free public schools along with libraries. Classes were held in various buildings around town until 1909, when a large two-story public school building was constructed. Here, some students gather for a photograph, with a few showing off their bicycles. (Courtesy of Robert Berglin.)

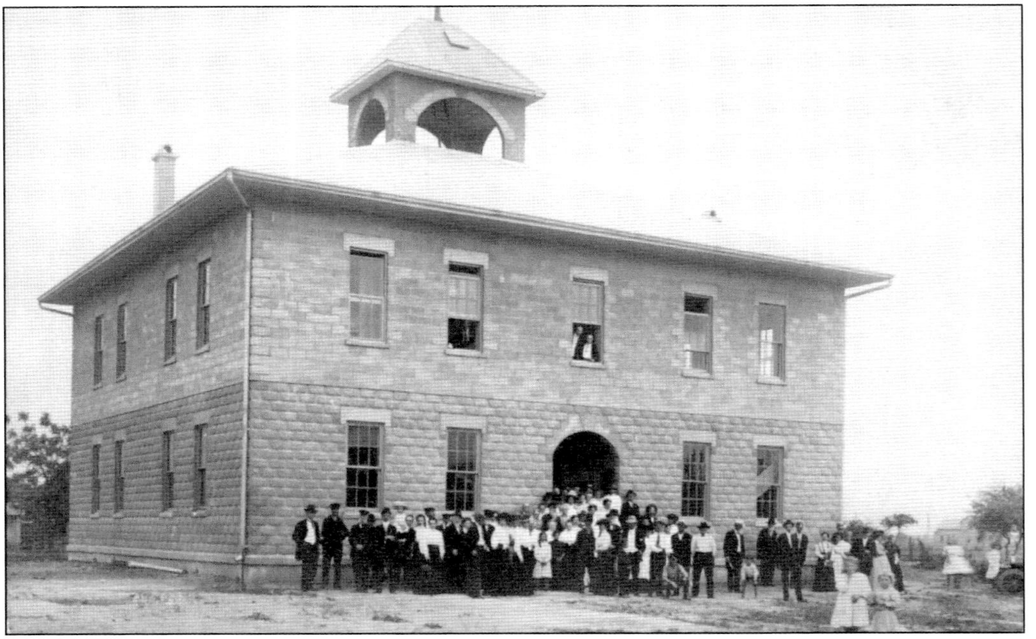

Coming of Age. These Fairhope School students, who would grow into adulthood during the 1920s, gathered with the grown-ups for the opening of their handsome new public school. Decades later, the masonry-block school they attended at the corner of Church Street and Morphy Avenue would be razed to make way for the Fairhopers Community Park. (Courtesy of Reed Myers.)

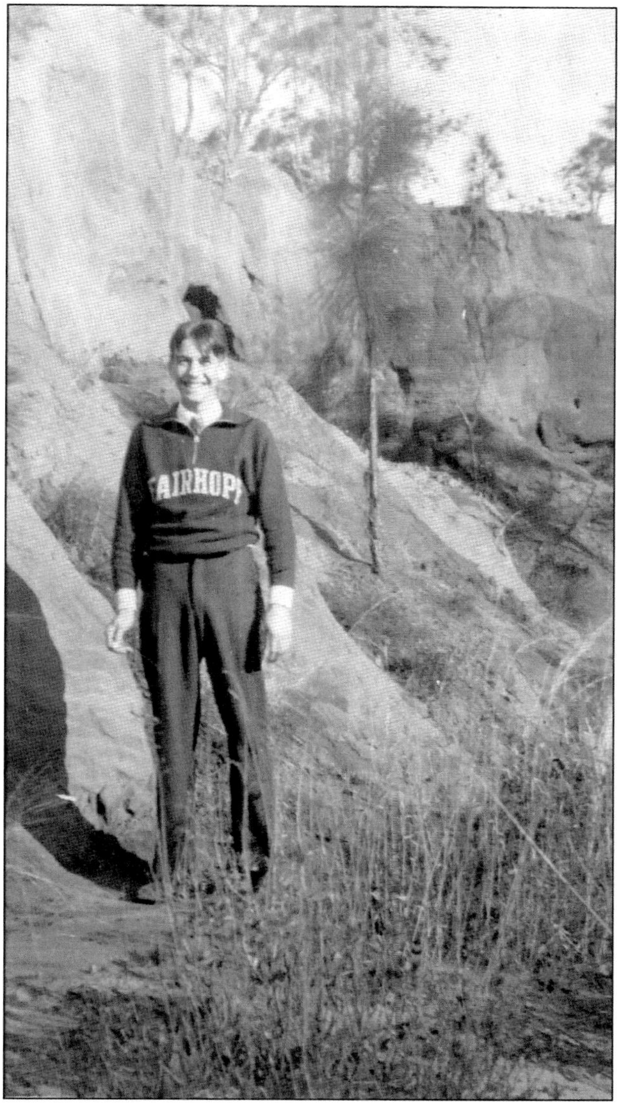

Lettered Sweaters in Style. Fairhope students spent many halcyon days having fun on the Mobile Bay beach, a gathering place for the local teenagers as well as for older residents and families. Here, Francis Malito, standing at the base of a town bluff, shows off his Fairhope jacket. (Courtesy of FMH.)

Fairhope's First High School. By 1925, Fairhope opened an accredited high school with 105 students. The landmark at 100 South Church Street served generations of students until it was closed in 2011. Its last school use was as the Fairhope K-1 Center. The present high school, built in 1993, is located at the edge of town on US Highway 98. (Courtesy of FMH.)

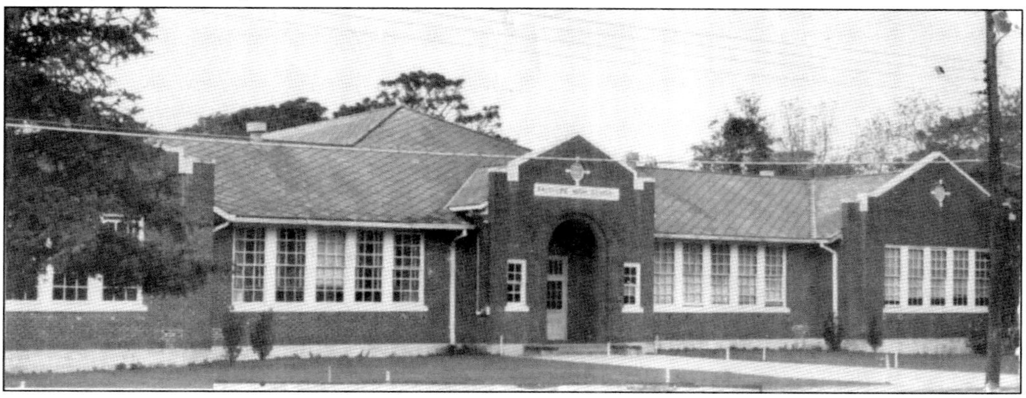

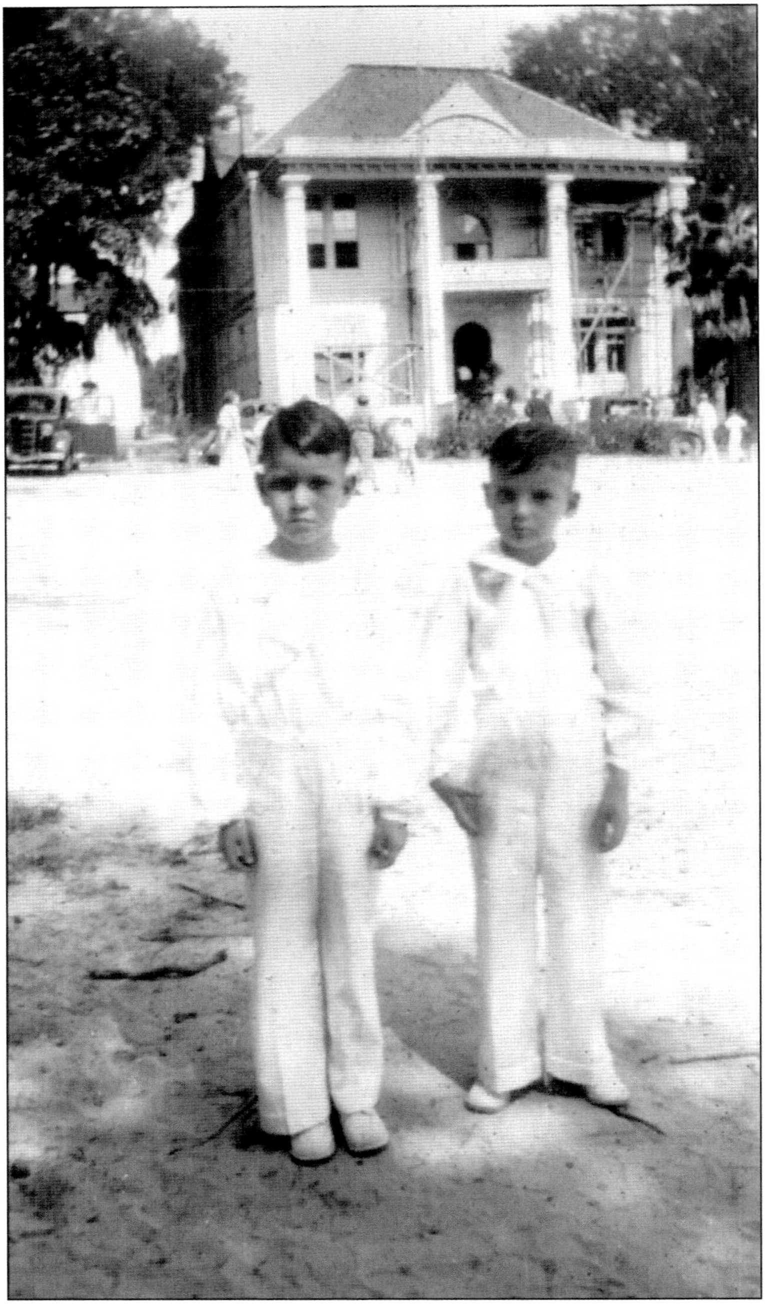

Teachers' College Nearby. The Daphne State Normal School, located near Fairhope, was the only state teachers' college in south Alabama when it opened in 1907, and many of the town's educators were trained there until it closed in 1948. It was housed in this former Baldwin County Courthouse, where Lavigne Berglin, left, and William Godard of Fairhope are pictured at a May Day festival. Daphne was the county seat from 1868, when it was decided that the seat should be moved to Bay Minette. Daphne resisted the change, so some men from Bay Minette stole the records at night and spirited them away to the present courthouse there. (Courtesy of FMH.)

Eight

Oh, You Kid

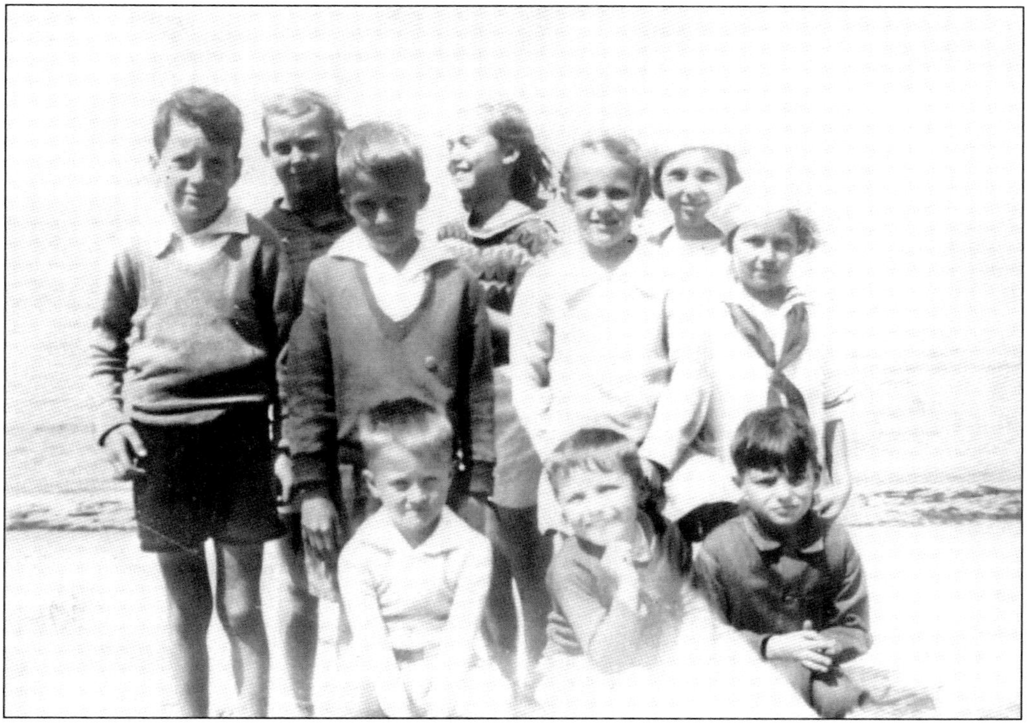

Fun in the Sun. Some Fairhope youngsters suspend their frolicking on the beach the promoters called the American Riviera in the 1920s to pose in the blazing sunshine. These children would become part of the new youth-based generation that brought its own sassy new slang, racy culture, and unprecedented freedoms. (Courtesy of FMH.)

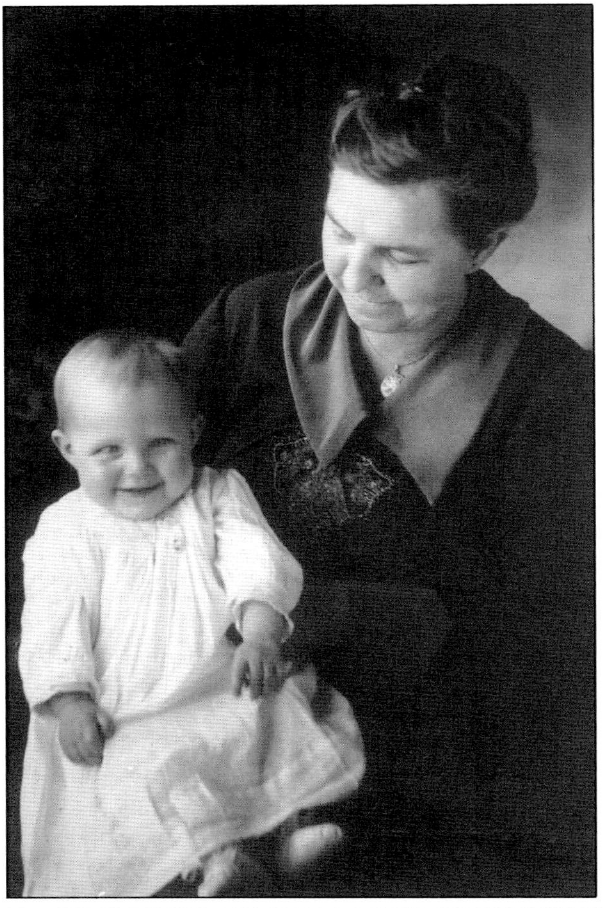

New Generation Welcomed. Little Olive Jean Gaston, the first grandchild of Fairhope's founding family, was born to James E. and Olive "Piney" Gaston in 1919. Pictured here being admired by her maternal grandmother, Emma L. Wood, Olive seems delighted to be facing a new decade. Emma Wood was always in demand for catering large community dinners and banquets. (Courtesy of Harriet Swift.)

Duck Pond Delightful Spot. The spring-fed pool on Fairhope's waterfront was an intriguing cypress glade for children to explore in the 1920s, and it remains so today. The rustic bridge has been replaced, but the beachfront park still draws families with toddlers, who bring bread to feed the seagulls, geese, and duck populations there. (Courtesy of Reed Myers.)

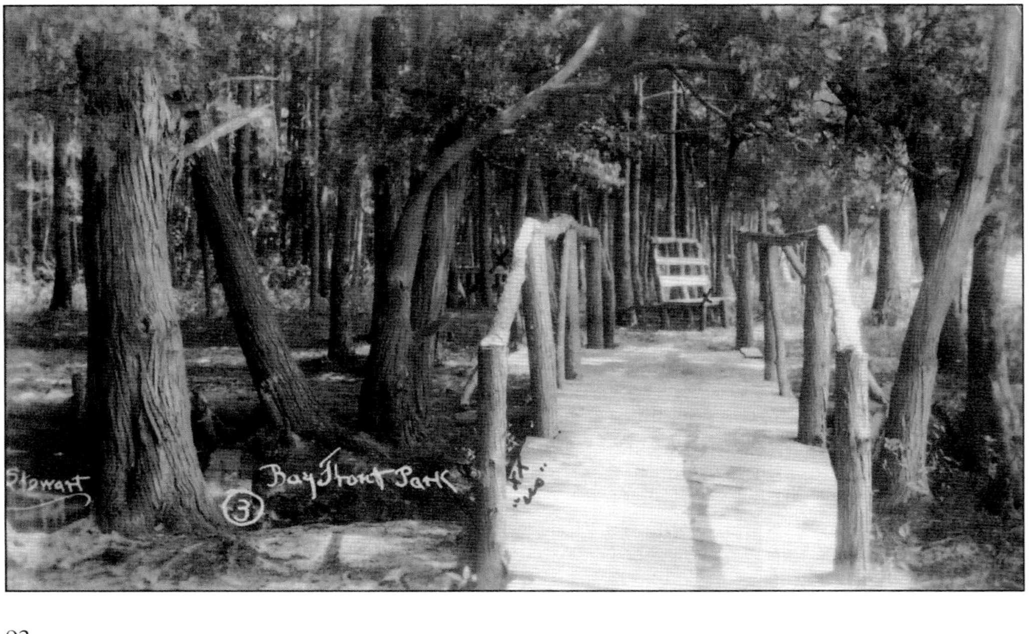

Yes Sir, That's My Baby. In 1922, Mary Gaston showed off waving daughter Mary, also called "Buddy." The child's father, Arthur (the first boy born in Fairhope) gave her the nickname because she was a little buddy he liked to take to work with him when he set type at the *Fairhope Courier*. (Courtesy of FMH.)

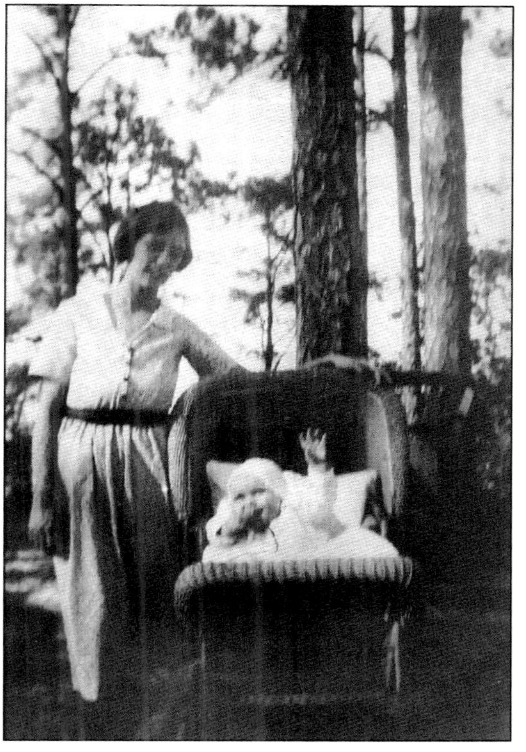

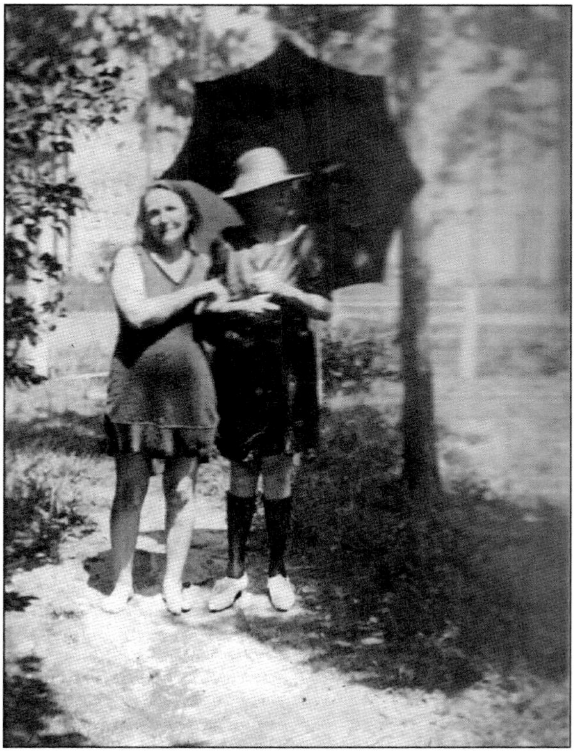

A Budding Flapper. An older Buddy Gaston poses with her grandmother Mary Price near the same location on the Fairhope bluff. Her younger brother Ernest B. "Barney" Gaston, a fighter pilot, was killed when he was shot down over France in World War II. He was later declared a war hero. (Courtesy of FMH.)

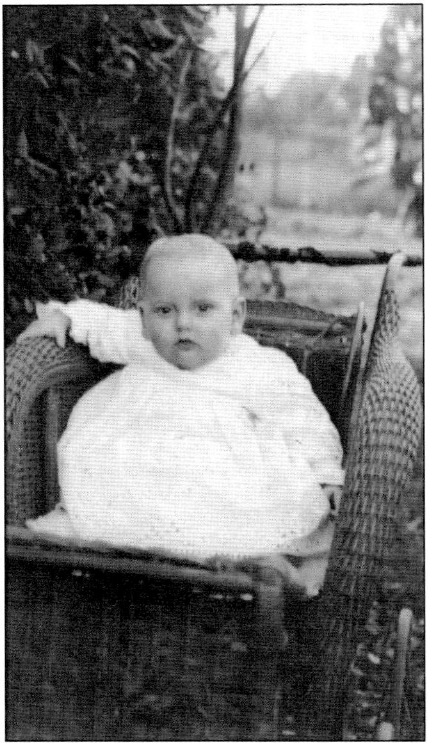

THE BOY WHO WAS. Dudley was the youngest of four sons born to William and Alice Webb Stimpson, the first couple to be married in the newly founded Fairhope. William established the town's sawmill, where all the boys worked. Dudley, however, was killed in a hunting accident in 1928. (Courtesy of Harriet Swift.)

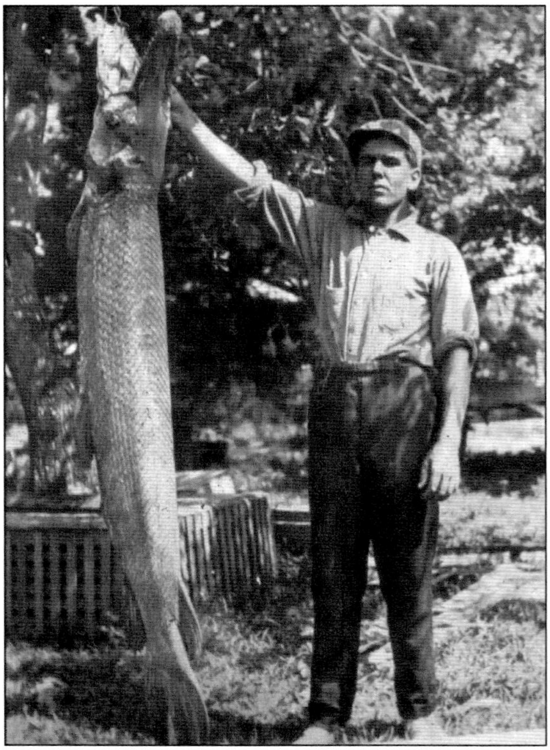

FISH BIGGER THAN BOY. Jesse Stimpson, the eldest son, who managed William Stimpson's Sons Sawmill after his father, an Englishman, died in 1923, displays a trophy alligator gar he caught. Jesse also played sports, leading the Fairhope Athletic Club during the 1920s. Stimpson Field on Morphy Avenue, now the city tennis courts, was named for him. (Courtesy of FSTC.)

Live Hood Ornament. Robert Dean Swift perches on the hood of the family automobile in the late 1920s. His grandfather had arrived in the Fairhope settlement in the late 1890s and purchased a large tract of land on the bay bluff on the north edge of town. The privately held Swift property was not a part of the FSTC. (Courtesy of FMH.)

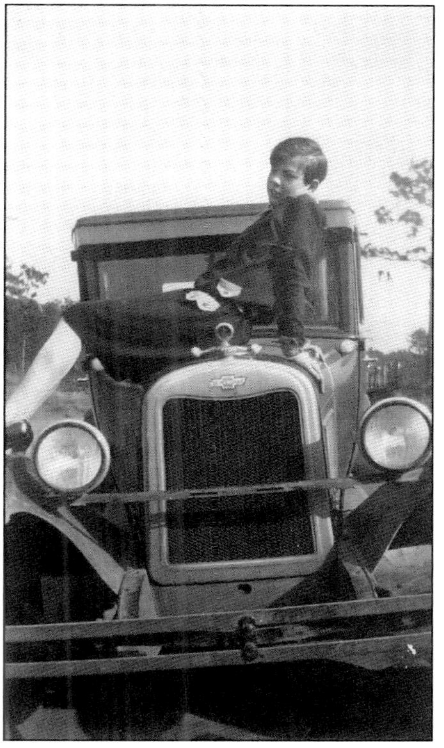

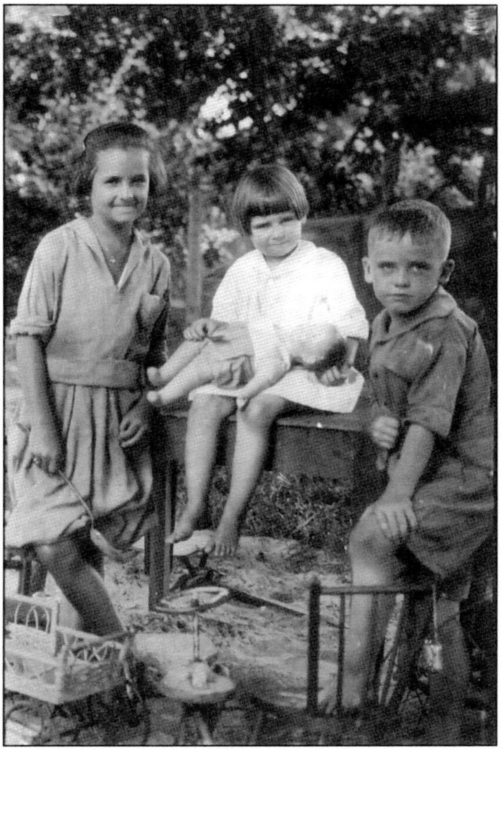

The Watched Pot. In this 1922 image, the Swift children have been busy making mud pies. Pictured are, from left to right, Jane, Harriet (holding her baby doll), and Robert. The children of Ernest and Jennie Swift were often seen about town riding on their pet pony. (Courtesy of Harriet Swift.)

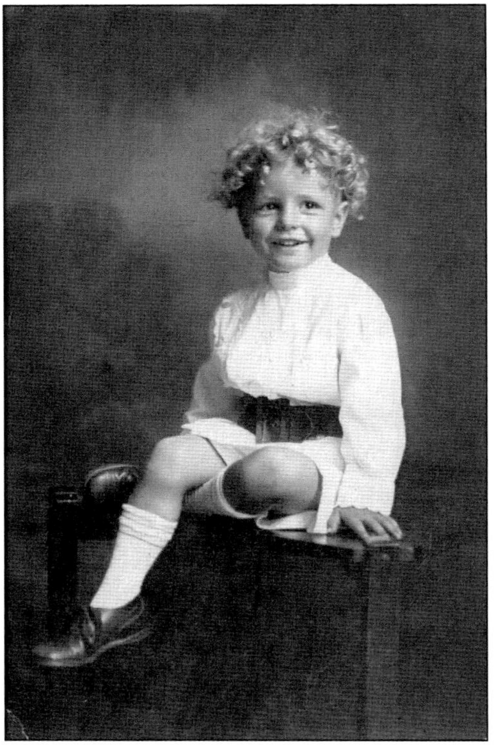

Everybody Loves My Baby. George DuBrock, three years old in 1920, is dressed for his portrait as a little golden-haired cherub with a head full of curls. When he came down with tonsillitis a few years later, his progress was reported in the local newspaper. He became a master woodworker and clockmaker. (Courtesy of George DuBrock collection.)

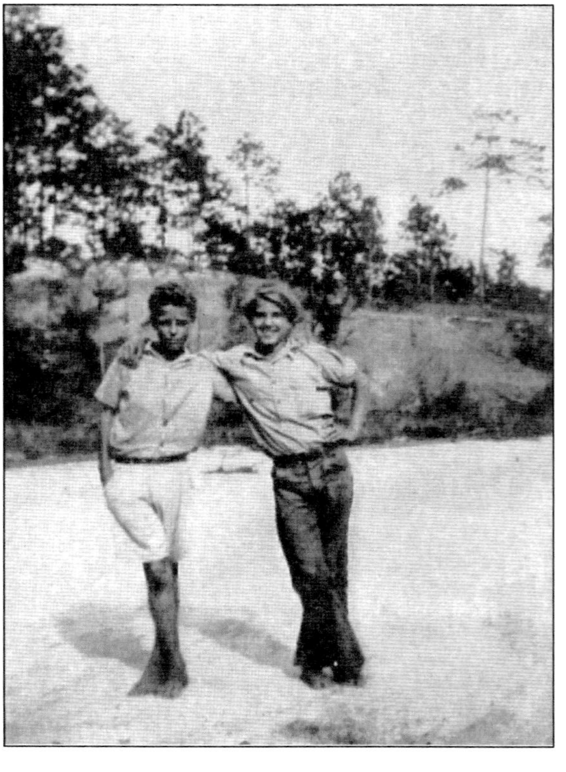

Ain't Misbehaving on the Beach. An older George DuBrock, left, and his pal Raymond Flagg seem to be having fun on the Fairhope beach. They were part of a generation of youngsters who grew up in the carefree 1920s only to come of age and struggle through the Great Depression of the coming decade. (Courtesy of George DuBrock collection.)

THE SMALL BACHELOR. James "Jimmy" Price is immaculately dressed to have his picture taken. In the 1920s, ready-to-wear clothes were available for the first time for children as well as grown-ups, and Fairhope offered them early on. Ellen Anaker opened her Kiddie Clothes Shop on a town corner in 1923. (Courtesy of FMH.)

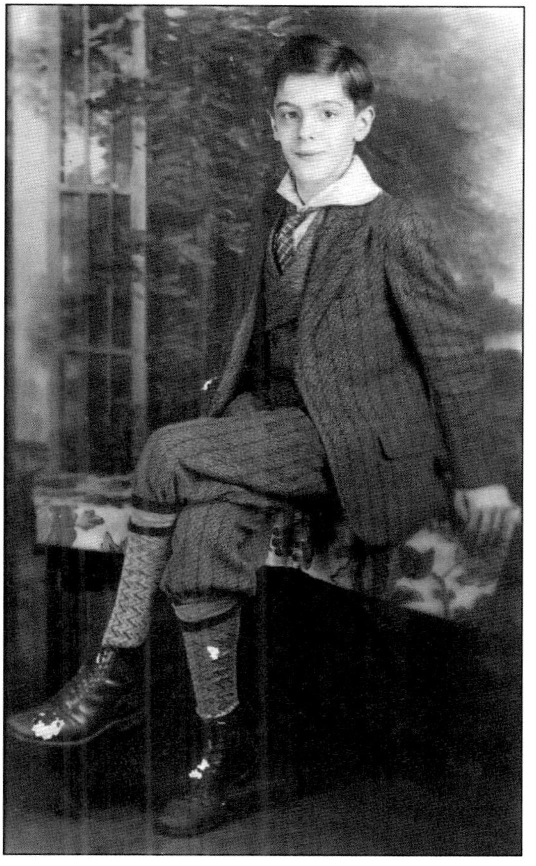

IT'S PARTY TIME. Along with all the party hats worn at this birthday celebration, the mother of the honoree (standing on a chair) is sporting a newly fashionable cloche hat. Children's parties were also a part of the social scene in Fairhope which, if not Gatsby's East Egg, was at least the biggest town on Alabama's Eastern Shore. (Courtesy of the WOFC.)

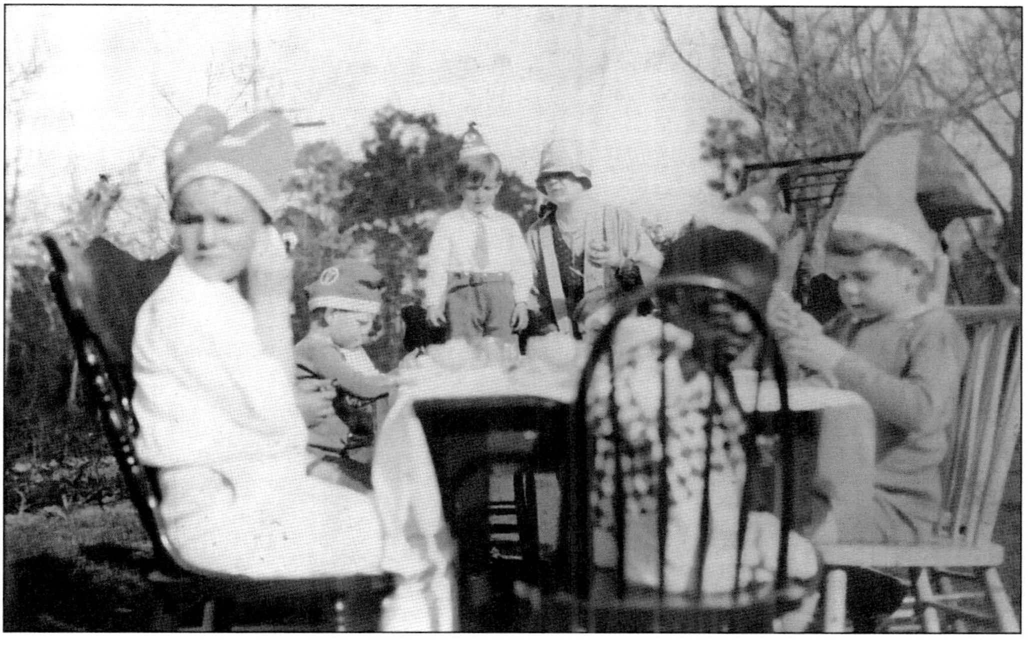

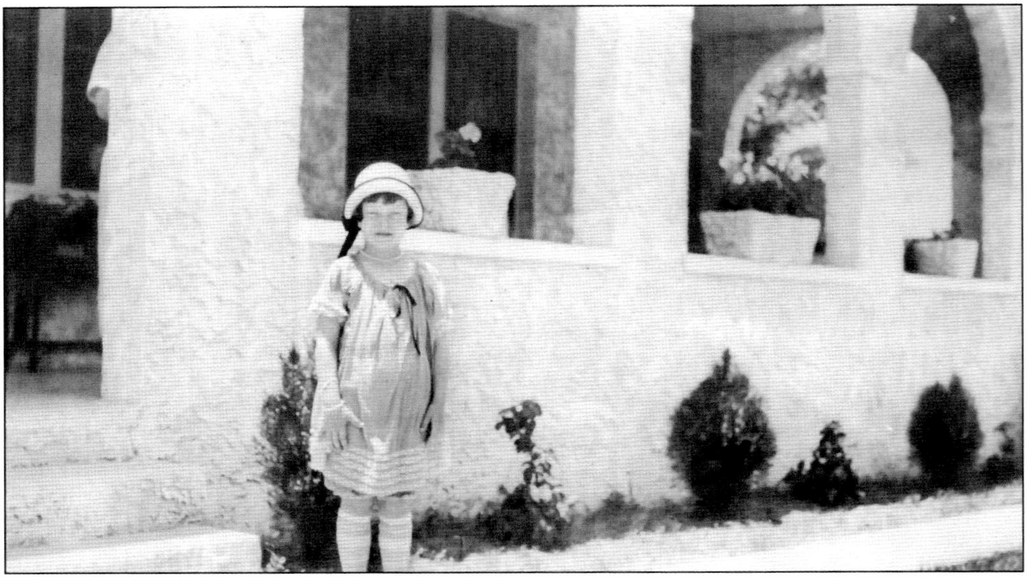

AIN'T SHE SWEET? Little Hazel Martha Forster, age six, is all dressed up for some special occasion in 1925. Her family's home, the first house on Fairhope Avenue at the top of Wharf Hill, is still standing. Her father, Herbert, helped his in-laws build a new casino to replace the one destroyed in the big storm of 1916. (Courtesy of Flora Maye Simmons collection.)

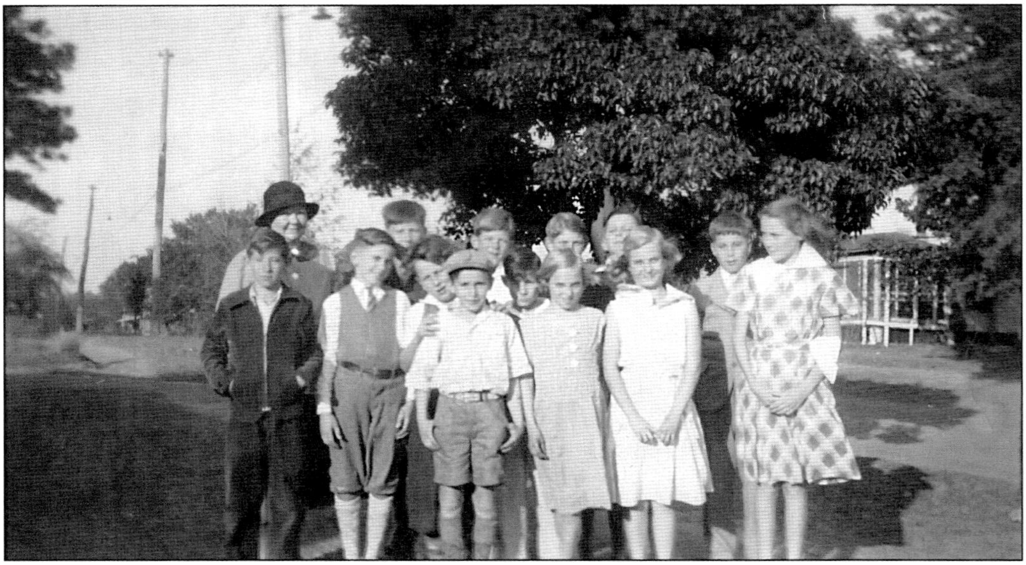

THE AGE OF INNOCENCE. A Sunday school class from the Fairhope Christian Church poses on the street with their teacher. By the 1920s, Fairhope had churches of all denominations. The boy in the center is Reed Myers, whose donation of his family's collection of early photographs and postcards to the Fairhope Museum of History made this book possible. (Courtesy of Reed Myers.)

TOWER TEMPTED YOUNG DAREDEVILS. Climbing the water tower, a rite of passage for the more daring older students in town, became a risky feat when a big, new tank was constructed. Many old-timers around Fairhope recalled scaling the tower in their youth, out of general small-town boredom and just because it was there. Amazingly, no one was ever reported to have been injured in a fall. (Courtesy of FMH.)

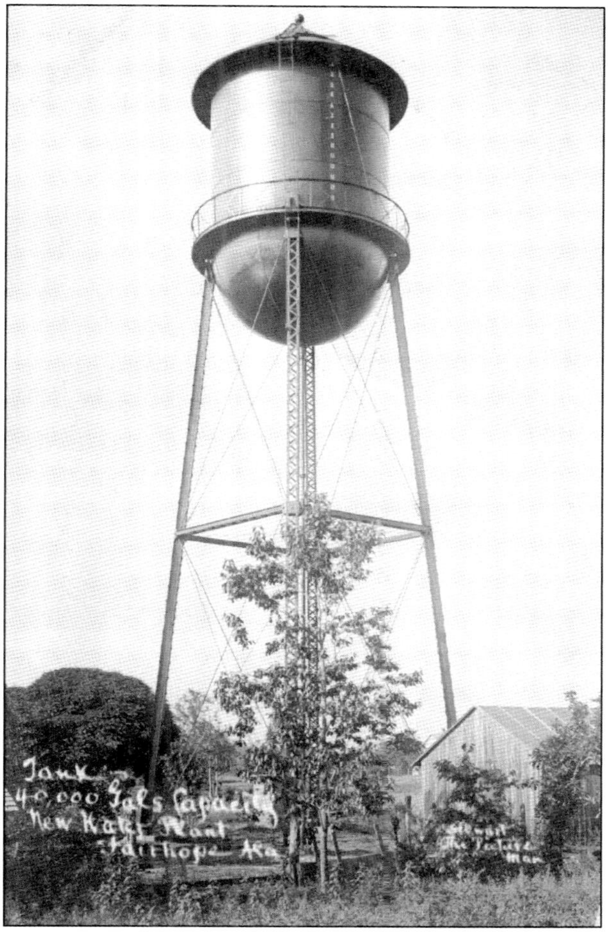

ANOTHER GOOD CATCH. The Berglin boys watch their father string up an ugly alligator gar for display in their backyard. Fishing for the gar, Alabama's largest coastal sports fish, was appealing because it could be caught on a hook and line. Marvin, at the right, would go on to serve as a Fairhope councilman for many years. (Courtesy of Robert Berglin.)

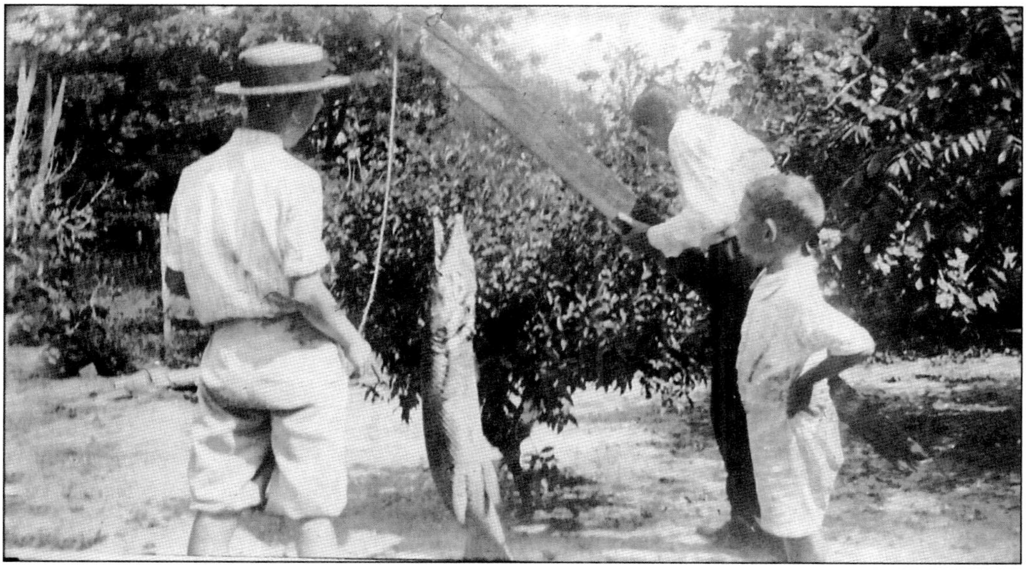

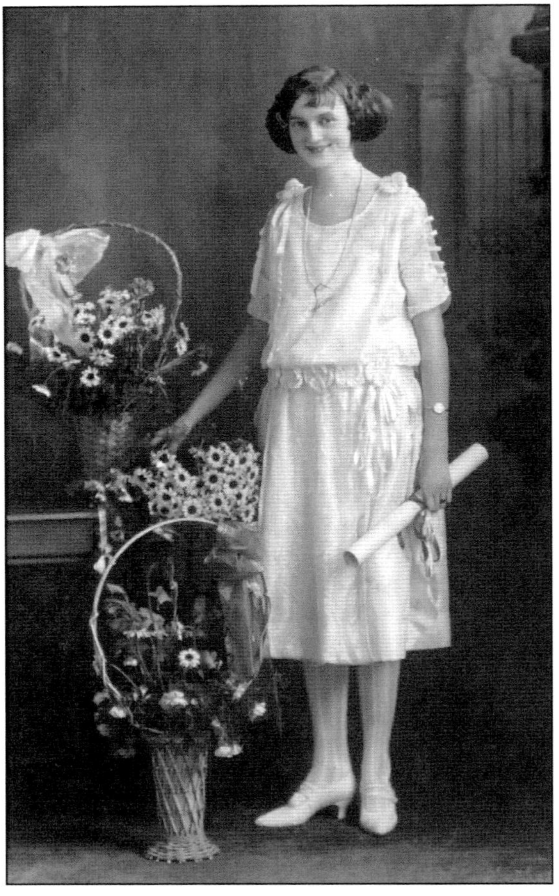

Glad Rag Doll. Irma Norden, a shyly smiling young graduate holding her diploma, is a vision of the latest high fashion of the 1920s in her silk stockings and drop waist dress. The decade would signal a new independence for girls, who had shortened their hair as well as their hemlines. (Courtesy of FMH.)

Visions in White. Wearing traditional graduation-day white, these 1921 Organic School seniors all appear a bit diffident. Perhaps they were, as F. Scott Fitzgerald wrote, "a new generation dedicated more than the last to the fear of poverty and the worship of success, grown up to find all Gods dead, all wars fought, all faiths in man shaken." Or were they wistful for the past? (Courtesy of FMH.)

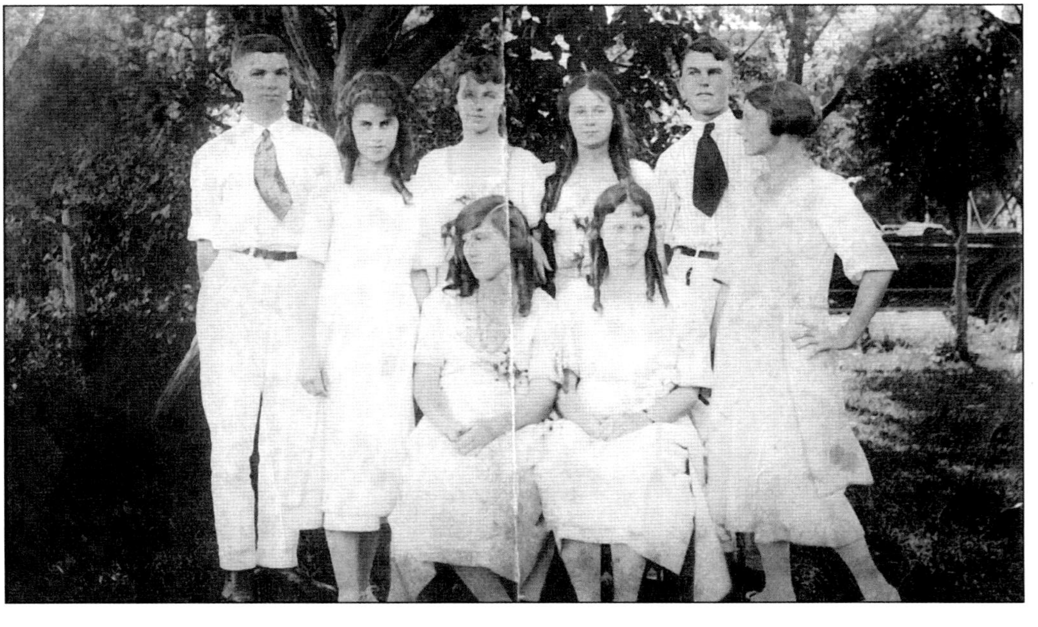

Cornelia Tone

"Cornee"

"Thou art a woman and that is saying the best and the worst of thee."

Harold E. Riegger

"Riegger"

"Oh music, sphere descended maid,
Friend of pleasure, Wisdom's aid."

Georgia M. Lloyd

"Georgia"

"Let us then be up and doing, with a heart for any fate;
Still achieving, still pursuing, learn to labor and to wait."

Monteith Albers

"Teets"

"Who can tell for what high cause this darling of the Gods was born."

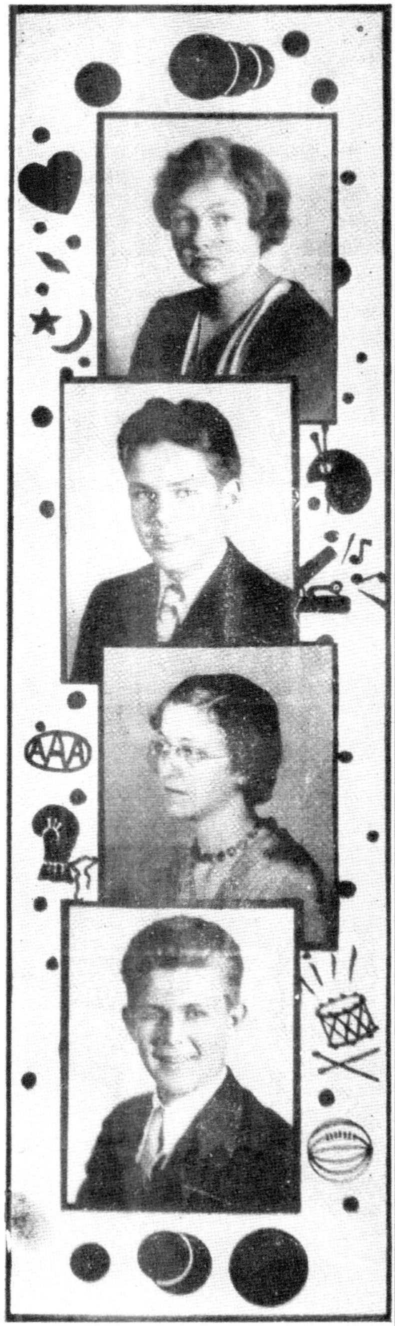

Coming National Names. The Organic School yearbook, *Cinagro* (*organic* spelled backwards), featured some future celebrities. Cornelia Tone was the daughter of a noted Chicago attorney, and Harold Riegger would introduce the lost art of raku pottery to America. Georgia Lloyd, whose millionaire father founded the American Communist Party, created the Campaign for World Government, while Monteith Albers remained in Fairhope. (Courtesy of the MJM.)

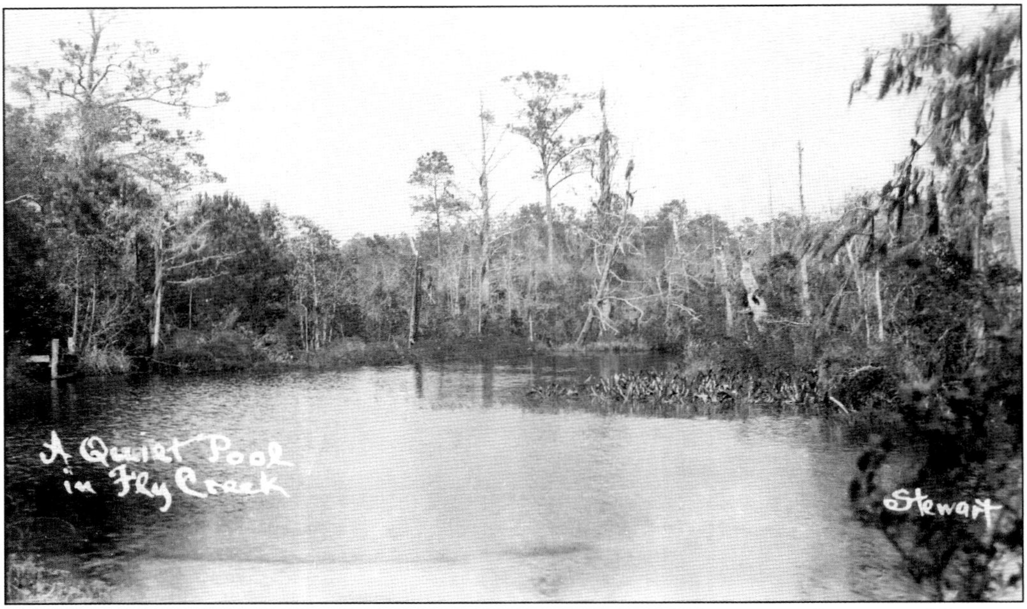

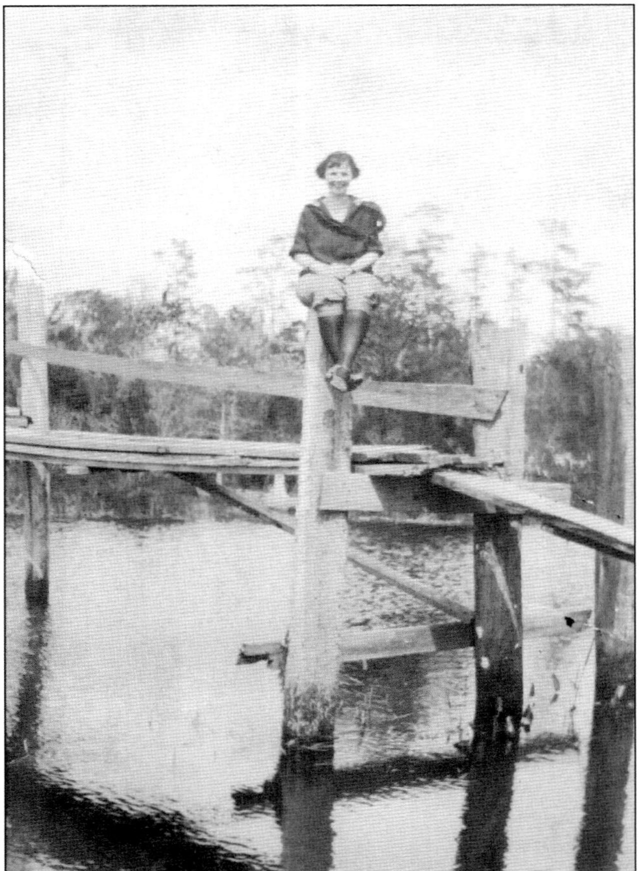

A SECLUDED SWIMMING HOLE. Fairhope's high schoolers would sneak off to Fly Creek for moonlit swims among the water lilies, often taking a wind-up Victrola so they could dance on the banks of the freshwater pool at the edge of town. Sometimes, they stopped on their way to play the Nickelodeon and dance at the Pink Elephant. (Courtesy of Reed Myers.)

ON TOP OF THE WORLD. Women were beginning to come into their own in the 1920s, no longer taking a backseat to the men. Perched atop a piling on a rickety Fly Creek diving platform, this Ms. Daughty, in a demure middy blouse, daringly displays the trousers that the new women fliers were wearing. (Courtesy of FMH.)

Nine

You Dirty Rat!

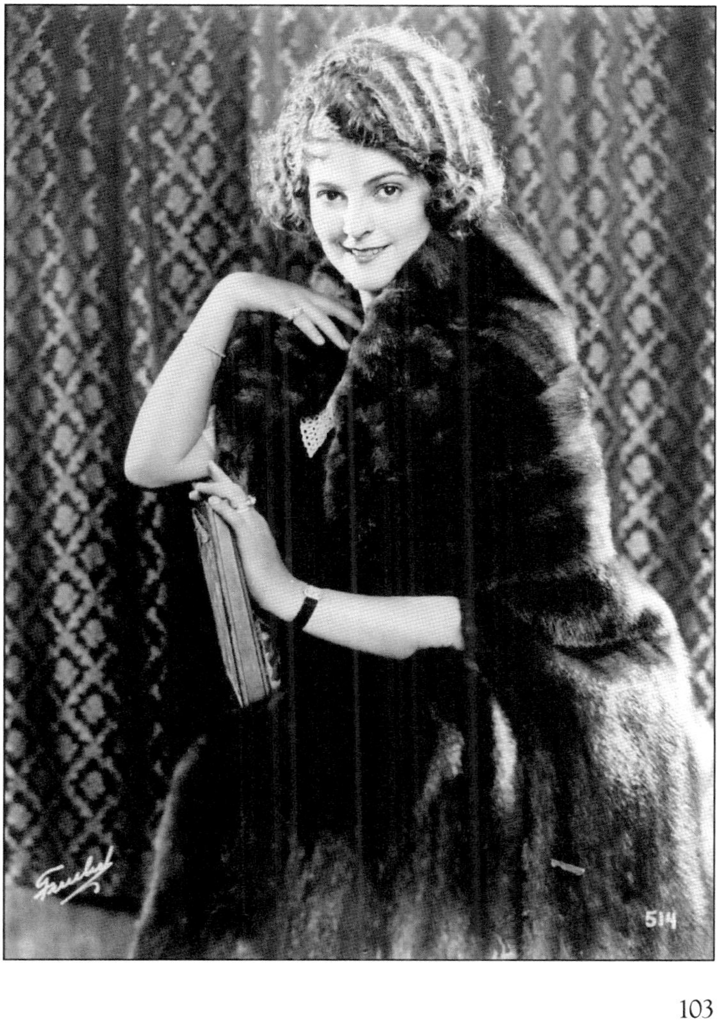

Fairhope's Own Movie Star. Priscilla Dean, an actress born in New York, lived in the Fairhope area for many years, according to the local newspaper. In 1920, she was Universal Films' leading lady, starring in *Outside the Law*, a classic in the then-new gangster genre. She appears with Lon Cheney, who first speaks the famous line, "You dirty rat!" (Courtesy of John Cork.)

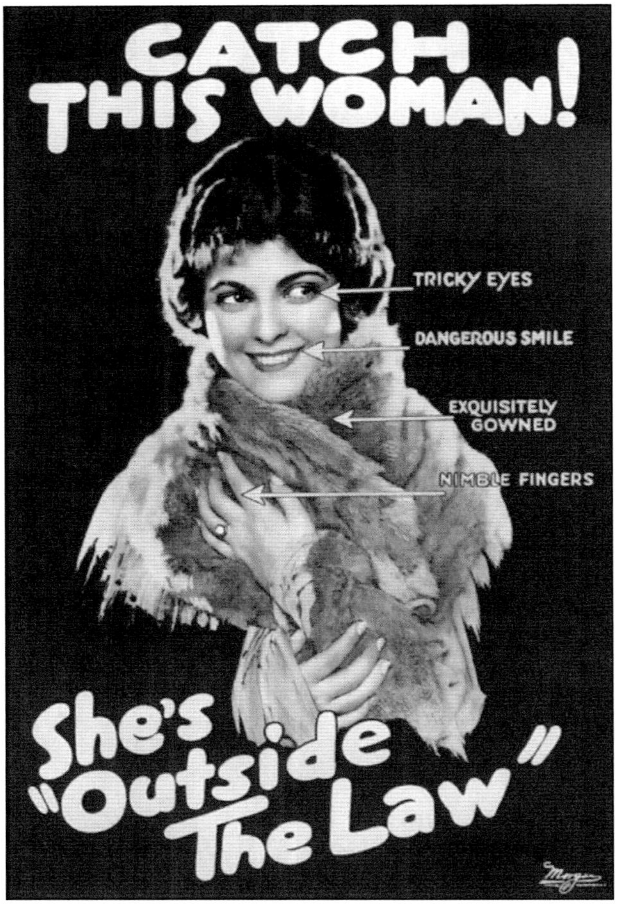

Silver Screen Moll. As the pistol-packing heroine Silky Moll in the silent film featuring the opium-smoked streets of Chinatown, Dean was the epitome of the 1920s flapper. She was in dozens of movies until the advent of the talkies, when her star faded, along with those of many other actors. When she appeared in a Fairhope photoplay, the newspaper urged a "rousing reception."

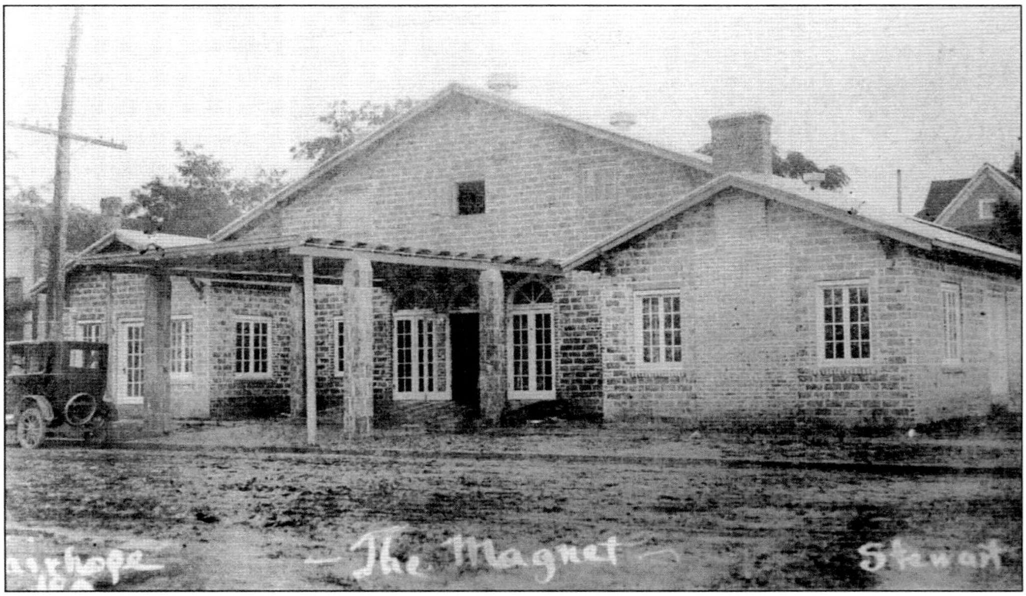

Magnetic Movie Theater. The Magnet Theater, built in 1924 and designed by a Mobile architect, had a sumptuous Egyptian Revival interior with balcony. Moviegoers came from miles around and paid 50¢ for admission. It was south Alabama's longest-operating movie house when it closed in 1974. The building burned in 2010. (Courtesy of FMH.)

Fascinated with Movies. Edward P. Totten, an English-born single-tax proponent and judge, moved from North Dakota to Fairhope in 1920 and began showing silent films at Comings Hall before building the Magnet Theater. An agnostic, he showed features on Sundays, despite the protests of local preachers. He also was rumored about town to be a nudist. (Courtesy of Camilla Bishop.)

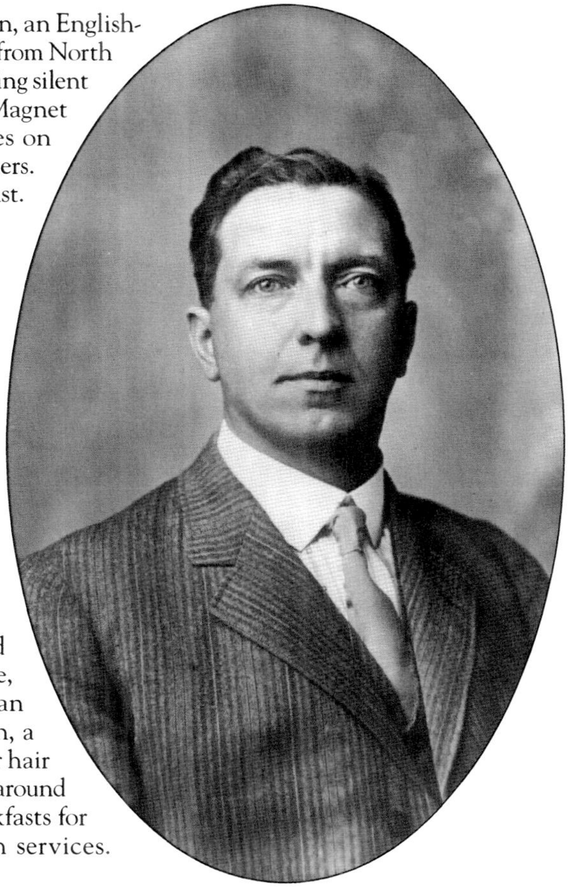

Out of the Picture. Totten (whose head did not make this photograph) and his wife, Lillian, play with their youngest child, Dan Edward, who was born in Fairhope. Lillian, a liberated woman, bobbed and marcelled her hair and was the first to openly wear riding pants around town. The couple hosted big Sunday breakfasts for many Fairhope friends in lieu of church services. (Courtesy of Camilla Bishop.)

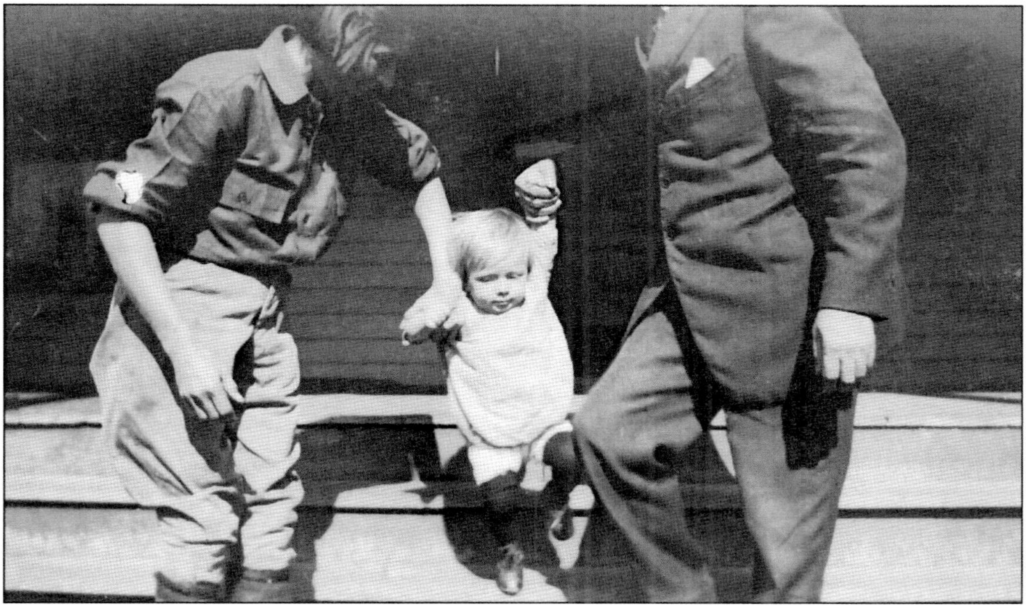

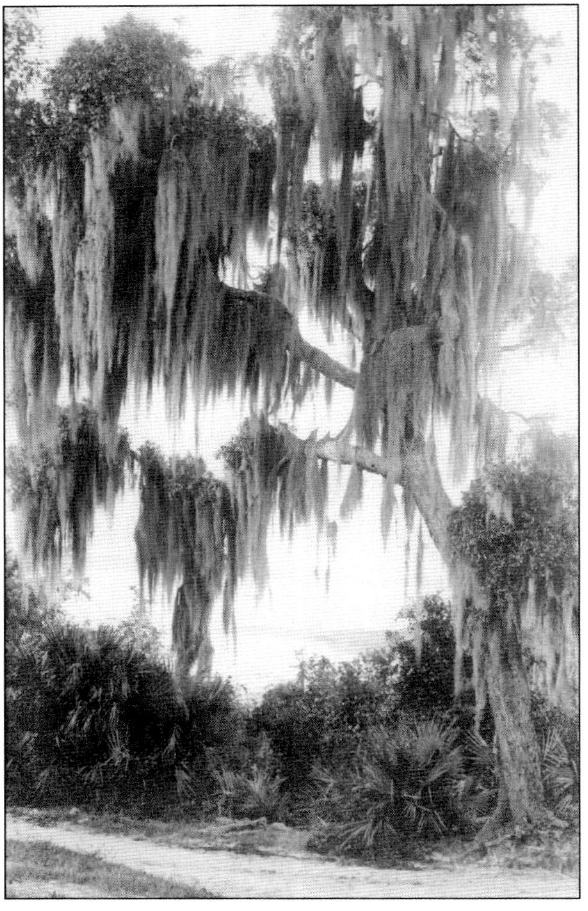

Beyond the Horizon. Entertainment took all forms in Fairhope, which offered a wide range of pleasurable pursuits for such a small town. Much like today, many people were just as content to spend their evenings strolling along the bluff, admiring the spectacular scenery and sunsets through gossamer veils of moss. (Courtesy of FMH.)

Shakespeare in the Sand. "A bank where wild thyme blows" made a natural amphitheater for Fairhope's annual Shakespeare festival productions, which were held for a dozen years. The whole town got in on the act, either performing or applauding. Shakespeare classes were held at the library, and many visitors came from across the bay for the plays performed in honor of Shakespeare's birthday. (Courtesy of Helen Dyson collection.)

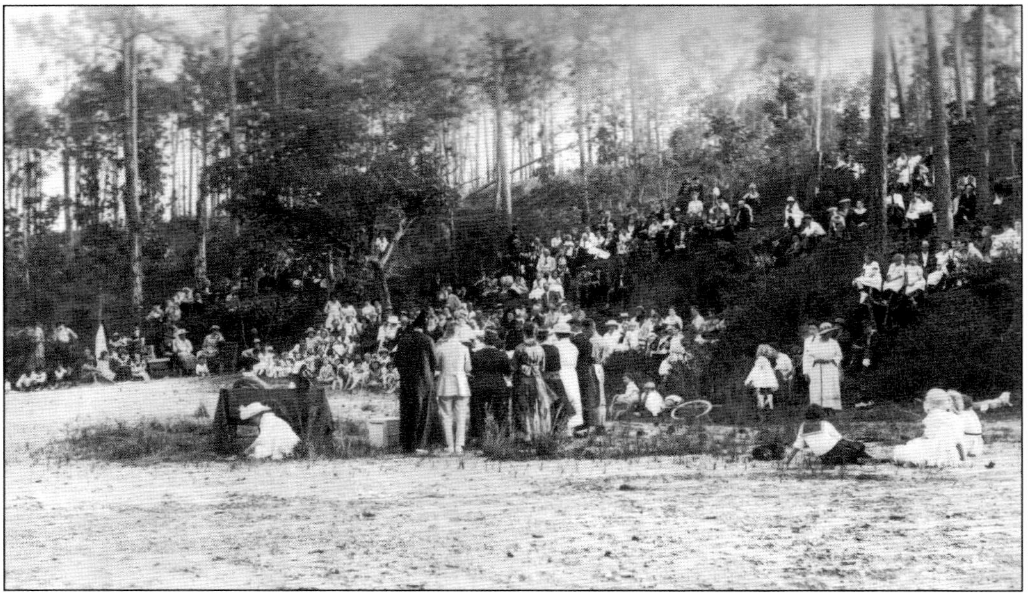

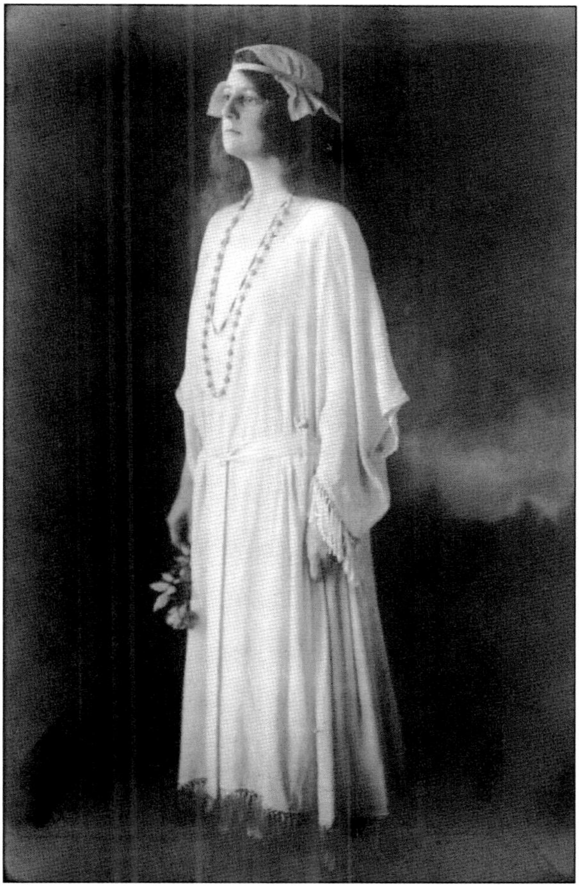

Some Divine Music. Rose Kamper starred in the first Shakespeare celebration in April 1922, which featured excerpts from *A Midsummer Night's Dream* and *The Tempest*. Known for her beautiful singing voice, she and her husband had moved to Fairhope from Mobile in 1920 to operate a grocery business called Kamper's. (Courtesy of FMH.)

Preparing for Mischief. These costumed Fairhope youngsters gathered for their roles in *A Midsummer Night's Dream*, in which the Bard writes, "Stir up the Athenian youth to merriments." This first play was staged in Davis Gully near the foot of North Section Street, which was later extended with a viaduct across the gully. (Courtesy of FMH.)

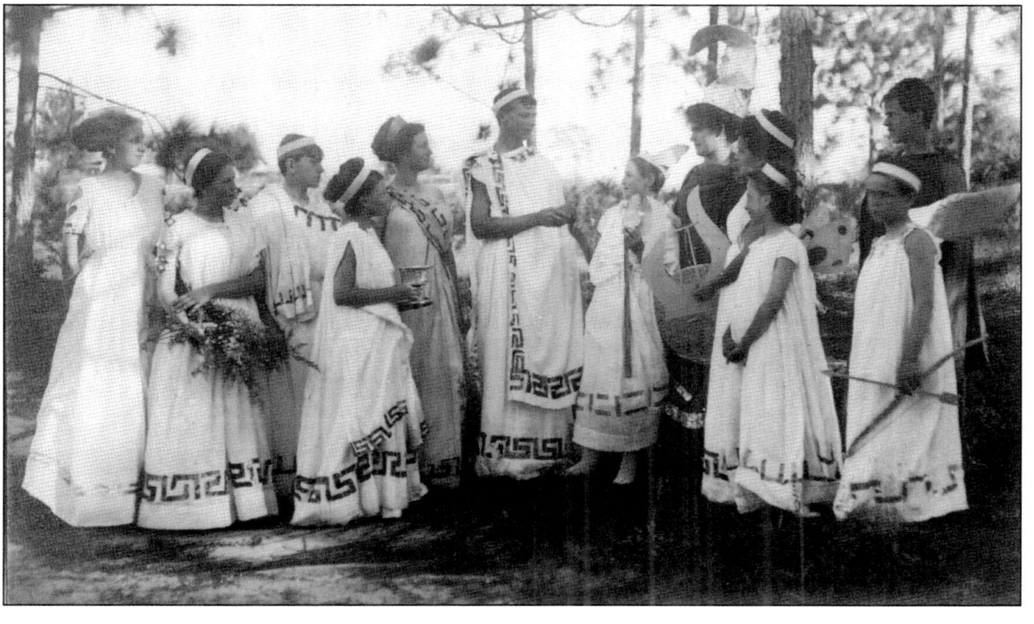

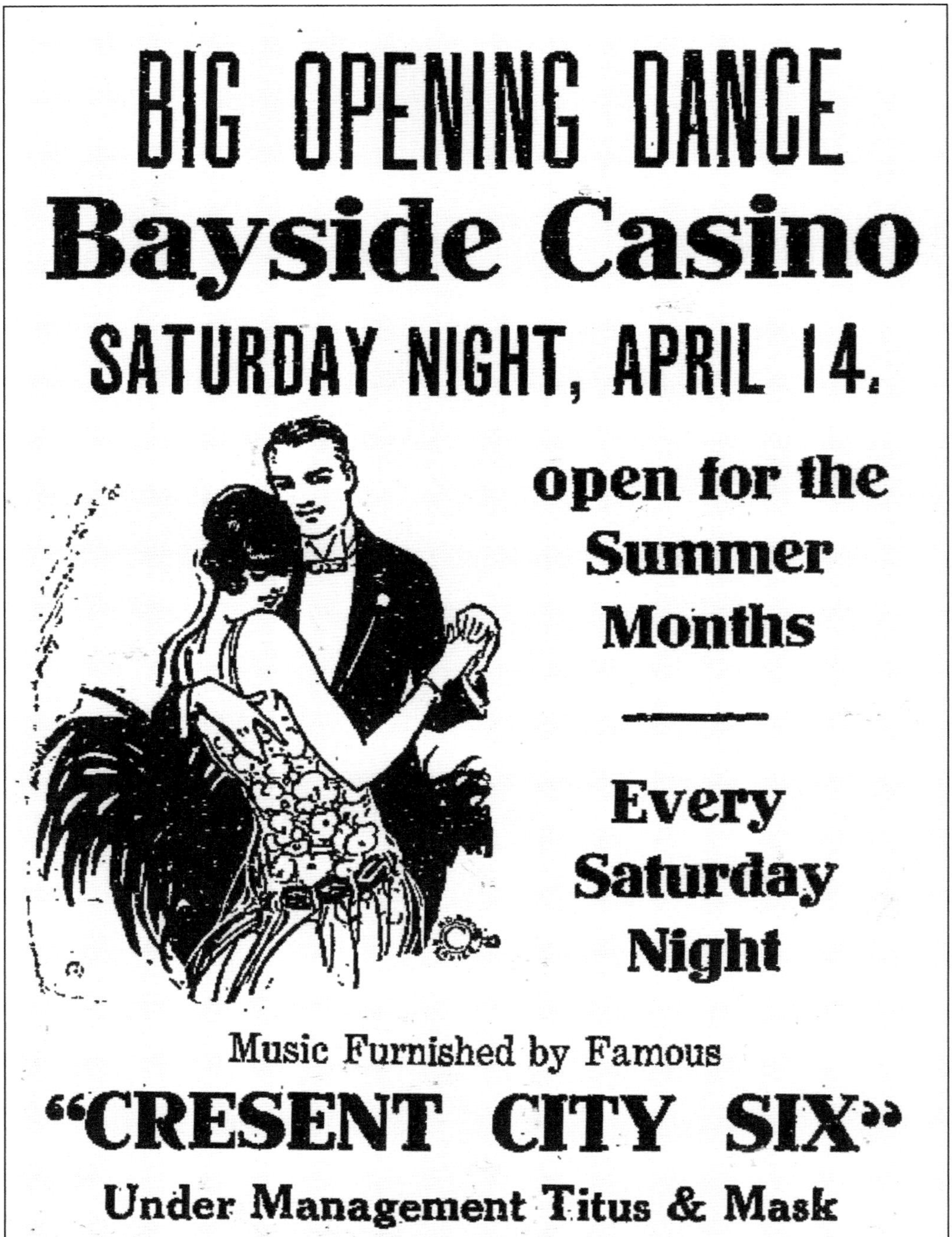

FAIRHOPE'S CASINO OPENS. A big new casino—a pleasure palace and not a gambling hall—opened on the waterfront in May 1921 and was advertised to rival the best in Miami. Every Saturday night, revelers could dance to jazz by groups like the five-piece Dixie Society Orchestra of Memphis, the Bayview Jazzers, the Battle House Eight, or the House of Joy. (Courtesy of the *Fairhope Courier*.)

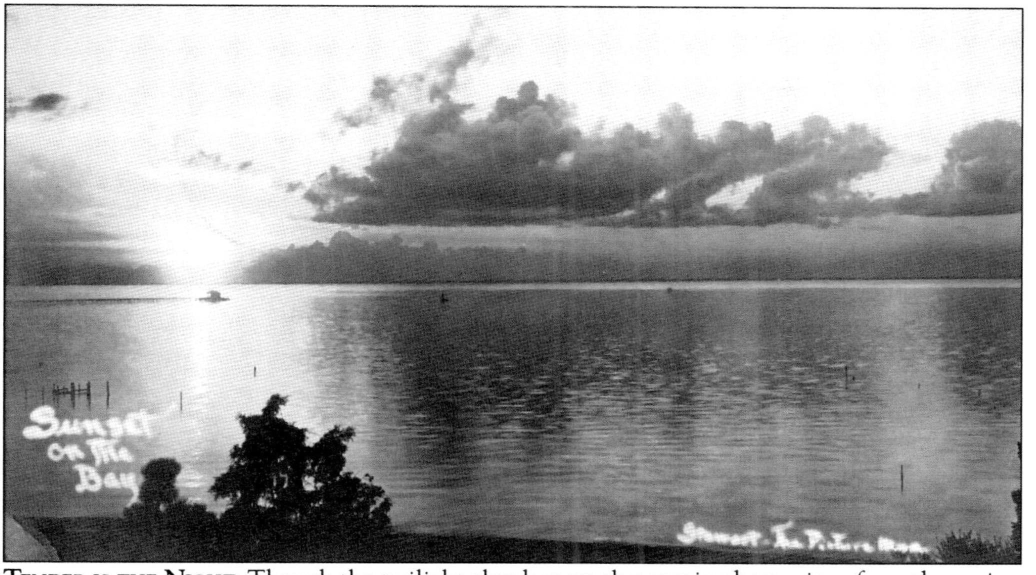

TENDER IS THE NIGHT. Though the twilight clouds seem threatening here, views from the casino balconies usually offered colorful sunset panoramas over the bay. The Bayside Casino advertised steamer excursion packages, windows that opened to "all the breezes that blew," a hardwood dance floor, bathing suit lockers, and even a bowling alley. (Courtesy of FMH.)

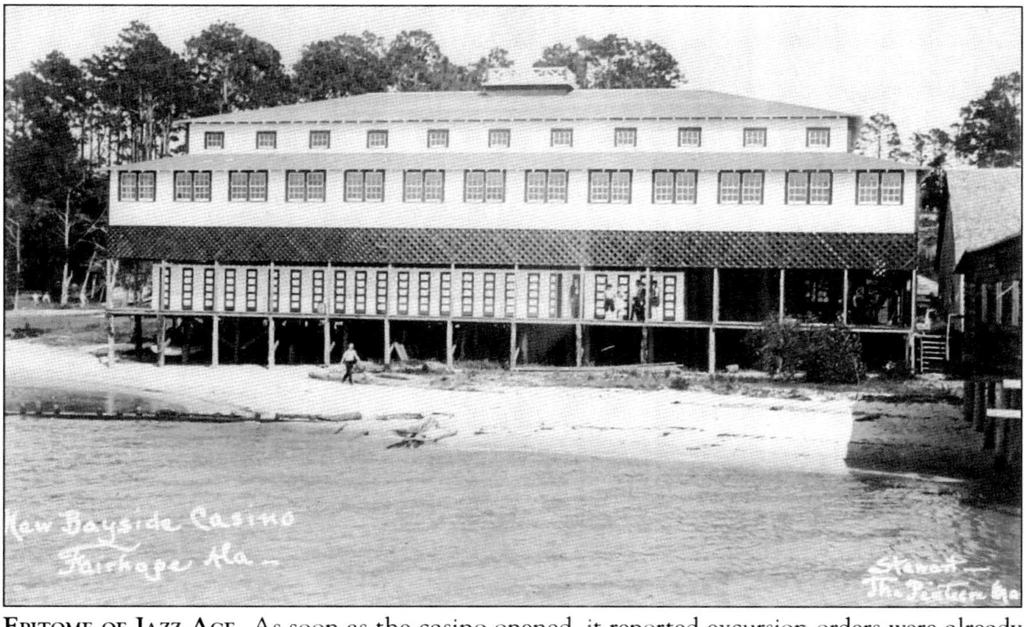

EPITOME OF JAZZ AGE. As soon as the casino opened, it reported excursion orders were already being booked for the next spring. As Fitzgerald says in *The Great Gatsby*, "All night the saxophones wailed the hopeless comment of the *Beale Street Blues* while a hundred pairs of golden and silver slippers shuffled the shining dust." (Courtesy of FMH.)

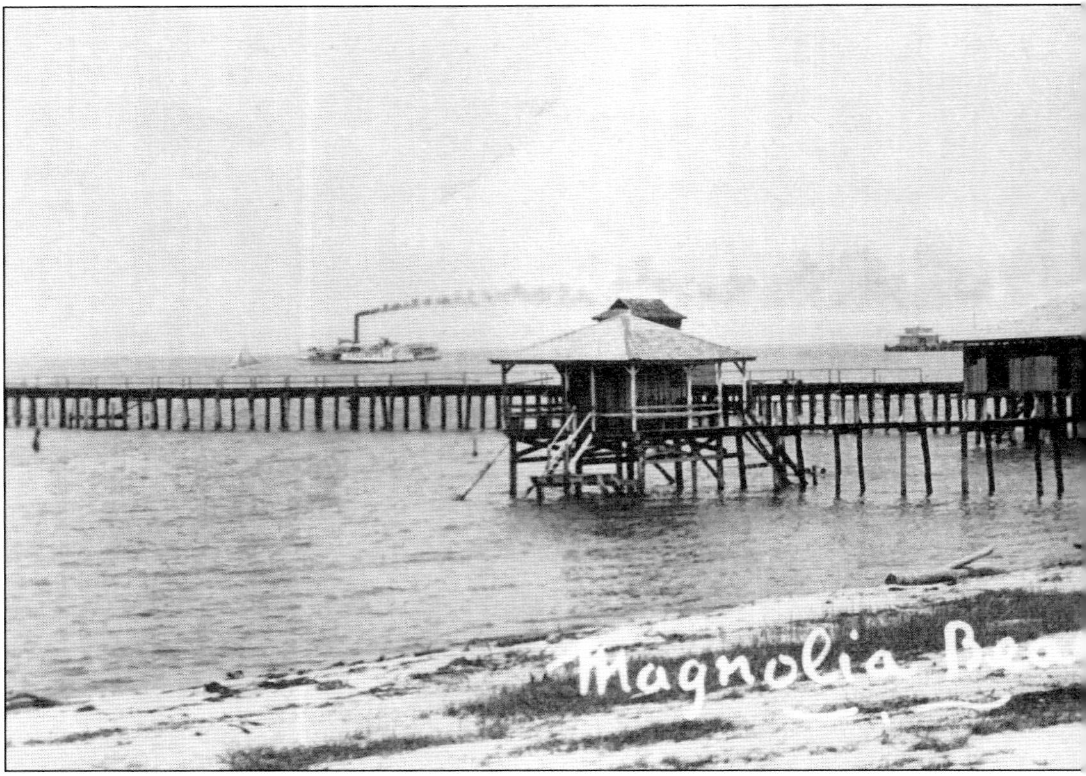

MAGNOLIA BEACH PAVILION. Burkel's pavilion on Magnolia Beach, south of the wharf seen in the distance, had a large dance floor that also doubled as a basketball court for big games. It was the center of the Fourth of July festivities in 1921 when a reported 3,000 visitors came ashore on the

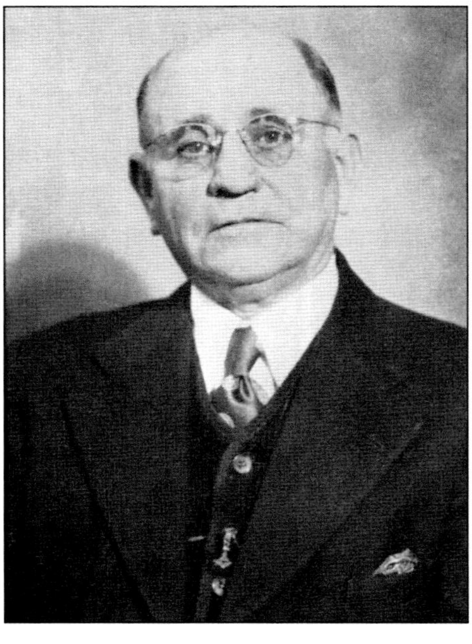

ENTERTAINMENT HIS CALLING. Charles Burkel, who ran away from his home in Germany when he was 16 to join the circus, traveled the world and was involved in the hotel and restaurant business until 1920, when he moved to Fairhope. He opened the Magnolia Beach Pavilion, usually just called "Burkel's," for entertainment. (Courtesy of Marie Bankhead Owen collection.)

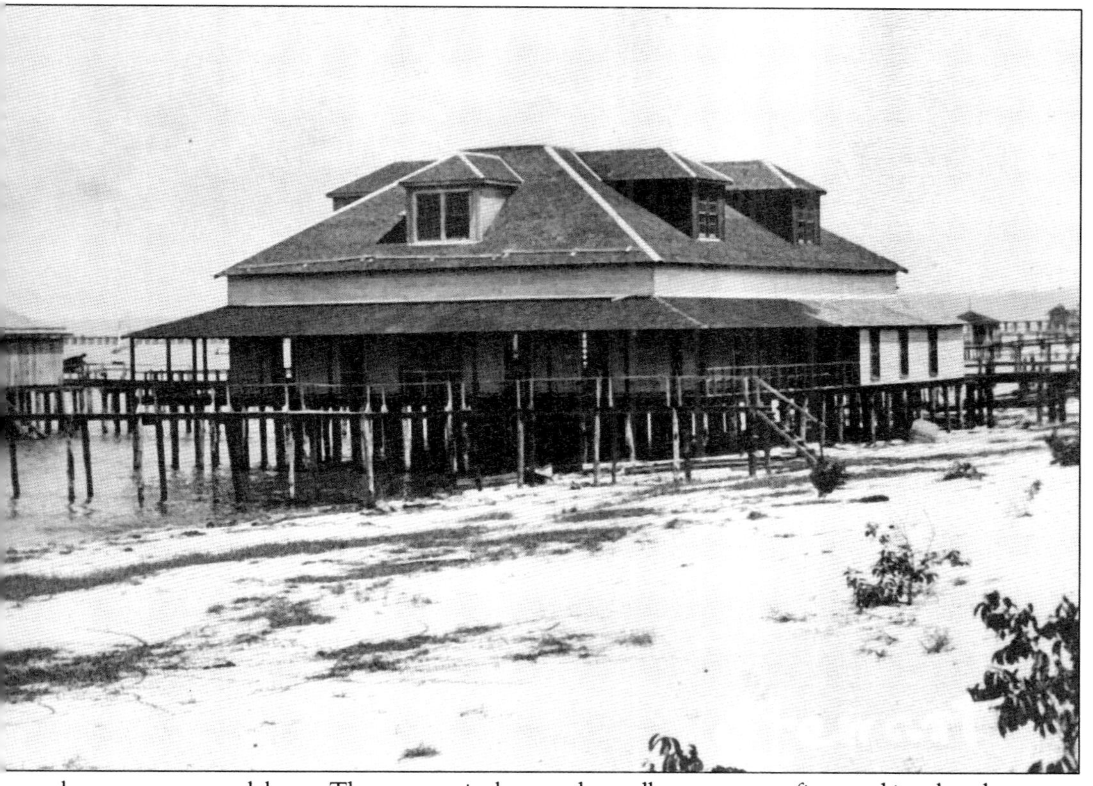

bay steamers to celebrate. There were airplane and speedboat races, surfing, and jazz-band contests all day long. Fireworks and boxing bouts also were featured. Since its earliest days, Fairhope has hosted an extravagant show for the national holiday. (Courtesy of FMH.)

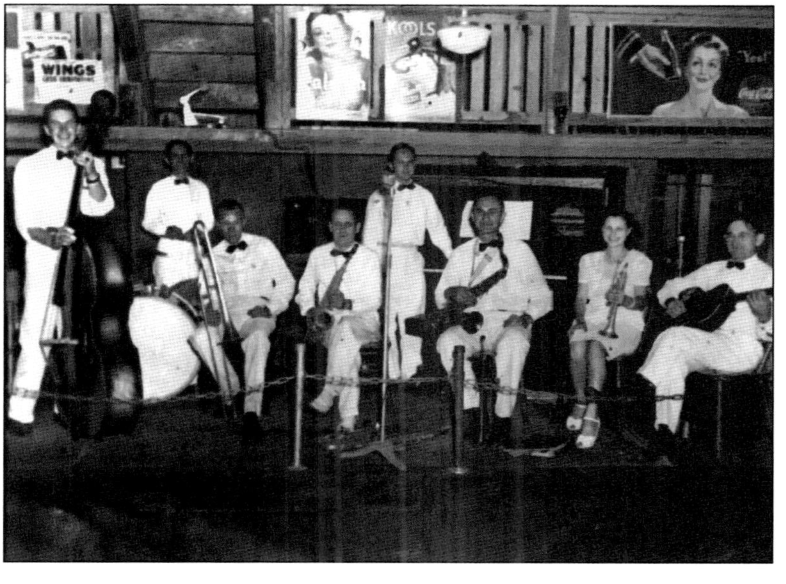

LOCAL MUSICIANS FEATURED. From the 1920s into the 1940s, the Fairhope Melody Makers played on Saturday nights at Burkel's pavilion. The band members are, from left to right, Billy Ruge, Abie Stratis, John Lucassen, Clyde Lowell, Jimmy Lowell, John Novak, Marie Novak, and Gordon Lowell. Gordon was usually on the piano. (Courtesy of Helen Garrett.)

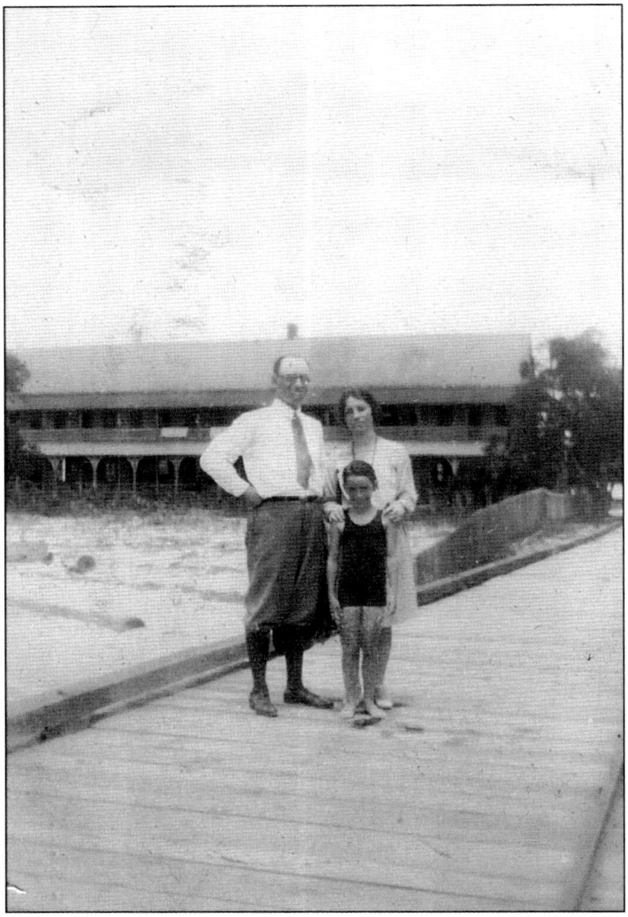

On the Boardwalk. These visitors maintain their sporty-but-proper 1920s dress for a beach outing with their son as they pause on the wharf in front of the Bayside Casino, a popular amusement spot for families. Although there were afternoon contract bridge parties held there, it was not a casino in the sense of the gambling establishments of today. (Courtesy of FMH.)

The Last Dance. Visitors head back down the pier to catch a steamer for the hour-and-a-half boat ride back home at the end of a pleasurable day at the state's premier beach resort. The men wear their straw boaters, and the women, their summer dresses, as everything they needed for swimming was available for rent at the casino. (Courtesy of FMH.)

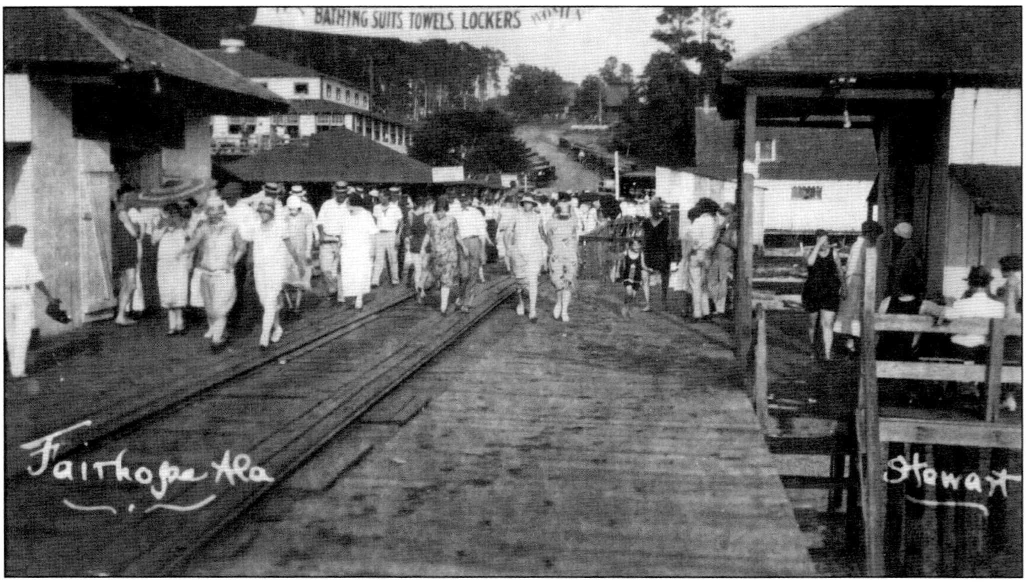

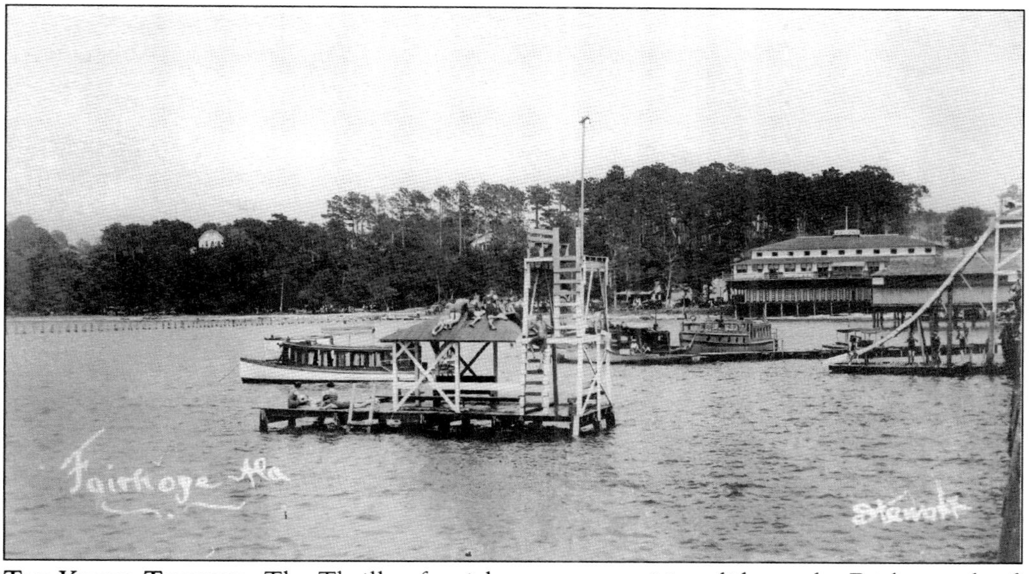

The Killer Thriller. The Thriller, far right, a steep, exciting slide on the Fairhope wharf, always drew a long line of adventurers. The daring diving platform is in the foreground with several pleasure motorboats moored behind. The Fairhope Casino overlooks the busy scene in the summer of 1924. (Courtesy of Edwin Skinner.)

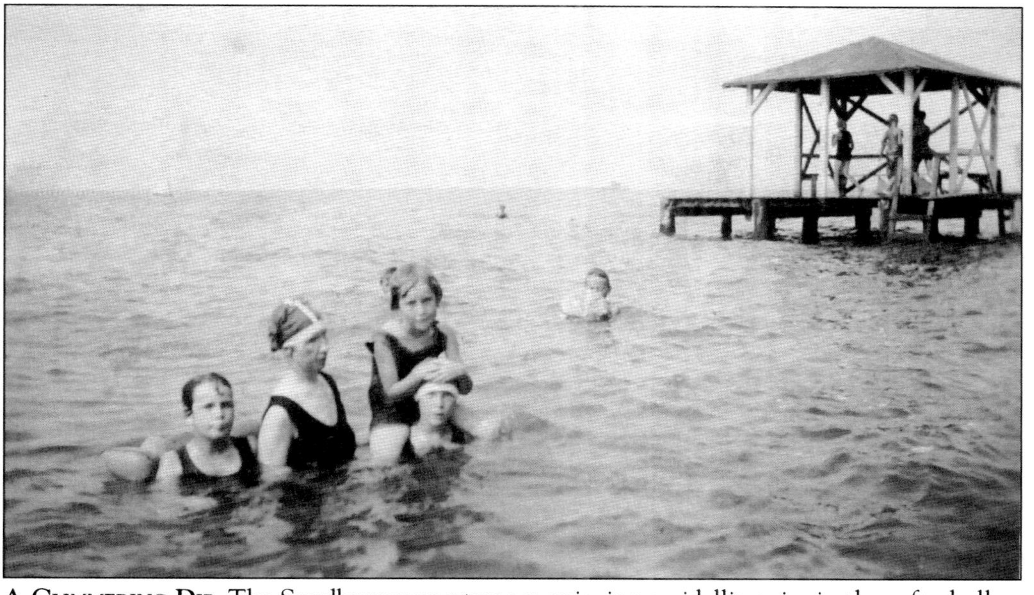

A Glimmering Dip. The Sundberg youngsters are enjoying an idyllic swim in the soft, shallow bay waters in the mid-1920s. Frances is floating on water wings to the far left, holding onto her aunt Nell, who is blind. Ruth is riding on the shoulders of her mother, Lois, and Edwin can be seen in the background. Others play on a platform. (Courtesy of Pinky Bass.)

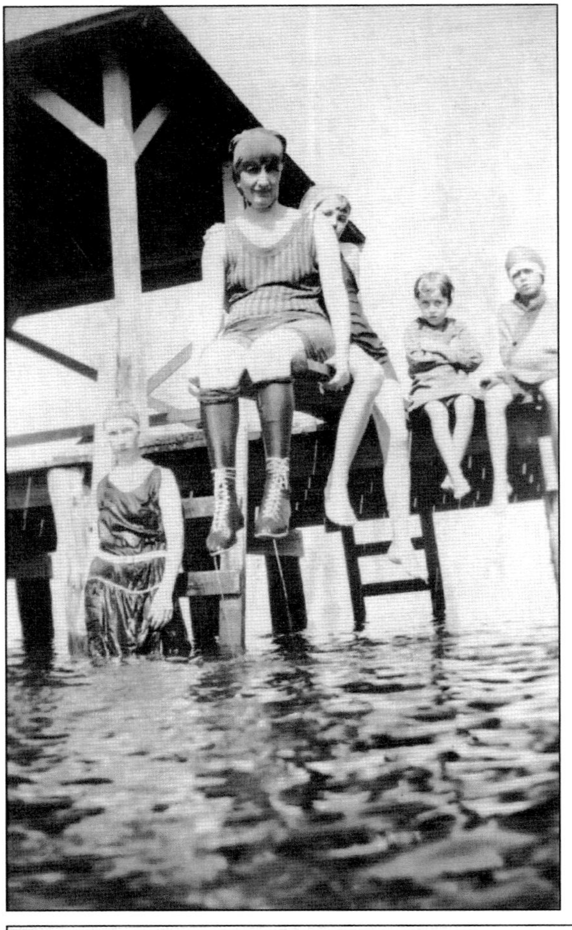

Poised for a Plunge. Sundburg family friend Mrs. McLaughlin, wearing dark swimming stockings, balances on the end of a wooden diving board on the pier, flanked by Marion. At left, Nell Slosson stands on the ladder, and on the pier Ruth and Frances are wrapped in towels. (Courtesy of Pinky Bass.)

Sandcastles on the Beach. A sandcastle with moats rises on an inviting crescent of the Fairhope beach. It is being built by Frances, left, Ruth, center, and Marion Sundberg, who frequently visited their Slosson grandparents in Fairhope before later moving there themselves. (Courtesy of Pinky Bass.)

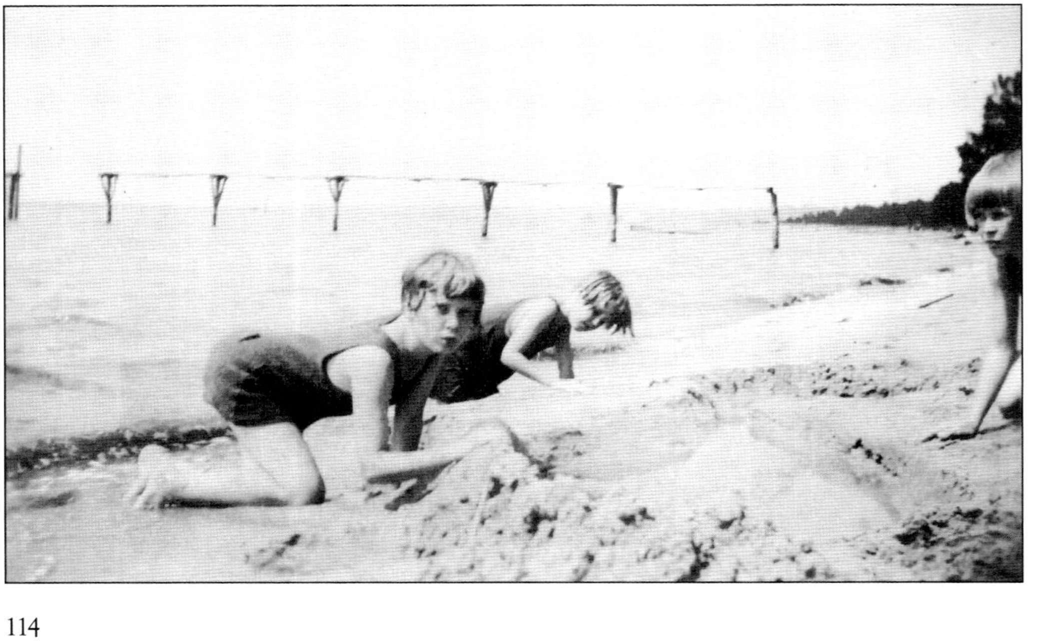

AIN'T NOBODY'S BUSINESS. This young trio cuts up for the camera, with the boy and girls swapping clothes and bathing suits during the 1920s. At least they bothered with wearing the woolen suits, as many folks in Fairhope preferred to just "air bathe," as they called it. (Courtesy of FMH.)

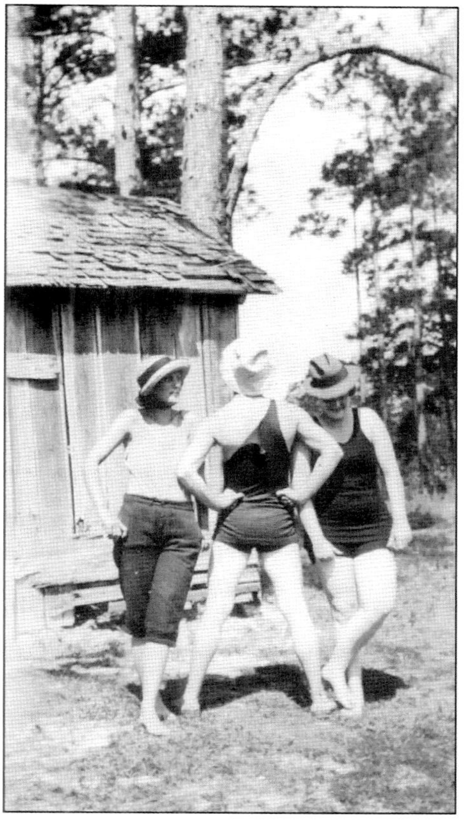

BATHING BEAUTY REVIEW. By the end of the 1920s, bathing suits had become shorter and more formfitting. This 1929 bathing beauty contest was held during Fairhope's sixth annual three-day Labor Day celebration, which marked the end of the summer resort season. That year, the redheaded Miss Fairhope, Gladys Grimes, No. 6, won. (Courtesy of FMH.)

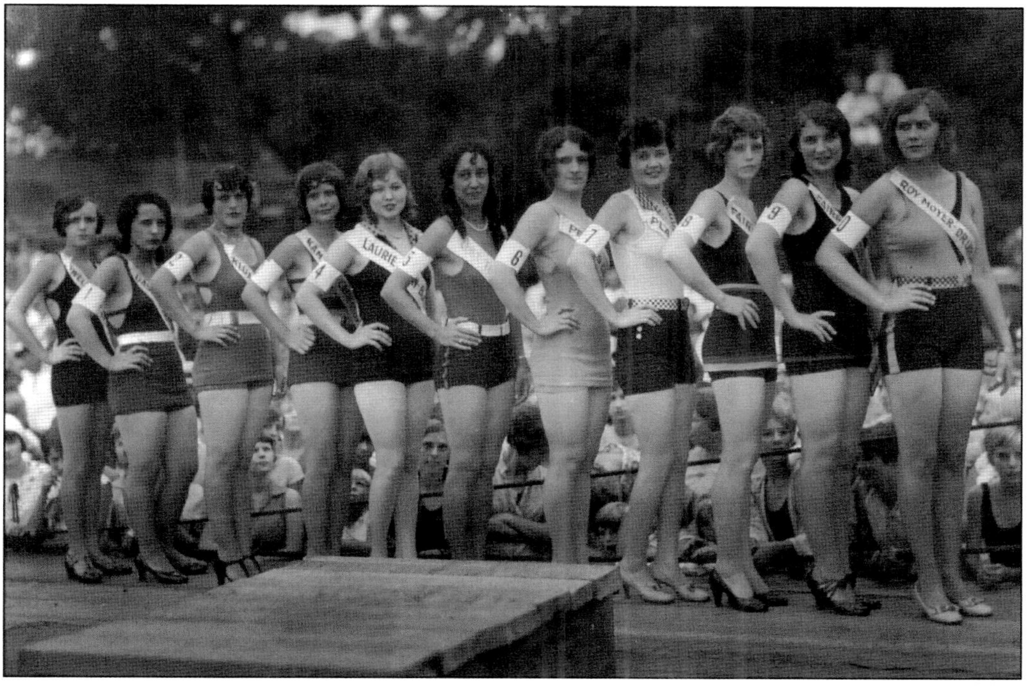

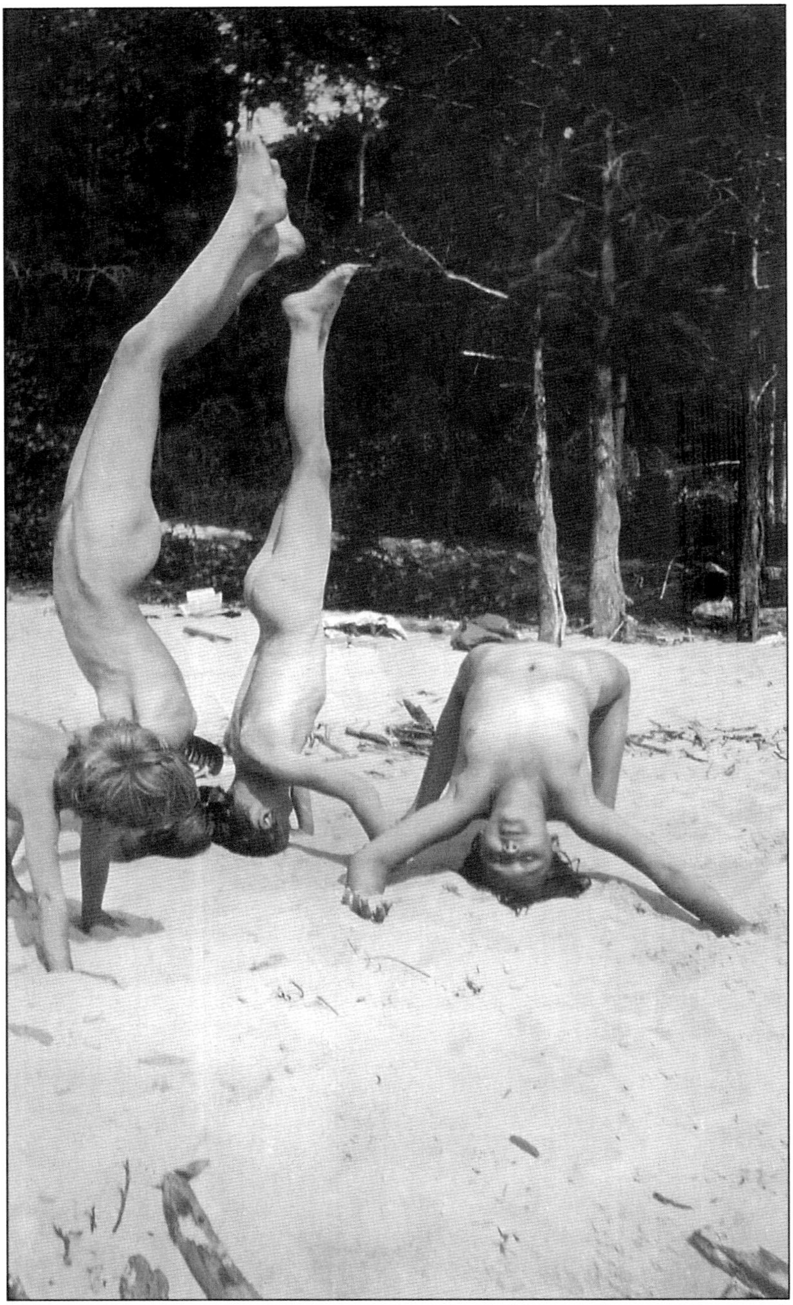

The Skin Games. Master craftsman Wharton Esherick's children and writer Sherwood Anderson's wife, Tennessee, frolic naked on the Fairhope beach in 1921. The two families, among others in town, were nudists who enjoyed swimming and sunbathing in the buff. The multitalented Esherick also was interested in theater and eurhythmic dance, which was harmonious movement as a form of artistic expression. He came to Fairhope to teach at the Organic School after hearing Marietta Johnson lecture in Philadelphia. At the school, he made woodcuts and carved wooden picture frames for which he would become famous. (Courtesy of the Wharton Esherick Museum.)

Ten

Flappers and Philosophers

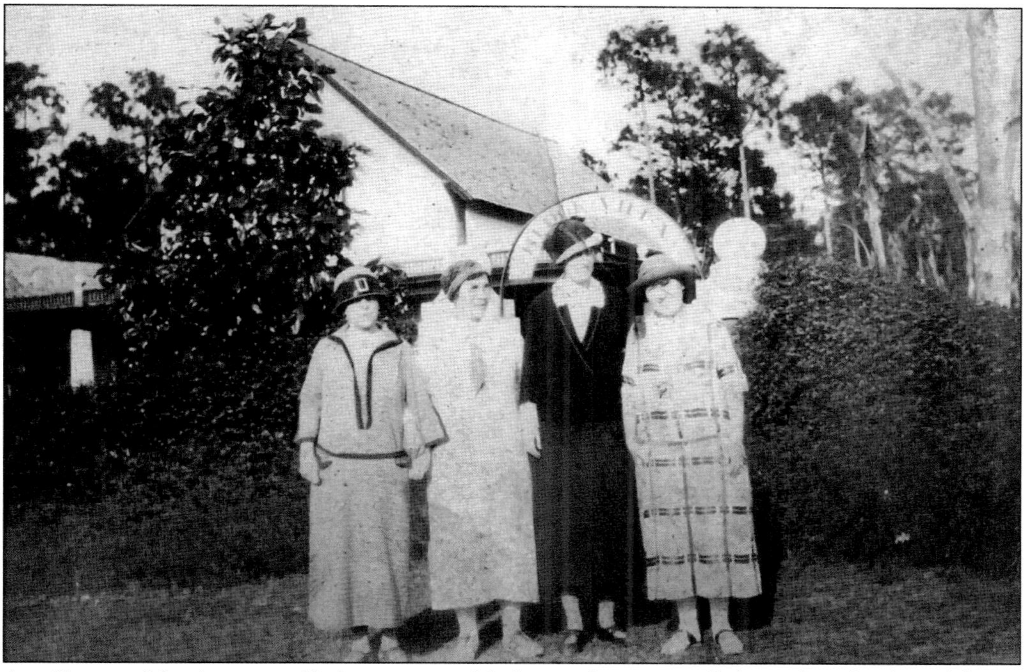

All Dolled Up. A group of ladies, presumably lawyers' wives, is all dressed up for the Alabama State Bar convention held in Fairhope in 1925. Their outfits and fancy headwear are symbolic of the Gatsbyesque era. Aside from just nudists, Fairhope's resort beaches drew many conventions during the 1920s, including the Alabama Press Association. (Courtesy of WOFC.)

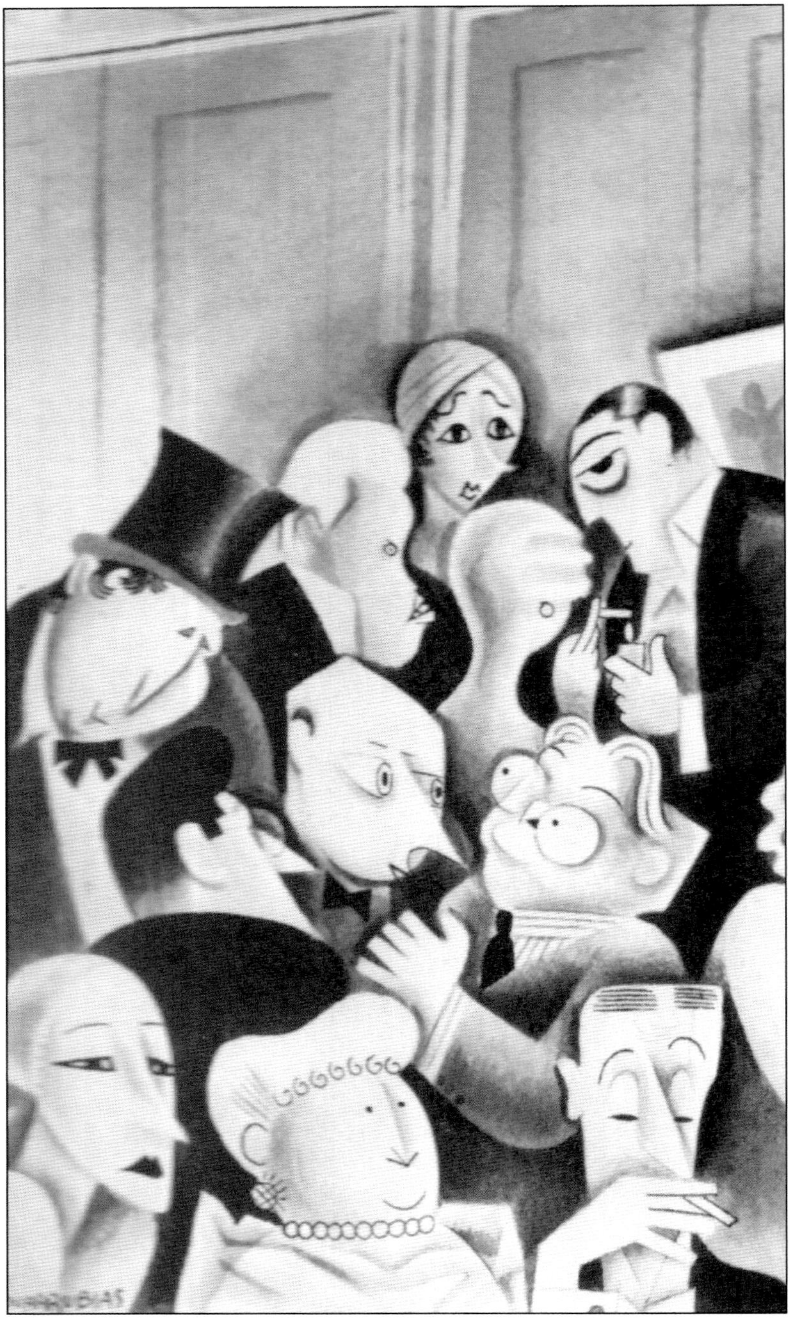

FAIRHOPE ATTRACTED THE CELEBRATED. Noted New York drama critic and 1920s Algonquin Round Table member Heywood Broun (depicted at left in top hat), sent his son Heywood Hale Broun to Fairhope's Organic School, as did many other Eastern notables. The liberal journalist unsuccessfully ran for Congress on the Socialist ticket in 1930. The younger Broun went on to become a well-known sports commentator and writer, penning *Whose Little Boy are You?* This drawing, titled *First Night*, was featured in *Vanity Fair* in 1930. (Courtesy of Library of Congress.)

A Grateful Guest. A satisfied visitor sent this elaborate card of thanks to Helen Sacriste, the owner of the Colonial Inn, after having what appears to have been a record fishing trip. The excellent weather and angling in Mobile Bay was a major drawing card for the coastal town in the winter, along with fresh seafood cuisine. (Courtesy of WOFC.)

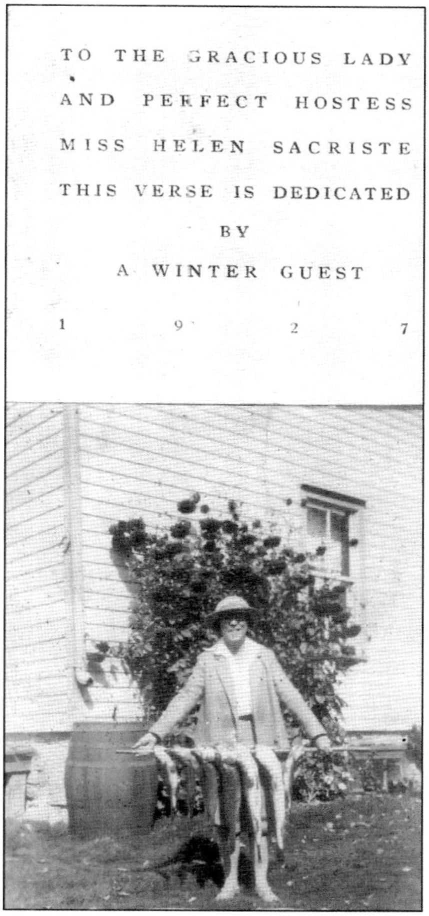

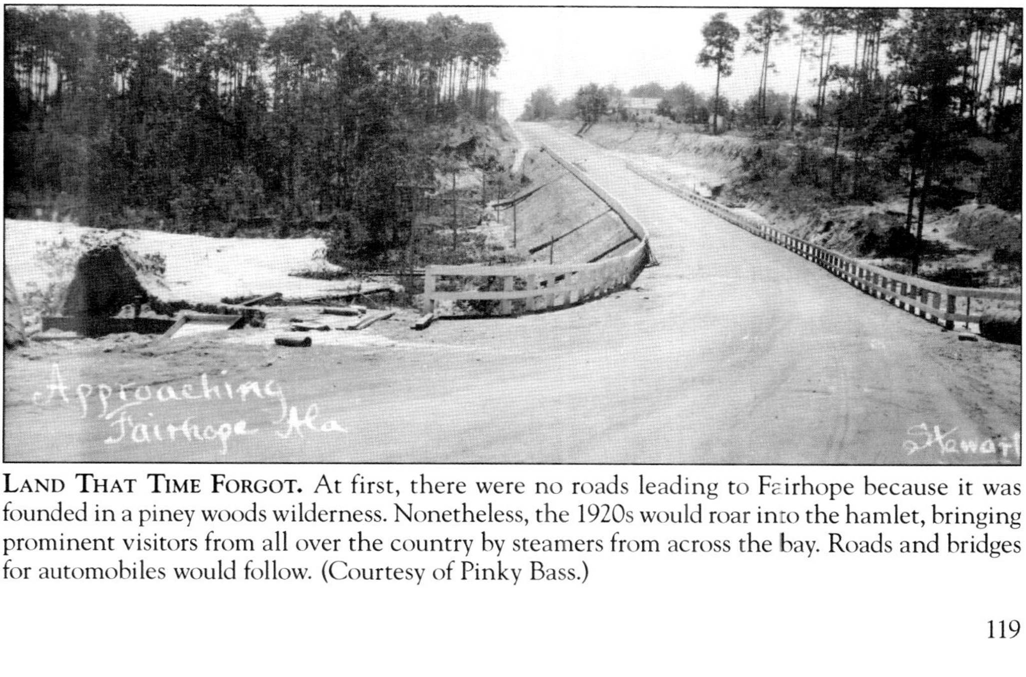

Land That Time Forgot. At first, there were no roads leading to Fairhope because it was founded in a piney woods wilderness. Nonetheless, the 1920s would roar into the hamlet, bringing prominent visitors from all over the country by steamers from across the bay. Roads and bridges for automobiles would follow. (Courtesy of Pinky Bass.)

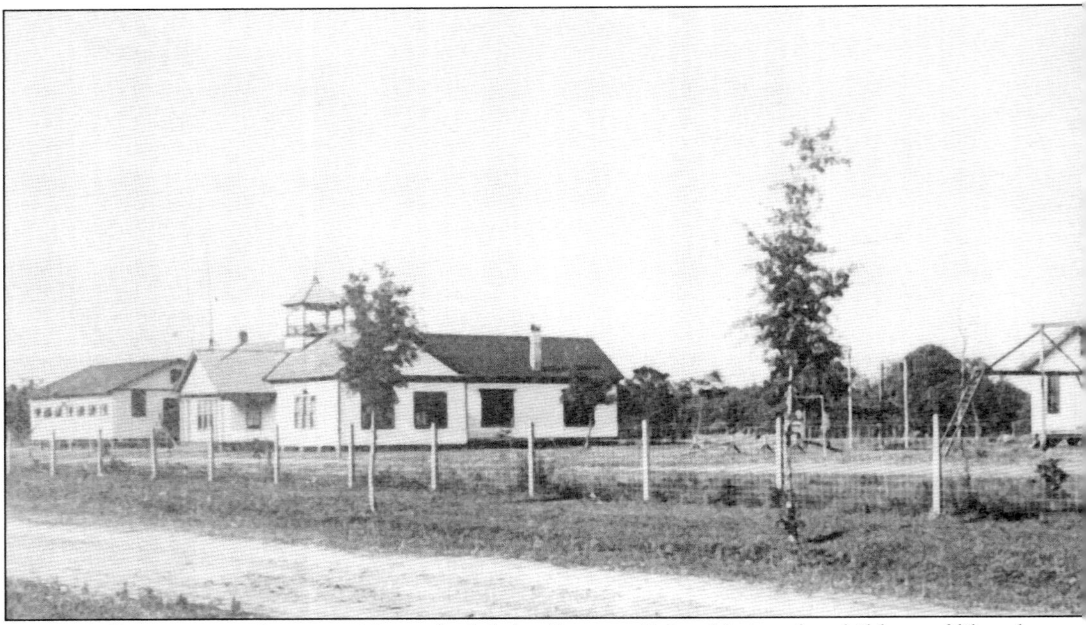

School's Reputation Spreads. Not only did the Organic School bring the children of liberal and influential figures to Fairhope, but faculty from Oxford, Yale, Harvard, and Cambridge Universities came to teach. Fairhopers and many friends financially supported the school, which was a symbol of progressive education. The campus, with the original Bell Building with tower

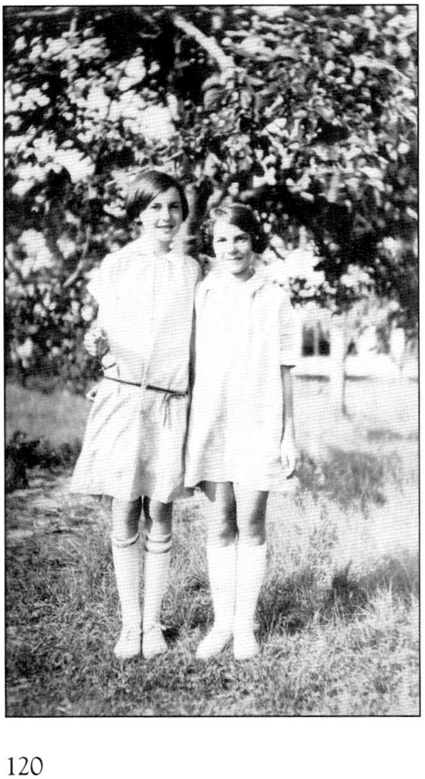

The Bee's Knees. Elizabeth Ann Klingensmith, right, and her fellow student are little flappers, showing their knees in the new short skirts of the 1920s. Elizabeth was a boarding student from Detroit, where her father, Frank L. Klingensmith, was second-in-command at Ford Motors from 1915 to 1921. He left the company after a falling-out with Henry Ford over Wall Street financing the company and next headed another automobile firm. (Courtesy of MJM.)

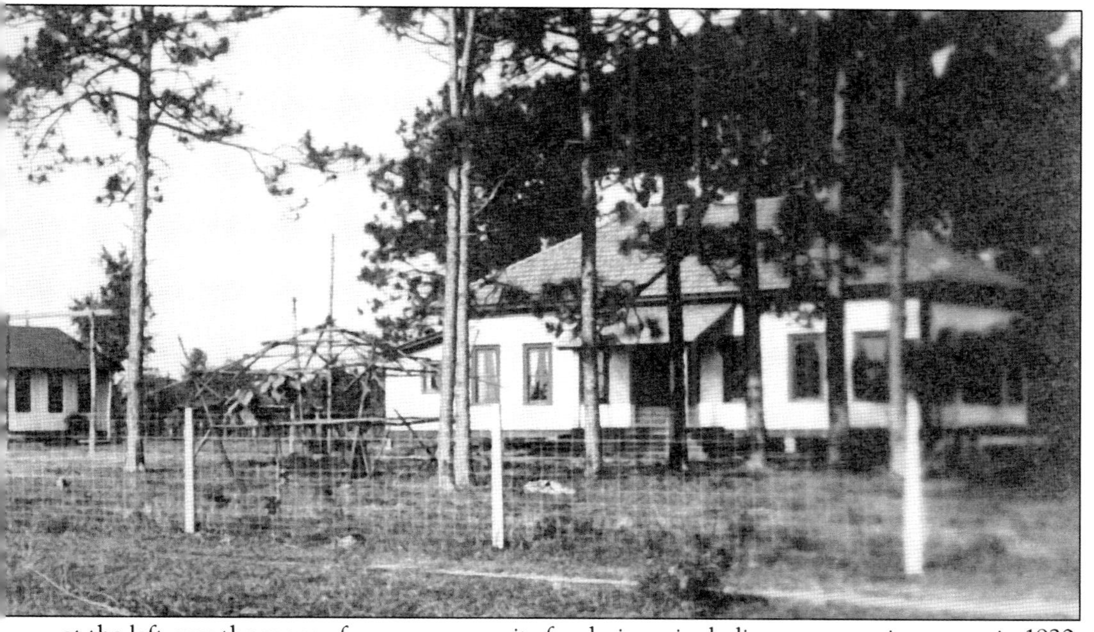

at the left, was the scene of many community fundraisers, including an open-air concert in 1920, which advertised performances by a Professor Zoelman, his violinist son Wotan, and a mezzo-soprano named Miss Trout. (Courtesy of Reed Myers.)

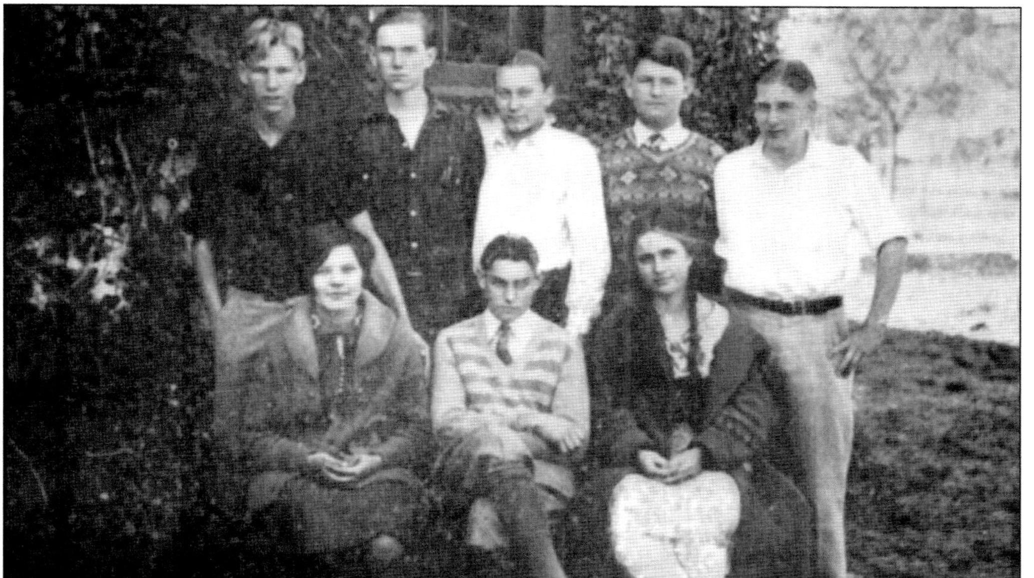

A Prestigious Class. A page from a 1926 Organic School yearbook includes Charles Klingensmith, son of a former vice president of Ford Motor Company, and Elizabeth Mead, sister of the famed anthropologist Margaret Mead. Elizabeth and her younger sister Priscilla attended the school while living at the Fairhope Hotel with their grandmother Martha Mead. (Courtesy of MJM.)

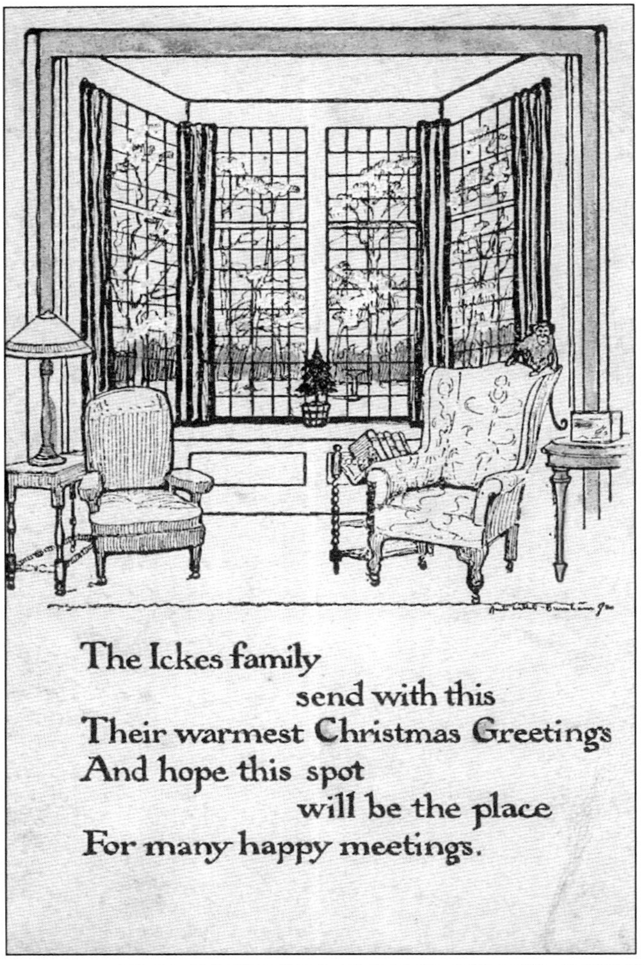

Greetings from National Leader. Harold L. Ickes, a future US secretary of the interior and second-longest-serving cabinet member in American history, vacationed with his family in Fairhope, where his son Raymond attended school. Ickes, a noted liberal, headed the Chicago NAACP. The family sent this Christmas card to the Colonial Inn in the 1920s. (Courtesy of the WOFC.)

Weathering the Storm. Organic School students made their own boats in shop class. On March 27, 1920, a storm brewed after a teacher took eight children, including Ickes's son, out into the bay. Little Claire Gray ran up the hill to alert townspeople, and Cornelius and Arthur Gaston rescued the children. Ickes presented them with a plaque of appreciation, now on display in the city's history museum. (Courtesy of MJM.)

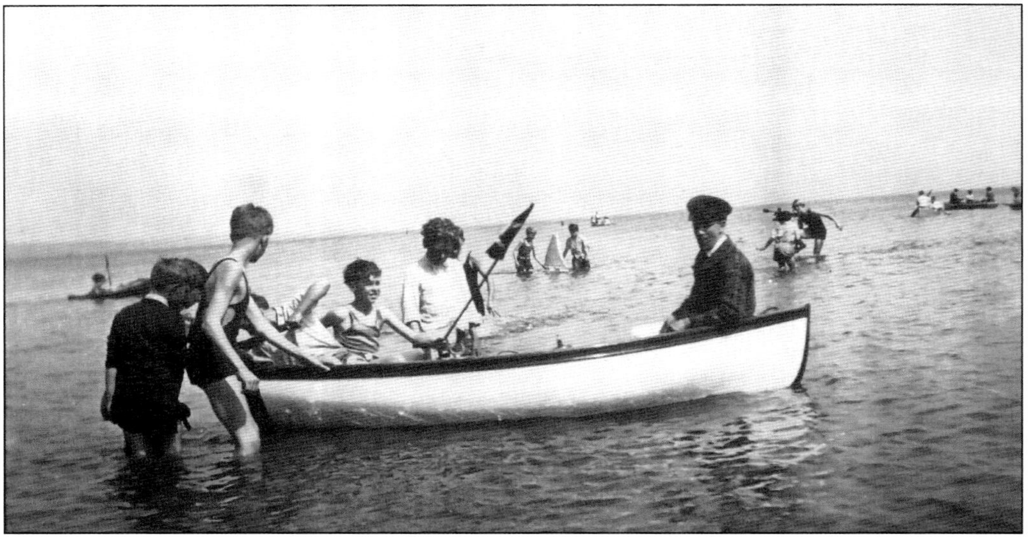

NOTED FAIRHOPE AUTHOR. Eleanor Risley, a Fairhope writer, published her local newspaper articles in a booklet titled *Real Fairhope Folks*. She left town in the 1920s, carting her belongings in a Chinese wheelbarrow, to hike the mountains of north Alabama and Georgia. Her stories of the trek were serialized in the *Atlantic Monthly* and published as *The Road to Wildcat*. (Courtesy of University of Arkansas.)

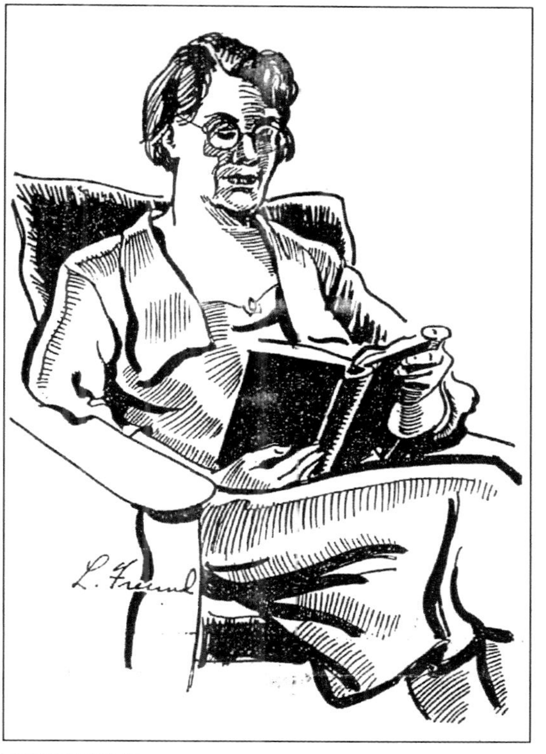

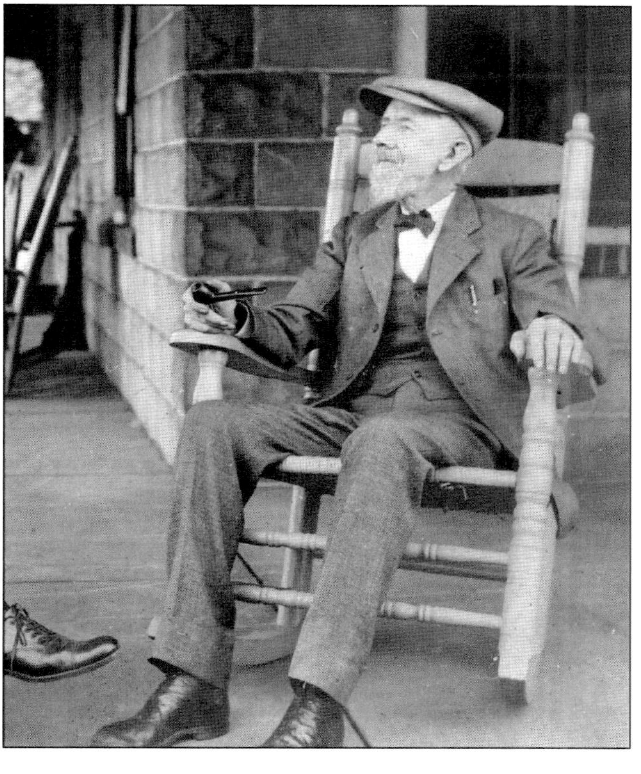

A FAIRHOPE PHILOSOPHER. Capt. Jack Cross, rumored to be a scion of a wealthy English lord, helped his wife run the Fairhope Hotel where he philosophized with guests. Fairhope author Francis Gaither, who moved to New York in 1929, dedicated her book *The Painted Arrow* to Cross. In the 1920s, the MacMillan Company also published a short history of his life. (Courtesy of Fairhope Public Library.)

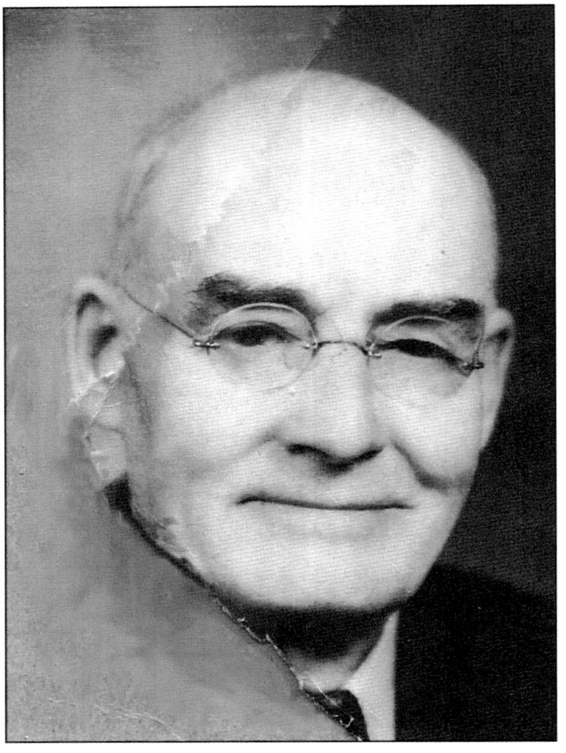

High Tones and Swells. Prominent Chicago attorney David K. Tone, a friend of Clarence Darrow, sent his five children to the Organic School in the 1920s. His 1924 address to the Fairhope Forum on the difficulties of the single tax is described in the newspaper as "a good and entertaining discussion with no acrimony or abuse." Apparently, that was unusual for the spirited community forums. (Courtesy of Thomas Ottinger.)

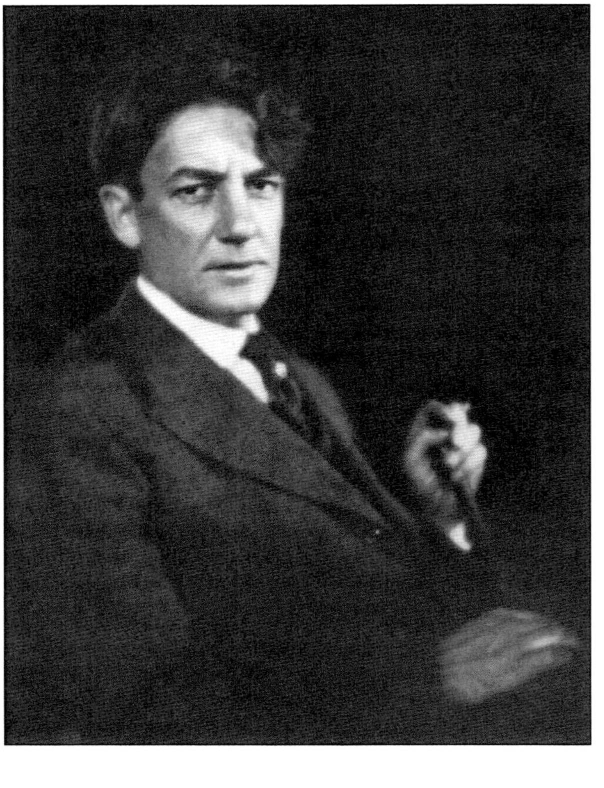

Author Retreated Here. Noted American author Sherwood Anderson, who has been called America's most distinctive novelist, escaped to Fairhope in the early 1920s to avoid the national acclaim of his *Winesburg, Ohio* stories. "This year it has been very hard for me to live in the Middle-West," he wrote in his journal while in Fairhope, where he wrote *The Triumph of the Egg*. (Courtesy of Newberry Library.)

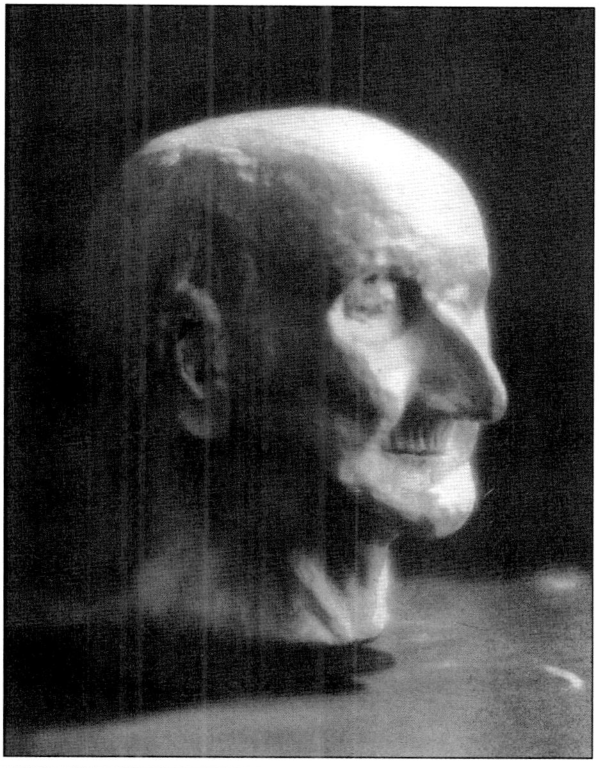

Old Scholar in Clay. Anderson's wife, Tennessee Mitchell, was a bohemian he had married at a quasi-nudist colony. She followed him to Fairhope, where she sculpted clay busts to illustrate his short story collection. A self-taught artist and eurhythmic-dancing teacher, her sculptures, captured by famed Chicago portrait photographer Eugene Hutchinson, appear in Anderson's book. (Photograph by Eugene Hutchinson.)

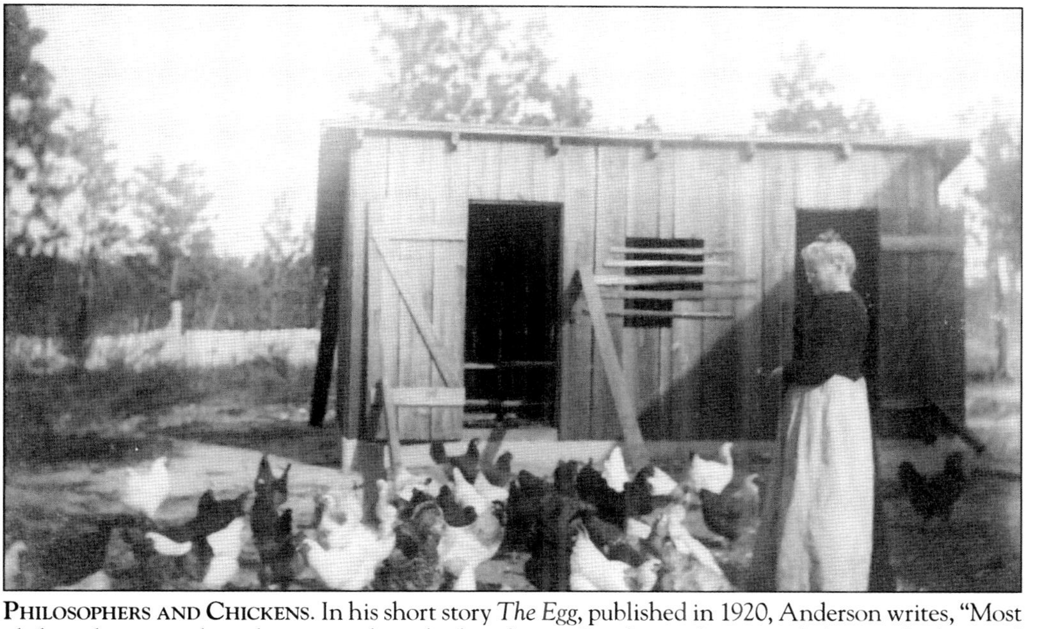

Philosophers and Chickens. In his short story *The Egg*, published in 1920, Anderson writes, "Most philosophers must have been raised on chicken farms. One hopes for so much from a chicken and is so dreadfully disillusioned." Fairhope had both plentiful poultry yards and philosophers. Here, a resident is feeding her flock. Or perhaps she is contemplating which came first—the chicken or the egg? (Courtesy of Reed Myers.)

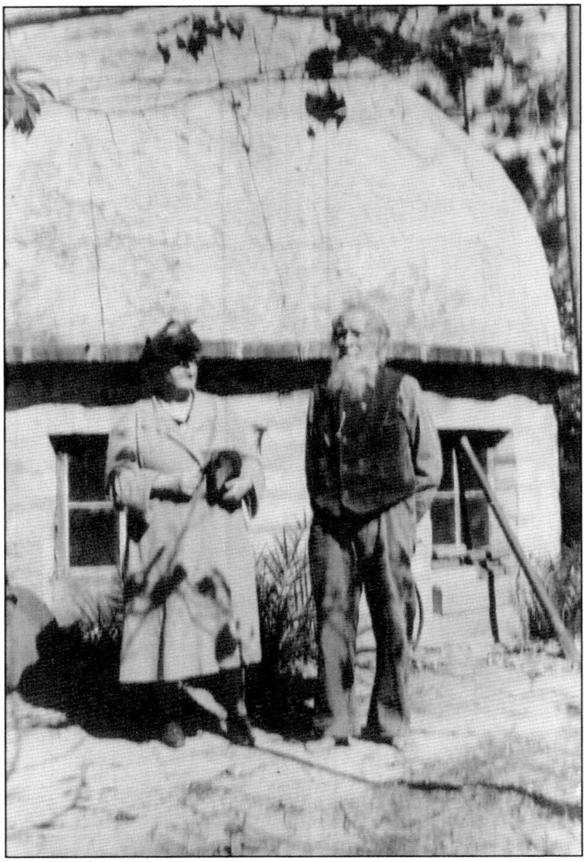

Life of Contemplation. The eccentric Henry Stuart, who built his hut near Fairhope, visits with a doctor's wife from Birmingham. Many seekers made pilgrimages to visit the hermit, who had 1,200 guests register in his log after he arrived in October 1923. People still visit his home, made legendary in the novel *The Poet of Tolstoy Park* by Fairhope author Sonny Brewer. (Courtesy of FMH.)

Another Fairhope Character. The children at right watch as "Aunt Ellen" Hill, as she was called, sweeps the yard in front of her cabin near Fairhope. She lived in the area before Fairhope was founded and later cooked for several local families. Until her death in 1924, visitors came to see the former slave and hear her stories about the old days in the South. (Courtesy of FMH.)

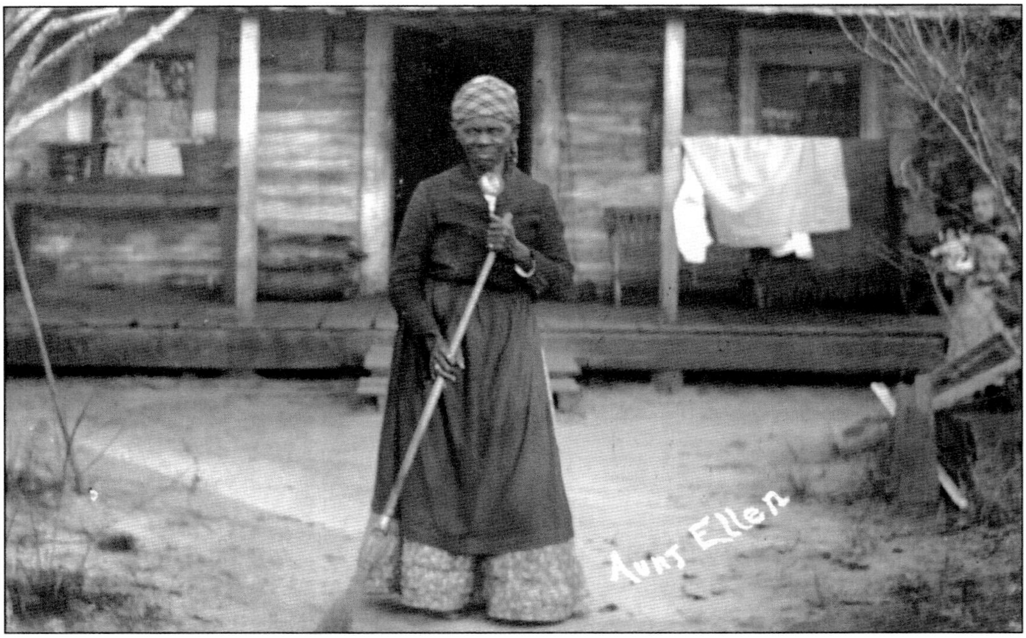

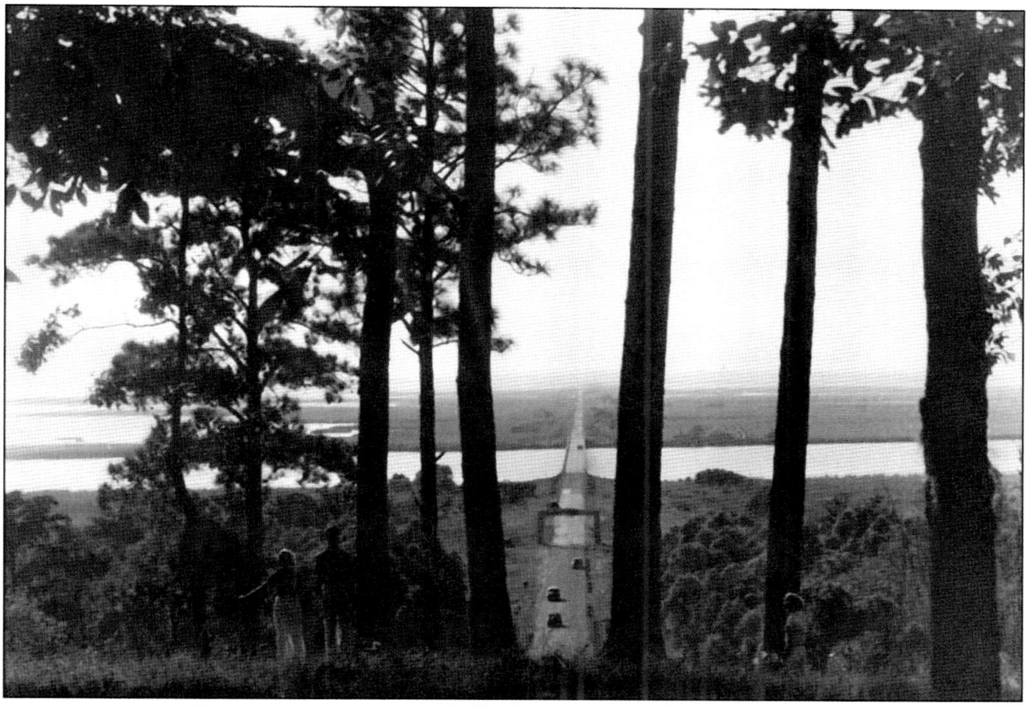

Beginning of a New Era. On June 14, 1927, the new Cochrane Bridge and Mobile Causeway, hailed as a modern engineering feat, opened. It provided a connection across the bay, and Fairhope, now a link for motorists traveling from coast to coast, would be forever changed. In the first year, nearly 200,000 vehicles crossed the seven-mile causeway that remained the only such crossing until 1978. (Courtesy of FMH.)

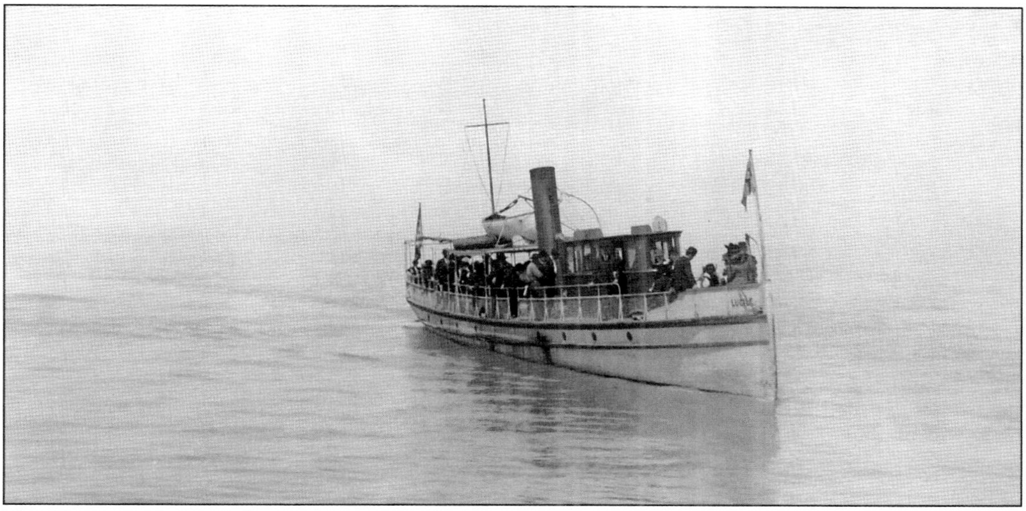

The Land of Mist. The steamers soon became a misty memory, as Fairhope's grand decade of the bay boats, like the fast mail steamer *Lucille*, ended. Wall Street crashed, and the Roaring Twenties would become a wistful, nostalgic interlude between hard times. "So we beat on, boats against the current, borne back ceaselessly into the past," writes Fitzgerald in ending *The Great Gatsby*. (Courtesy of Pinky Bass.)

Consistent with our mission to preserve history on a local level, this book was printed in South Carolina on American-made paper and manufactured entirely in the United States. Products carrying the accredited Forest Stewardship Council (FSC) label are printed on 100 percent FSC-certified paper.

MADE IN THE USA